Confessions of the Miner's Canary

By Allan White, MA

Published by Author

Dedicated to the memory of:

Allan Sheahen (June 28,1932 – October 29,2013),

Sheahen, was a long time and tireless campaigner of the basic income movement. Personal communication with Sheahen has provided me with many useful insights which have informed my discussion of basic income in this book

Table of Contents:

ACKNOWLEDGMENTS:

"I believe it is vital to identify disabling barriers and work towards their removal. But it is also necessary for us, as disabled people to share our experiences and develop accounts of our lives"

-Tom Shakespeare, disability studies scholar 1996

For the writing and production of this book, gratitude is owed to many. In no particular order, I would like to thank the following persons and entities who have helped along the way. First, I would like to thank visual artist, Holly White- Gehrt (of no relation to this author) for her exceptional and devoted work on developing the cover art. I would like to thank my long time friend, Clay for the many conversations over coffee, we have held, regarding this book. The dialogue between Clay and I has been Instrumental in enabling me to develop this project. Also, I owe many thanks to archaeologist and long time friend and colleague Cathy Jean (CJ) Anderson, for her assistance in editing this manuscript. The 2nd edition of this book will be fully edited by CJ. Finally, I would like to thank the following university libraries for their provision of scholarly resources and quiet place to work. These libraries include; the Collins Memorial Library at the University of Puget Sound (UPS), Tacoma, Washington, the Evans Memorial Library at The Evergreen State College (TESC), Olympia, WA, and the Brooks Memorial Library at Central Washington University (CWU), Ellensburg Washington.

"The reasonable man adapts himself to the world; the unreasonable one persists in trying to adapt the world to himself. Therefore, all progress depends on the unreasonable man."

—George Bernard Shaw

The author of this book is among countless victims of misdeeds perpetrated by neoliberal society and it's institutions that dismiss disabled citizens. I have been mislead by the deceptive and empty promises of vocational rehabilitation, and robbed of opportunities for genuine learning through oppressive market centered pedagogies. Further, I have waged disputes with employers, backed only by toothless equal opportunity statutes, and have endured degrading treatment from Social Security Administration while vying, along with others like myself, for protection under an increasingly porous social safety net. Yet the above scenarios I describe are more than mere examples of "personal struggles". Like the especial hardships endured by many disabled persons, these are manifestations of political systems and economic structures that are fundamentally flawed, which fail to provide a valued place for so many of society's members. Those operating under so much as a minor functional difference are particularly vulnerable to the specter of disposability, brought on by wasteful and destructive neoliberal capitalism. As canaries in this coalmine, the struggles of America's disabled citizenry must be regarded not as mere accounts of personal tragedy but as fuel for critical examination of our social structures, institutions, and of the basic values and mores upon which they are based. In order to progress toward equitable inclusion of citizens at every level of ability, we must reject the antiquated fallacy of personal responsibility and diligent work as the cure to all hardship.

Moreover, this author is among the growing legions of those who comprise a "new sector of disability" in America. As I describe it, this "new sector of disability" consists largely of individuals of average or higher measured intelligence, who enjoy reasonably good physical health but are afflicted with comparatively minor neurological impairment(s), which create seemingly disproportionate hardships with social and career functioning. Throughout this book, I argue that our hardships are not merely consequent to our impairment(s) but rather are an outcome of a harshly competitive society and economy stemming from the present global capitalist order. In her book *The Overworked American*, which addresses the issue of time famine, sociologist Juliet B. Schor describes this phenomenon as "an economy and society that are demanding too much from people". The very nature of such a society will invariably exacerbate hardships incurred by even seemingly mild organic impairments.

Now more than ever, we inhabit a place in history, where we must collectively grapple with fundamental questions regarding how to promote a culture that fosters mutual respect among all members, despite intractable differences among us, attributable to organically based variations in talent and ability. Such an objective is imperative to creating a valued place for everybody, and nurturing the best in each and every one of us. This is a central question proposed in Richard Sennett's book, *Respect, in a World of Inequality*, a work that served as a major source of inspiration for this book. Having been born with multifaceted neurological impairments, in the form of a clinically non-specifiable learning disability, Sennett's book resonated sharply with me. In particular, I was taken by Sennett's discussions of the unequal distribution of talent among individuals and how this fact must be reconciled with any ethos of unconditional respect for all. Sennett's discussion of adult dependence is also a familiar theme in the struggles of many disabled adults, who yearn for both self respect and respect from others despite functional compromises. Yet we presently live in a society where the respect afforded to individuals is based on the social currency of individual talent. It's as though respect were some scarce resource with not enough to go around.

My interest in the sociological inquiry of disability was ignited while residing in Exeter, United Kingdom, working towards my MA degree in experimental archaeology. I was increasingly drawn to the university library's literature on disability studies. Such literature, while irrelevant to the subject of my Master's course, was highly relevant to my new focus and direction in life. For numerous reasons, the subject of disability studies increasingly became an interest of mine. I felt disenfranchised by both the academic structure and social climate of my Masters program. My Master's course was little more than an intensified version of the vast majority of my undergraduate education. That is, I achieved little aside from frantically spinning my wheels, towards earning a degree, while learning nothing I didn't already know. Making matters worse was the fact some of my colleagues were narrow-minded and highly intolerant of my unique proclivities as a differently-abled person. I felt alienated by the elitist one-upmanship mentality of my class.

After earning my MA, I immersed myself in readings on disability studies, sociology, economics, and political science, all in an attempt to make sense of and come to terms with the world which denied me a respectable place in society for much of my adult life. Naturally, I yearned for answers as to why I had always struggled so with basic social integration despite impairments which should (at least hypothetically) create no major hindrance. Why is it so difficult to break out of the glass bubble that I long remained trapped within?

So after having defied seemingly unbeatable odds to complete two BA degrees and a MA degree, I grew to question the values I had been brought up with and blindly accepted as fact. Why is it that more and more people, particularly the disabled, will find that hard work, disciplined focus and determination fail to pay off in ways that we are often lead to believe? These very questions were the starting point for the critical social examination and reflective observations forming the basis of this book's subject matter.

INTRODUCTION:

"If we are to achieve a richer culture, rich in contrasting values, we must recognize the whole gamut of human potentialities, and to weave a less arbitrary social fabric, one in which each human gift will find a fitting place"

— Margaret Mead,
Sex and Temperament in Three Primitive Societies

"It is a sin to waste talent; do not let your potential go to waste". This simple but powerful advice from Mr. DiTulio, a middle-aged social worker and pen pal, conveyed to me many years ago at the age of 21, proved an effective catalyst for prompting a major life transition. At the time, I was taking refuge with my parents, very much cloistered from the outside world, and mainstream society. Taking Mr. DiTulio's words of wisdom firmly to heart, I endeavored to leave the netherworld of my creation to embark on a quest to secure the precious jewel of an ever so elusive dignified and comfortable social niche. Yet in my ceaseless quest for this artificially scarce gem, I grew increasingly weary and abundantly familiar with processes by which our society callously squanders the potentialities of its members. The primary agency of the waste I refer to, resides not in the domain of individual choice and action, but rather in public policies grounded in a quasi-utilitarian logic, that primarily serve the interests of an elite capitalist ruling class. Such institutions fail to take account of natural variation in human abilities, and the significance thereof, with regard to a given population's capacity to flourish under the disenfranchising societal conditions they create. Among the populations most susceptible to deleterious effects of prevailing social and economic conditions are those of us imbued with unique organic variations and resultant functional differences. Too often such individuals find that neoliberal capitalist modes of production have little or no economically viable purpose for them.

This is an increasingly frequent reality among those of us who

1

constitute the growing number of neurodiverse individuals in society. The terms "neurodiverse" or "neurodiversity", were coined by autism advocate Judy Singer who postulates that atypical (neurodivergent) neurological development (resulting in clinically recognizable brain differences, such as dyslexia, ADD, autism, etc.) is a normal human variation that should be respected as any other difference. Many neurodiversity advocates assert that society should strive towards being more structurally inclusive of neurodiverse individuals.

Depending on one's actual diagnosis, individual variation thereof, overall severity, and social environment, many neurodiverse adults are able to lead productive lives with successful careers. However, a preponderance of data posits that we remain disproportionately represented among America's growing post-industrial underclass, saddled with chronic unemployment, underemployment, social exclusion, low achievement, and welfare dependency. Such is increasingly the case even among neurodiverse adults with relatively minor impairments such as specific learning difficulties and mood disorders. This may come as no surprise among social service workers or those in the profession of clinical psychology. In such professional circles, increasing social exclusion among even mildly impaired neurodiverse adults, has been known for years. Yet many among the general public fail to understand our struggles, the social and political ramifications of them, and their relevance to society at large. It is precisely these issues that I seek to address in this book.

While it has long been known that cognitively impaired adults struggle economically and socially, relatively little has been done politically to address the social and economic ramifications of this issue. Based on the dominant medical model of disability, such hardships are considered an unfortunate but natural consequence of living with any type of impairment. Hence we commonly posit the solution to the struggles of disabled persons in both the advancement of medical interventions and the free will of impaired individuals to secure appropriate clinical treatments and to "rise to the occasion" and work harder to "overcome" their disability. Such assertions, while culturally palatable, and sentimentally appealing to the masses, are unrealistic, based on ignorance, undue faith in modern medicine as well as an untenable belief in the omnipotent human will.

Many of us are naturally awestruck and inspired by isolated

accounts of disabled individuals who overcome seemingly insurmountable obstacles to achieve great things. Such accounts while inspirational, do not represent the reality of neurodiversity, or of disability in general. Often missing in these isolated accounts is any acknowledgment of the various means of outside support available to these triumphant disabled heroes. Also absent in such accounts is a detailed analysis of the person's particular disability and it's specific limiting effects, relative to their achievements. Not all persons with the same basic diagnosis will have the same specific limitations. For every successful computer technician afflicted with autism, there are many others whose unique autistic variation severely limits nonverbal cognitive skills, rendering them technically illiterate and perhaps virtually unemployable. And while it may be truly inspirational to hear of a double amputee marathon runner, we must not forget the concrete reality engendered by specific technological advancements. With today's prosthetic technologies, a well conditioned amputee can potentially run just as adeptly as an athlete with all limbs fully intact. And it is indeed commendable that such athletes are afforded the opportunity within our society to publicly compete in athletic competition as these endeavors serve to de-stigmatize specific disabilities. However, in the process of de-stigmatization, we must be careful not to transform theirs and similar accounts into a type of hero worship. Such attitudes potentially ignore the hardships experienced by all disabled persons, and foster a "blame the victim" attitude towards the multitudes of disabled people who remain disadvantaged because of our disabilities.

It is erroneous to celebrate the achievements of the disabled as entirely individual triumphs. Equal recognition must be accorded to the advancement of adaptive technologies, and the myriad environmental and social supports that enabled the impaired individual to achieve to the level that they were able to. By fully examining outside factors, attributable to the achievements of specific impaired individuals, it becomes possible to glean insights as to how we can engender a culture and society that nurtures the best in us all, despite whatever amalgam of talents and limitations an individual may naturally possesses.

In contrast to popular inspirational anecdotes, an examination of any official statistics on labor market participation, social integration and neurodiversity illustrates a far bleaker picture of hidden disability in America. For example, using two separate data collection programs, both the decennial census survey, and the annual American Community Survey (ACS) the US Census Bureau collect data relative to standards of living for disabled populations within the US. Both surveys include data pertaining to those with cognitive impairment. Findings from both types of Census Bureau data indicate that underemployment is potentially commonplace even among neurodiverse persons who have completed a Bachelors degree or higher. Moreover, during the past three decades, both state and federal social service agencies have witnessed a drastic uptick in caseloads, based on seemingly benign impairments, usually of mental or psychological origin. Many such conditions, attributable to this uptick, would have been virtually unheard of generations ago. Since the late 1980s, SSI recipients, under age 65, awarded based on mental and psychiatric impairments, other than intellectual disability, have grown at a rate nearly twice that of the overall growth of SSI rolls. From 1988 to 2010, numbers of such beneficiaries grew by a six fold, or 83% increase. By comparison, the population of non-mentally impaired SSI recipients grew only 2.5 times[1] in that same period. Thus overall SSI rolls have increased by 3.5 times with much of the increase attributable to growth in caseloads relating to mental or psychiatric impairment. In 1988, persons receiving SSI on the basis of mental or psychological impairment constituted merely 20% of SSI rolls. By 2010, such SSI beneficiaries comprised 42% of SSI rolls. Moreover, while numbers of SSI/DI beneficiaries show substantial documented growth, most statistics focus only upon those receiving benefits and say nothing of the many thousands of SSI/DI applicants who, while suffering from highly debilitating conditions, are denied benefits based on failure to meet SSA's unduly stringent eligibility criteria. Research on populations served by other welfare programs may provide insight into this matter. For example, state administered Temporary Aid to Needy Families (TANF) program, does not consider the presence of disability, for eligibility, yet very telling trends can be ascertained among its case files.

A recent study conducted by Mathematica™ Policy Research, Inc. was conducted to address potential eligibility of TANF recipients for other aid programs. The study indicated that many TANF recipients

[1] Increase of SSI/DI caseloads related to physical or sensory handicap is believed to simply be resultant of the general aging of the American populace. Advances in medical technologies enable not only people to live longer but to live longer, even given the presence of illness or disability.

might be better served by SSI or other disabled income support. However many such individuals are handicapped by impairments that fail to meet federal criteria for disability.

Implemented in July of 1997, TANF was created under the Personal Responsibility and Work Opportunity Reconciliation Act, instituted under President Bill Clinton in 1996. The goal of this measure was to provide temporary financial assistance while aiming to get people off assistance primarily through employment. The program imposes time limits, and job search requirements to limit the amount of time families remain dependent on public assistance. Since its implementation, the TANF program has seen sharp general decline in those receiving cash assistance, due to its temporary nature. However, in the midst of this overall decline, recipients with mental disorders or other challenges affecting their ability to work, tend to remain on the rolls and are served for longer durations by this temporary aid than non impaired recipients. Recent studies, aimed at assessing potential eligibility of TANF recipients for means tested disabled income support, have found mental disorders to be the most common among TANF recipients, with 1/3-1/4 of such individuals having symptoms associated with a mental condition. While these estimates can differ slightly depending on how disorders are defined and measured and the data collection strategy and methodology used, one study estimated that specific types of mental disorders are especially common among TANF recipients. Findings indicate major depressive disorder to be most frequent at 26.7%, followed by post-traumatic stress disorder at 14.6%, and generalized anxiety at 7.3%.

So contrary to exaggerated populist charges of disability based welfare programs, largely serving malingerers undeserving of such assistance, the TANF statistics on mental health diagnoses among recipients, indicates quite the opposite. There is likely a significant faction of the mentally impaired population, gravely disadvantaged with regard to employability, yet remain underserved by available social services and left to their own devices to survive. For some this may include marginal sporadic employment, and adult cohabitation with family members. For those without such support systems, chronic homelessness may be problematic. As a society we must do better than this. Nobody chooses to be disabled. And persons with disabilities should not be left to the mercy of highly variable and often fragile resources of private individuals, for support. We must create a system that provides for the basic needs

5

of those among us who are unable to work, without compromising their dignity or self determination.

Political conservatives erroneously attribute growth of disability based welfare dependency, to unduly lax disability determination criteria. Such ideologues may also blame opportunistic lawyers who seek to profit by enabling unscrupulous malingering idlers to leisurely subsist off the public dole. I maintain that such an argument presupposes a false causal relationship and that nothing could be further from the truth. It is significant that the unprecedented growth in this population of SSI beneficiaries has occurred despite welfare reform legislation in the mid to late 1990s which enacted more stringent disability determination criteria for SSI/SSDI qualification.

My contention holds that such an uptick, in the face of more stringent qualifying criteria is best explained by conditions inherent to the typical post-industrial economy, and society and their impacts upon neurodiverse adults. Work intensification, long working hours and a complicated, competitive, and exclusionary "workplace culture" are typical features of the workplace under neoliberal capitalism. All of these features render the modern workplace virtually forbidden territory for many workers with the slightest disability. Furthermore, the decision to drop out of the workforce, among disabled workers, is typically followed by years of attempting to attain self sufficiency. Eventually disabled workers may see no other life options but to surrender to the inescapable reality that society has no economically viable use for them. Throughout my college years, I personally befriended many people in my same situation - pursuing higher education as a means to surmount the social disadvantage incurred by our impairments. Yet many of these dear friends found their efforts entirely in vain, leaving them with no recourse but to remain dependent on the public dole, despite impressive academic achievements. Such accounts should really give pause for thought. Pursuit of college degree is no easy undertaking and to do so with any sort of disability typically requires an effort well above and beyond the norm. Such cases stand in stark contradiction to the notion that anyone would simply attempt to "cash in" on some *ad hoc* diagnoses they were given, seeking disability benefits as a ticket to a comfortable, leisurely life. This is an even more egregious misconception, given that living off of paltry disability benefits, is anything but a comfortable, existence that anyone would actually strive for. Add to it, the stigma and marginalization, associated with welfare dependency and it is even more difficult to fathom how anyone would actually aspire for such a life.

As a neurodiverse person, I metaphorically liken the experience of neurodiversity, in our time, to proverbial canary in a coalmine, hence the title of this book. This metaphor originates from pre-industrial, and early industrial times, when coal miners brought caged canaries into the mineshaft as a live carbon monoxide indicator, that warned of gas leaks within the mineshaft. Canaries being more sensitive to even minute traces of the toxic gas would die and cease chirping well before the gas reached sufficient concentrations to harm humans. Thus when the canaries died, the miners knew to exit the mine. In an analogous way, neurodiverse adults are more susceptible to potentially deleterious social, political, and economic conditions that threaten life quality for the general population if intensified or left to fester unmitigated. And it is indeed tragic that society at large has never sought to critically examine the neurodiverse experience to glean insights for potential societal and economic reforms that will not only improve our life prospects but also improve living standards for non-neurodiverse people as well. Preindustrial miners knew to step out of the mine when the canaries quit singing.

Laypersons and even many professionals often regard seemingly minor neurodiverse states as benign conditions, amenable to successful treatment through medication and simple lifestyle adjustments. There is no shortage of self help literature on the market which makes it seem as though such conditions can be merely turned "on" or "off", just like a switch. Yet too often clinical interventions and self help measures are simply ineffective. Sometimes even "relatively minor" organic brain dysfunctions, lead to disastrous consequences in the lives of the patient, their families, and their loved ones. In such cases, we commonly attribute such tragic misfortune to the impaired individual, and their lack of adequate "coping mechanisms", personal integrity or willpower. Yet when any identifiable segment of the population is disproportionately afflicted with disadvantage it defies logic and basic humanity to adhere to obsolete, unworkable ideals, which posit full responsibility upon individuals within the population in question, for their lot in life. No humane and civilized society should accept this. When any specific group within a population is afflicted with disproportionately afflicted with hardship, there are clearly external causal factors at fault. Few people, if any, choose a life of hardship and exclusion. In identifying causal factors attributable to such vast achievement gaps, we must reject popular one sided explanations based on an individualistic rationale of just deserts. By extension, we must then ask how social and economic restructuring can not only serve as a more effective antidote to the frequent social exclusion of the differently-abled, but also engender a society that is conducive to optimal thriving, growth and self determination of all members. These are not contradictory mutually exclusive ends, but interrelated, mutually compatible ones. And so it naturally follows that this should not be an issue of concern specific to neurodiverse individuals, their families, and their loved ones; it is an issue that should concern all of humanity.

The social exclusion, incurred by neurodiverse people is merely a byproduct of a fundamentally ailing social order that diminishes, or potentially diminishes the quality of life for all of society's members in ways that most remain comfortably anaesthetized to. We all pay the price, when one segment of humanity is either intentionally or unintentionally relegated to marginalized status. Extraneous public welfare expenses, higher enforcement costs, and diminished personal security, and the overall lack of cohesion and trust, are but a handful of concrete examples of consequences indicating compromised quality of life for all, when we accept marginalization and vast inequities as integral, unavoidable aspects of dynamic free market democracy. Abstract ethical imperatives notwithstanding, the internal peace, long term stability, and sustainability of any nation state depends to a great extent upon the capacity to ensure that most if not all citizens are accorded a comfortable and dignified place without undue hardship of inordinate, often counterproductive and self defeating toil and effort. Simply finding a comfortable niche in life should not necessitate an act of heroism on the part of any person, disabled or otherwise.

An understanding of social interpretations or "the social model" of disability is imperative to better inform discussion surrounding this issue. A key concept of the social model of disability is the distinction between impairment and disability. Such a distinction enables critical examination, with an eye towards reform of exogenous social factors, which impart disadvantage onto impaired persons. As per the social model of disability, the designation of impairment describes exclusively organic and consequently functional difference. For example, a spinal cord injury or deformity, resulting in any measure of paralysis is an impairment. Disability, on

8

the other hand is a form of social oppression, embodied in the functional hardship, social exclusion, economic disadvantage, chronic dependence, and poor health often experienced by disabled persons. The exclusion and consequent disadvantage may be either attitudinal in origin, such as overt discrimination against those with known impairments, or structural in origin, stemming from barriers in the physical or cultural environment, that inadvertently restrict a disabled person's life. Such structural barriers hamper daily activities, and restrict access to economic opportunities or other venues to meaningful social participation.

For example, a paraplegic equipped with a mechanically sound mobility aid, residing in a municipality, where wheelchair accessible infrastructure predominated and inhabiting a culture tolerant of diverse physical abilities; will most likely benefit from such an environment in a way as to actually diminish their disability. Such a person can enjoy reasonably unimpeded access to public buildings and spaces, and relatively unfettered access to educational opportunities, paid work, and other venues for social participation. When coupled with availability of technologies that enable her to do her job effectively, it can be said that such a person has the *impairment* of paraplegia, yet enjoys an environment, conducive to optimal thriving, enabling a full and productive life. In this respect, such a person may not be considered *disabled*. In a starkly contrasting scenario, that same person becomes disabled when unable to benefit from available assistive technologies, and/or lives in a community that fears and shuns the physically impaired, and lacks modern architecture and physical infrastructure to facilitate wheelchair access. A paraplegic in this scenario is most likely doomed to lead a highly restricted life marked by dependence, social exclusion, mitigated personal achievement, poor health and economic hardship and thus by definition is *disabled*. Strictly biological definitions of disability which posit the locus of disability solely in the dysfunctional individual can easily make it appear that impaired persons are 'naturally' and therefore, justifiably excluded from social participation. As such, striking parallels can be drawn between the use of such social Darwinian 'logic' in the oppression of disabled people, and pseudo-scientific justifications for the oppression of women, persons of color, and other historically subjugated groups. It is precisely this mode of thinking that most scholars of disability studies seek to combat.

With regard to neurodiversity, a social model of disability, taking

9

account of role functions of individuals and society, posits that the transition of the US economy from one based primarily on physical labor to one based on service and information processing has profoundly influenced the definition of disability in much of the developed world. In earlier economies based on physical labor, many individuals with cognitive disabilities such as learning disabilities or mild intellectual disabilities could easily serve as successful workers. However, in such of economy, an individual (particularly a male) with a physical disability would have been severely limited, with regard to employment prospects. However, in today's economy, disabilities impacting any aspect of cognitive functioning are often said to be much more limiting than a physical disability, as service and technical/information processing jobs require high levels of cognitive functioning.

Fordham University Sociology professor, Micki McGee posits that the emergence of the neurodiversity concept coincides not only with the mobilization of the disability rights movement but also the ascendance of neoliberal policy during the last three decades. The dismantling of government provisions for the care of the most vulnerable, and the valorization of individual responsibility are the hallmarks of conservative political discourse over the last 30 years. The above trends coincide with enormous speed up in the labor market. Increases in the pace of production entail expectations that one should be available to employers or clients across what was the previous divide of work and family, and the related demand for multi-tasking, as well as ever more emphasis on flexibility and sociability as prerequisites for employability. These transformations have rendered many who were formerly within the broad continuum of normal functioning "handicapped" in an accelerated and unpredictable production cycle that aims to compete in global labor markets. This factor alone accounts for the substantial recent growth in welfare dependency among those with relatively minor cognitive impairments, placing us within the world of disability.

Philosopher and disabilities rights theorist Susan Wendall, in her 2006 book, *The Rejected Body*, argues that just as the built environment handicaps the mobility impaired, the temporal environment of accelerated work schedules makes formerly acceptable levels of production deficient, rendering those who cannot maintain the new speed of production debilitated. The speedup in production in the past two decades has created an entirely new sector of disability: those with deficits in attention, flexibility, or sociability.

Concurrent with our changing conceptions of disability, to include various 'hidden' neuropsychological handicaps, recent decades have seen moderate increases in the general public's awareness of neurodiversities such as ADD, bipolar disorder, and the varying degrees of autism, just to name a few. As clinical psychologist Thomas Armstrong, points out in his 2010 book *Neurodiversity*, the past 60 years have also witnessed unprecedented growth in actual numbers of individual clinically recognized psychiatric illnesses. Specifically, Armstrong notes that when the first edition of the *Diagnostic and Statistical Manual* (DSM) of the American Psychiatric Association was published in 1952, only 100 categories of psychiatric illness were listed. By 2000, that number had tripled. Now even newer disabilities have been added to the 2012 edition of the DSM, including Illness Anxiety Disorder, Mixed Anxiety/Depression, Social Communication Disorder and many others.

The drastic growth of recognized mental disorders, and concerns as to their innate legitimacy, remains a source of controversy within lay and professional circles alike. The controversy relates to frequent skepticism, often manifest as populist suspicion concerning ulterior profit motives of a "psychological industry" that seeks to bolster revenues by "creating" new disorders to diagnose and treat. Another popular charge is that the recognition of such disorders is nothing more than a manifestation of a culture obsessed with strict conformity to a narrow set of rigidly prescribed norms that seeks to arbitrarily "label", and hence stigmatize those who deviate ever so slightly. However, in accordance with social interpretations of disability, upon which the neurodiversity movement is philosophically underpinned, I maintain that the current growth in clinically recognized disorders is directly related to increased socio-cultural relevance of clinically recognizing and attempting to treat these conditions.

Postindustrial life in much of the developed world is marked by a competitive fast paced tempo, technical complexity, and unique social challenges. These social conditions select for an agile, rapid processing neuro-cognitive wiring, a robust psychological constitution, and extroverted interpersonal style. Any deviation from these socially selected norms becomes a problem to be dealt with. This is not simply due to an idle obsession with conformity, but

11

rather to societal conditions that select a narrow range of functional types for success and penalize those who deviate with failure and exclusion. Underlying organic differences accountable to many presently recognized brain differences have always been present among the population. Yet they are far more likely prove problematic in today's society. In the cruelest of ironies, recent growth in both popular awareness and clinical understanding has not been matched with commensurate changes in public policy to confer significant improvements in life prospects for neurodiverse individuals. This I believe to be due to the prominent and highly influential medical model of disability which focuses on treating the "defective" individual. Such a focus negates the objective of social modelist thought, which seeks to improve popular attitudes toward the disabled and reform social structures and institutions that are fundamentally ailing. Inclusion is only one facet of this objective. One integral component must also involve the improvement of social welfare for those so severely disabled that they will never attain self sufficiency despite all available medical treatments and environmental modifications.

So why does society at large continue to expect the disabled to achieve feats of heroism that few will ever accomplish? Wouldn't it be more advantageous if disabling barriers were simply removed or attenuated to the greatest extent possible? What about re-structuring economic systems in ways that would confer greater economic opportunities for most people, regardless of their relative capabilities or lack thereof? What about improving physical infrastructures in ways that enhance physical mobility for impaired people and enhance quality of life for non impaired persons alike? It's all possible.

Empowerment of disabled people is not a zero-sum game that translates to corresponding hardship on the non-disabled. It is often the case that structural improvements that mitigate hardship for the disabled also enhance quality of life for the non-disabled as well. For example wheelchair access ramps and elevators in public buildings not only facilitate public access for wheelchair users, but also improve access for parents with strollers, injured able-bodied persons using crutches, or workers carting unwieldy objects within buildings. Improved bicycle access in major urban streets not only has potential to enhance physical mobility and independence for physically robust neurodiverse individuals, but also lends a low cost, economically viable, healthy, and environmentally sound transportation option to non-disabled commuters. And academic adjustments that enhance the learning environment for neurodiverse (aka "learning disabled") learners also have the same effect on neurotypical students. The list goes on.

My Disability

At this point, I shall describe my specific diagnoses and then illustrate how they relate to my unique life struggles and challenges as a neurodiverse adult, in a global capitalist world. In the foregoing discussion, I shall describe my disability largely from a clinical standpoint. However, given the preceding discussion, I invite you the reader to consider the present neoliberal cultural and economic climate with regard to disabilities similar to mine.

My most recent official diagnosis is a multifaceted one including; learning disorder - Not Otherwise Specified (NOS) with slow cognitive processing and impaired fine motor speed, Developmental Coordination Disorder (DCD) by history, and possible ASD (Autism Spectrum Disorder) traits. I have been told that for all intents and purposes, the combination of my non specifiable learning disorder and motor deficits is effectively the same clinical entity that UK researchers and clinicians refer to as dyspraxia. The term "dyspraxia" is derived from the two Greek words, "dys", meaning impaired or abnormal, and "praxis", meaning action or deed. Thus "dyspraxia" simply refers to an impaired ability to carry out an action or deed. Of all known impairment categories, the criteria for dyspraxia, seems to most closely match my actual range of symptoms. For this reason, I will describe it in some detail.

It is estimated that dyspraxia affects about 5% of the general population with about 70% of afflicted individuals being male. Dyspraxia, as epitomized by the co-occurrence of motor and perceptual deficits, was first identified and described by Collier in the early 1900s as "congenital maladroitness". Soon thereafter, Dr. Samuel Orton declared it to be 'one of the six most common developmental disorders, showing distinctive impairment of praxis'. Since then it has been described and labeled by many, such as Jean Ayers, who in 1972 called it a disorder of Sensory Integration, or Dr Sasson Gubbay who in 1975 called it the 'Clumsy Child

Syndrome'. Other labels have included developmental awkwardness, sensory motor dysfunction, minimal brain dysfunction, motor sequencing disorder, and most recently Developmental Coordination Disorder, though this latter condition is becoming increasingly recognized as an entirely distinct entity, apart from dyspraxia.

 In accordance with standard American psychiatric diagnostic protocol, however, my neuropsychologist could not legally diagnose me specifically with dyspraxia, as it is not yet listed in the DSM IV. In casual conversation, however, I often simply refer to my condition as dyspraxia, as it is less of a mouthful and easier to describe than my actual myriad diagnoses. What's more, my functional limitations seem to match those of dyspraxia to an absolute T. Therefore I feel that this gives me some license to casually identify myself under this diagnostic category.

Though the term dyspraxia is often used synonymously with DCD, controversy exists, regarding the interchangeability of both respective terms to describe the same condition. According to many experts, dyspraxia, as commonly understood, is its own distinct condition characterized, primarily by the presence of motor deficit, but by definition also involves a unique gamut of sensory integration, sensory processing, and cognitive impairments. In this way dyspraxia can easily have functional consequences beyond simply eliminating all prospects of becoming a world class athlete or a graceful dancer. Developmental Coordination Disorder, on the other hand is also its own distinct condition affecting specifically motor co-ordination. With DCD, motor difficulties can either occur independently of the presence of other impairments, or is frequently co-morbid with ADD, autistic spectrum disorders, and other organic mental impairments. Though DCD is highly co-morbid with specific learning and developmental disorders affecting cognitive processing, it does not actually entail any sort of cognitive processing disorders to necessitate diagnosis of the condition. Dyspraxia too can either occur singularly or comorbidly with other specific learning disorders and autistic spectral disorders. Currently, DCD is the closest related condition to dyspraxia listed in either the DSM IV or DSM-IV-TR and is categorized under the rubric designated for disorders usually first diagnosed in infancy, childhood, and adolescence. Official diagnostic criteria for DCD includes:

14

A) *Performance in daily activities that require motor coordination is substantially below that   expected given the person's chronological age and measured intelligence. This may be manifested by marked delays in achieving motor milestones (e.g. walking, crawling, sitting), dropping things, "clumsiness", poor performance in sports, or poor handwriting.*
B) *The disturbance in Criterion A significantly interferes with academic achievement or activities in daily living.*
C) *The disturbance is not due to a general medical condition (e.g. cerebral palsy, hemiplegia, or muscular dystrophy) and does not meet the criteria for a Pervasive Developmental Disorder.*
D) *If mental retardation is present, the motor difficulties are in excess of those usually associated with it*

       Coding note: *"If a general medical (e.g. neurological) condition or sensory deficit is present, code the condition on Axis III"*

Axis III of the DSM IV designates general medical conditions. The World Health Organization currently lists it as Specific Developmental Disorder of Motor Function.   The ICD 9-CM designates dyspraxia as a condition that includes many of the criteria for DCD (ICD code 315.4), that is considered to have two primary characteristics:

- Loss of ability to perform familiar purposeful movements in the absence of paralysis or other neural sensory-motor impairment.

- Inability to execute complex coordinated movements resulting from lesions in the motor area of the cortex but involving no sensory impairment or paralysis. Apraxia, is another term that is sometimes synonymously with dyspraxia, but is an entirely different condition altogether. Here, an understanding on clinical terminology helps to clarify the distinction. In clinical jargon, the prefix "a" refers to the absence or loss of a function, whereas "dys" is simply an impairment or disruption of function. When combined with the root word "praxia", meaning to carry out a deed or action, apraxia defines a complete lack of ability to plan and carry out muscle movement and occurs in the absence of severe muscle weakness.   Verbal apraxia affects muscles involved with speech production, including the jaw, lips, tongue, and respiratory system. Unlike dyspraxia which is by definition always congenital, apraxia usually occurs as a result of a stroke, or may be acquired from birth.

The Dyspraxia Foundation, based in Herts, England, currently hosts a website containing a detailed list of commonly identified traits and symptoms researchers attribute to dyspraxia, including deficits in gross motor skills, speech and language, perception, learning, thought, and memory, emotional functioning, as well as confused lateral dominance (i.e. interchangeable preference in the use of right or left hand), difficulties in modulating eye movements, hence visual tracking difficulties, and secondary emotional adjustment problems, stemming from hardships of living with the condition. Very few dyspraxics will exhibit every single known symptom, but most dyspraxics will have a few traits under each category thereof. Additionally, four basic subtypes of dyspraxia have been identified, based on the presence of specific symptoms. These four subtypes include:

- Ideo-Motor Dyspraxia: Inability to complete single step motor tasks, such as combing hair and waving goodbye.

- Ideational Dyspraxia: Difficulty with multi-step tasks like brushing teeth, making a bed, putting on clothes in order, as well as buttoning and buckling.

- Oromotor Dyspraxia: Difficulties coordinating the muscle movements required to produce words.

- Constructional Dyspraxia: Problems with establishing spatial relationships, as in the ability to accurately position or move objects from one place to another.

With most forms of dyspraxia, it is the combination of sensory integration, perceptual, and sensory processing disorders along with psychomotor deficits that often negatively impacts the efficiency with which one can execute 'simple' mundane activities of daily living. Many adults with dyspraxia and related disorders report difficulties with driving, cooking, housework, personal grooming and other "simple tasks".

Sensory processing and sensory integration difficulties are also an aspect of my disability. Typical problems associated with these particular dysfunctions, involve a subnormal ability to simultaneously process two or more forms of incoming sensory stimuli. This capacity is critical to manipulative processes germane to the execution of many activities that non-affected persons do with little or no conscious effort. As an example, fully intact sensory integration enables one to visually recognize and appropriately respond to road signs and markings while driving a car; an activity involving the simultaneous processing of both visual stimuli (e.g. the signs/markings) and tactual stimuli (e.g. the perception of your body in space/time while traveling at a given speed).Any dysfunction in sensory processing/perceptual ability essentially means that the basic senses hearing, vision, touch, smell, and taste are fully intact, but are filtered and interpreted in a very idiosyncratic way. There may be oversensitivity, or diminished sensitivity to specific sensations (i.e. touch, smells, or visual stimuli such as excessive light) or incoming stimuli may be mentally interpreted quite differently altogether.

Visual and auditory perception both are highly problematic for me. For example, if searching for a specific coffee cup placed on a shelf among several, I may need to gaze at the entire assemblage long and hard before finally spotting the cup I need. I also have grave difficulty understanding "highly accented" English or speech that is too rapid, loud, soft, highly inflected, or lacking distinct standardized annunciation of all syllables. In other words, the best way to communicate with me is to speak like an American English speaking news reporter.

In an abstract sense, the combination of motor and sensory processing deficits often hampers one's ability to effectively and productively interface with their external environment. Such difficulty often manifest as the impaired communication and interactive ability, and/or inefficiencies in manipulating one's external physical surroundings, hence impediments with expediently executing even mundane daily tasks. For example, it can easily take me around 45-50 minutes to simply get cleaned and dressed in the morning. Such marked slowness stems from impairments in fine motor functioning, with consequent manipulative limitations, and inefficiencies in motor planning[2].The words of this book you are reading (and hopefully enjoying) have been orally dictated with voice recognition software. Despite my best efforts I have never been able to develop adequate keyboarding skills. When walking or running on level ground, I frequently out-pace many people, but if you were to see me walking down a flight of stairs, you would think I had severe arthritis in all

---

[2] Also called motor praxis. This refers to the ability to plan and execute a non-habitual task, based on a mental conception of it.

lower body joints. I also fumble and drop objects constantly, and this slows down many activities I might do. I have never been able to obtain a driver's license, even after two unsuccessful attempts at doing so. In all likelihood, I never will drive or own a car. I avoid chaos and crowds like the plague, and cannot function as part of a team, or follow large group conversations. I find waiting at slow cycling crosswalk lights or having my eardrums blasted with the roar of a poorly muffled vehicle engine, to be tantamount to forms of torture banned by most international governmental accords. I basically seem to function best in environments with a level of intellectual and sensory stimulation, found in a university library during summer session.

While late adolescence was when I first became aware that I most likely suffer from a specific learning difficulty, it has only been relatively recent in my life, that I believe myself to have arrived at a most fitting diagnosis, emphasizing motor, perceptual, and sensory integration dysfunction. These functional differences accord more closely with the nature of difficulties I experience.

At 22, I was given a diagnosis of ADD-predominantly inattentive type, but the neuropsychologist who performed my most recent examination, felt that the diagnosis was no longer applicable. Either I once had ADD but have since outgrown it, or I never had it in the first place, and was simply misdiagnosed. That was his impression. Reflection of my academic and other life experiences leads me to believe the latter might be the case.

During my years of college/university education, I quickly came to realize that the origin of my academic challenges stemmed not from impaired concentration or difficulties with comprehension or retention of subject matter. Rather, my greatest source of difficulty stemmed from impairments of motor planning, and the manipulative and organizational abilities, germane to the efficient completion of essays and other academic products, traditionally assigned to assess student learning. This realization never occurred for me as a schoolboy during my compulsory 12 years of pre-college education. Though my college essays and presentations typically earned stellar marks, organizing and composing them required an effort well above and beyond simultaneously maintaining two full-time jobs. As a second year undergraduate, I calculated that I spent anywhere from 70-85 hours per week, just in working on assignments. I literally had to eat, drink, sleep, and breathe the completion of coursework, often compromising my focus on the actual subject matter(s) I was researching. I never had difficulty in developing ideas for academically worthwhile essay topics. Moreover, I always had a clearly defined thesis for every paper, understanding fully what needed to be written, to support it. Yet extrapolation of all of my thoughts, ideas, and research data in the form of a coherent essay or presentation was nothing short of an epic struggle. Typically, I would begin writing a 1500-2000 word essay 3 weeks prior to its due date, whereas most students could complete the same assignment in a matter of days. One would never think that an impairment affecting mostly psycho motor processes could negatively affect performance in a sedentary activity like writing and composition, do we? Quantitative skills classes were the only ones where comprehension of subject matter was problematic. This was due to challenges with the manipulation of the many complex rules and principles involved in higher level mathematics. However in subject areas capitalizing on crystallized verbal intelligences, such as social science and history classes, only minimal study was required for me to earn high marks on in-class tests. This was especially true of multiple choice, short answer, and true/false tests, having no requirement of written expression in the form of full essay questions.

My particular range of impairments, indeed seem to represent a unique case, among those classed as "learning disabilities" or "specific learning difficulties". Generally these conditions are still, even among many professionals, considered to primarily affect academic learning, such as a dyslexic student who struggles to read and write, or the learner suffering from AD/HD who cannot focus and concentrate on class lectures and academic work without the aid of medications. Yet of all areas of mental functioning, traditional academic learning seems least affected by my condition. In fact many of my undergraduate colleagues frequently opined that my academic presentations - especially those pertaining to the subject of stone tools or *lithics*, presented as though rendered by an Ivy League professor than by any undergraduate student. However, functions such as task organization and completion, technical literacy, active problem solving, social functioning, interactive abilities, and communication behaviors seem to be most adversely impacted, by my condition. My areas of impairment seem to be mostly in the realm of normal day to day functioning. As such, I almost feel as though I relate perfectly to that archetypical professor, or academic who can't make a cup of coffee.

19

As one can see, I am a prime example of the entirely new sector of disability created by the present neoliberal order which sets the pace of the world to a freakishly rapid pace. The speed-up not only takes place in production but also in social relations. An inability to keep up with the accelerated pace of social interaction leaves one at a grave disadvantage with regard to social integration.

As one reads this book, it becomes apparent that I frequently identify myself as neurodiverse rather than by any actual diagnosis. I do this for several reasons. For one, because of the mixed and unspecified nature of my neurological impairment(s), I have no definitive diagnostic axis to align with. Asking me to do so would be somewhat akin to asking a person of mixed racial ancestry, to identify by one specific race or another, corresponding with each respective component of his or her heritage. Also because my diagnoses are so multifaceted, it seems that the term "neurodiverse" is more all encompassing and accounts for all facets of my impairments. What's more, this is a book dealing with political and sociological aspects of neurodiversity, and thus the term neurodiverse is more appropriate as it is more politically loaded. As a general descriptive term, encompassing multitudes of organically divergent (hence diverse) neurological conditions, it is potentially very unifying in a political sense, conveying unity and common bond among neurologically impaired persons, be they autistic, dyslexic, bipolar, etc. *E pluribus Unum*- from many, one. Such a common unity potentially serves as a starting point to rally around a common political cause of improved life prospects and self determination of neurodiverse persons.

For me, living as a neurodiverse person in a largely neurotypical centered world has been an amalgamation of multifaceted highs and lows. In some ways, my adult life represents one of the best possible outcomes, given my condition, yet in other ways it may represent one of the worst possible outcomes. This book chronicles my adult struggles to integrate into society and places these "personal struggles" in their relevant socio-political and cultural context. In doing so, it is my hope to present the reader with a different paradigm of disability; one that places the primary locus of causation and responsibility not on the impaired individual and their dysfunctional body, but on the body politic at large and its structures and institutions. In essence, this book is no lofty philosophical account of how I "overcame" adversity, nor is it a memoir of "personal tragedy". It is a call for structural, institutional and social reform. It is also my hope to illustrate that effective social integration of the differently-abled is something that we all have a stake in.

Additionally I wish to introduce social modelist thinking on disability to the general public at large, and to stimulate popular discussion on neurodiversity and increase awareness surrounding the plight of neurodiverse adults. It is also my hope to empower many neurodiverse men and women to critically examine their disabled status in society for what it is, a form of social oppression. Moreover, such critical examination must necessarily entail the identification of those external oppressive elements in their lives.

From this realization, through *concientization*[3], the oppressed become moved to organize and advocate on their behalf, a process that the late Brazilian reformist educator Paulo Freire refers to as *Praxis,* in his seminal writing, *Pedagogy of the Oppressed.* My advice to any neurodiverse individual is to not only seek any effective clinical intervention available, but also to become involved politically and do your part to promote neurodiversity awareness and to champion for your unique rights as a neurodiverse adult in society.

This book is written with a somewhat experimental approach employing a combination of personal memoir and independent research on neurodiversity in contemporary American society. My intent is to present the reader with a perspective on this issue, different from those typically presented in memoirs of this sort. This is an account of how a seemingly minor neurological impairment has lead to disproportionate social and occupational consequences, placing my challenges, struggles, and triumphs in their relevant socio-political context. In doing so, I examine prospects for reform of some of our basic institutions (i.e. education, welfare, etc.) in ways that would promote appropriate "niche construction" and self determination for neurodiverse adults in both the occupational and social realm. With the topic of this book primarily concerned with

---

[3] Grounded in Marxist critical theory and developed by Paulo Freire, this is the process by which the learner advances toward critical consciousness, permitting an in-depth understanding of the world, allowing for the perception and exposure of perceived social and political contradictions. This leads to taking action (or *praxis*) against the oppressive elements in one's life that are illuminated by that understanding

neurodiversity in adulthood, I discus little of my childhood, instead primarily focusing on my adult life experiences as a neurologically impaired individual navigating both the social and vocational spheres in a world structurally unsuited for those who function as I do.

My intent in writing this book is to highlight the disabling effects of social and economic circumstances encountered by neurodiverse persons in a neoliberal global capitalist world. I thus invite you, the reader to focus not on specific functional attributes of my impairment, but on the social context of life events that I describe.

The first Chapter describes a pivotal moment while coming of age, when I discovered my impairment and simultaneously discovered the world of primitive technologies[4]. Both discoveries enabled me to improve my lot in life, and the latter, awakened a dormant intellectual curiosity, which opened the door to enrichments that otherwise may never have not occurred. Chapters 2 and 3 describe my devotion to craft and my isolation from the world as a young adult. Yet my retreat from society and pursuit of an unrealistic life plan was motivated by a fear and mistrust of the world around me. My fear and mistrust, stemmed from frequent misunderstanding and mistreatment from others I had endured throughout my childhood and adolescence. The fourth chapter deals with my epiphany at age 21 to change my life course, seeking a seemingly more realistic path. Yet, despite my confidence and determination, I would run into frequent structural barriers prohibiting my rehabilitation into society. Chapters 5 and 6 describe my hard earned but superficial success in higher educational settings, and my initial entry into the normal workaday world. Both chapters also describe two different pedagogical approaches I undertook during my college years. While I succeeded in both settings, the system at large, permitted only a superficial level of success in the form of a high GPA, with none of the rewards, too often promised by higher education. The 7th chapter, entitled "Concientization" describes my transformation while pursuing my MA degree in England. During this transformative process, I came to recognize my disability as a form of social oppression, giving me a new focus and direction in life. In the 8th and final chapter, I discuss at length, the feasibility of an

[4] Ancient, usually 'Stone Age' living skills such as stone tool making (or flintknapping), fire by friction, natural fiber cordage and basketry weaving, archery bow-making, primitive fish and game procurement, etc.

unconditional basic income guarantee[5] and its potential to become a catalyst to promote self determination and to facilitate effective niche construction among neurodiverse adults. Within this chapter, I offer a scenario in which the collective niche construction and political organization of neurodiverse individuals, leads to other social reforms and cultural transformations, thereby generating a more neurodiverse friendly culture and society. Moreover an unconditional basic income may even obviate many of the ineffective and costly targeted social programs that attempt to serve the disabled.

An unconditional basic income accords with the canary in the coalmine paradigm, in the way that it is not a specifically targeted welfare state provision aimed at the disabled. I think of it as an improvement to the economic environment. Moreover it is an improvement that carries every potential to serve as an important catalyst towards systemically restructuring society in ways that dismantle structural inequities that negatively impact the neurodiverse especially hard and diminish opportunities, life prospects, and quality of life for many others as well. In essence, I propose a systemic transformation of culture and society. What I propose is a revision of the social contract and the formation of a new less competitive social order, one by which individuals are valued as much more than a mere means to an end but as an end in and of themselves. As such, I invite the progressively minded reader to think beyond the traditional disability centered social policy paradigms of civil rights, awareness, or income support. More broadly, and perhaps most critically, we must examine prospects for slowing down the current hyper-paced temporality that global capitalism has imposed on humanity. This is a discussion for which I do not profess to have all of the answers, but is one that I hope to

---

[5] The unconditional basic income is a proposed system that regularly provides each citizen with a sum of money. Other than citizenship, receipt of this basic income is unconditional. Because there is no means testing nor eligibility requirement, such a basic income could be more cost effectively distributed without agency of a large inefficient bureaucracy (e.g. SSA) ,and thus would also lack the built in "poverty traps" of means tested welfare, enabling disabled recipients to achieve varying levels of self sufficiency without penalty. Because these cash transfers could never be large enough to obviate earnings from paid work, such a system would be unlikely to promote idleness, with consequent threats to productivity.

contribute significantly to, as an author.

No longer shall it suffice to continue treating this social issue of neurodiversity, in accordance with the traditional individualistic and family centered approach that has been allowed to unsuccessfully prevail for far too long. Now, more than ever, America has reached a critical moment in history where social thinkers from the gamut of disciplines must examine critically the meaning of neurodiversity, in society. This is the starting point towards development and implementation of humane solutions to this potentially contentious issue; solutions that will more than merely improve economic prospects and life quality for neurodiverse adults, but enable society at large to benefit from the unique riches that we can potentially offer the world at large.

CHAPTER 1-A RANDOM DISCOVERY:

"Any situation in which some men prevent others from engaging in the process of inquiry is one of violence...to alienate humans from their own decision making is to change them into objects"
-Paulo Freire

On a chilly, crisp and dry late autumn Saturday afternoon, I sit in a local D&M coffee shop in Ellensburg, Washington, developing this manuscript and making plans for the upcoming week. My cell phone vibrates and I am prompted to check it. Upon doing so, I receive an excited text message from one of my comrades in the Tacoma Washington branch of the Socialist Alternative (SA) political organization. His message informs me of a small but telling victory of an SA candidate, Kshama Sawant, who won a seat in the Seattle city council, running as an open socialist. This improbable victory of a rogue political candidate holds great social significance in our time. For it is one exemplary manifestation of a new consciousness awakening across the nation, one incited by growing income inequality and uncertainty, which have recently become a household words. More than ever, Americans are growing to question the neoliberal free market fundamentalism, at the root of their declining living standards and working conditions.

Viewed through my eyes as a politically conscious neurodiverse person, the burgeoning anti-corporatist sentiment holds further significance. Sawant's victory occurred on the heels of the Occupy Movement for which the city of Seattle became a major hotbed. The Occupy movement was borne largely on the backs of those once comfortably middle class, now thrust into hitherto unknown despair, all too familiar among the neurodiverse. For the formerly middle class persons involved in the Occupy Movement, their new reality has been merely an inevitable consequence of an intensification of neoliberal policies. Didn't anyone hear that the canaries have stopped singing ages ago? So might Sawant's victory in Seattle signify that after over 30 years of unmitigated free market fundamentalism, the rest of the world is now starting to "get it"?

My political and social consciousness was fostered largely out of reflection upon the course my adult life has taken thus far, given the socio-political context I inherited. Like many neurodiverse adults, I have been relegated to a rather unconventional life. Despite many episodes of despair, I have always maintained an intellectual curiosity and a quest for dignity that has served as my driving force to keep me going despite all hardships.

Late adolescence was when I became aware that I likely have suffered from a lifelong organic learning disorder, suspecting either dyslexia, ADD, or some combination thereof as the culprit. As I later learned however, my actual condition is a different entity altogether with motor and perceptual impairments as primary features.

By late adolescence though, I knew that whatever my condition was, it will always impact success in established vocational niches, higher educational settings, and the general ability to interact with the world around me. Like many LD adults diagnosed late in life, I wondered if some early effective diagnosis and intervention would have made a positive difference in my latter adjustment. Yet no longer do I ponder on this matter. My involvement with clinicians, has only taught me how incompetent many such professionals are with regard to neurodiversity. Thus I now doubt that any early treatment could have mitigated my struggles as an adult. The true enemy is global capitalism and its structures and institutions.

At any rate, I entered adulthood as an alienated young man, disconnected from the external world. I was without context or normal acculturation. Moreover, I was laboring under a confused intrapersonal awareness, resulting in my highly problematic transition from adolescence to adulthood. Without such an understanding of one's natural proclivities, it is virtually impossible to formulate a sound life plan.

Discovering that I have a specific learning difficulty was one of two life changing discoveries that made a positive difference for me, despite grave social adjustment difficulties. The other such discovery for me was a completely happenstance introduction to the world of primitive technologies. These are essentially Stone Age skills and craft such as stone tool making (known as flintknapping), friction fires, the weaving of natural fiber cordage, shelter construction (i.e. huts, igloos, etc), and the manufacture and use of

26

ancient weapon systems like atlatls[6],throwing javelins, and archery equipment consisting of wooden bows with stone tipped arrows and sinew bow strings. These are essentially the very technologies which sustained all of humanity several millennia before the advent of the plow, the loom, the forge, and the potter's wheel.

My introduction to the world of primitive technologies was entirely random, materializing through one of my normal adolescent weekend visits to the Sea-Tac mall in Federal Way, Washington. Being an avid lifelong angler and shooting sports enthusiast, I browsed the sports section of Waldenbooks and stumbled across a text by Larry Dean Olson, entitled; Outdoor Survival Skills. The book promptly caught my attention as I was enraptured a few days prior, by a televised news broadcast about the discovery of a 5,400 year old frozen mummified corpse uncovered in the Austrian alps. It was the autumn of 1991 and this find made headlines across the globe.

The frozen mummy was later dubbed "the iceman" or Ötzi, after the

Ötztal Alps where his body had been recovered. Among the artifact finds described in the broadcast, were a small hafted bifacially flaked flint dagger, a copper axe hafted in a yew wood handle and several items of clothing, including a woven grass cape, and cured leather, deer and goat skin garments. As an outdoorsman, the news report naturally engendered curiosity on my part as to how entire cultures could sustain themselves largely through fishing and hunting. More specifically, how would they do so, with Stone Age technologies? While in the Waldenbooks browsing the pages of; Outdoor Survival Skills, the black and white photos and profuse illustrations of stone tools, thatched huts, snares, steps of hide

---

[6] An ancient hunting device predating the bow and arrow, that is used as an extension of the thrower's arm, to enable throwing a spear, with greater velocity and momentum than what is normally achievable with the naked arm alone. As part of a duo-component weapon system, the atlatl (or spear thrower) is simply nothing more than a length of solid material (i.e. wood, antler, bone) with a prong or cup affixed to the distal end and a grip enhancing aid (i.e. finger loops and or a knob) at the proximal end. Spears thrown with the aid of an atlatl are seated onto the prong or cup, and the thrower grasps the proximal end (or handle), and lobs the spear with a swift overhand motion, similar to throwing a baseball.

curing processes, saturated every fiber of my concentration, drawing me in like a vortex. I purchased the book without hesitation, and voraciously devoured all contents cover to cover that evening and the following day. I eagerly awaited the opportunity to fashion my first atlatl and dart set or primitive bow and arrow with which I would harvest a deer or perhaps an elk, just as my forefathers had done thousands of years ago.

By this time, I had developed a considerable level of upper body strength, despite being born with a baseline hypotonic muscular tension[7]. I thus felt confident in my physical ability to bring down any big game animal with a hand propelled dart. Hypotonia and muscular weakness are common among motor impaired persons. Hence, I learned early in life, the importance of exercising to stay fit. Physical fitness remains an important part of my life, to this day.

The hand of nature had dealt me an interesting "life puzzle" to solve, having a highly active temperament along with moderate to severe psychomotor impairments with sensory processing inefficiencies. The combined effects of both psycho-motor and sensory processing deficits had always negated my effective participation in many sports. This is especially so with activities involving any team effort. My inability to catch airborne objects, and to follow what others are doing and effectively co-ordinate my actions with theirs, rendered such sports forbidden territory for me. Thus, I long yearned for a truly recreational activity, demanding a degree of physical prowess, that involved no teamwork, physical contact with others, or intact equilibrium functioning. My choice of any such activity would have to be one in which and any difficulties resulting from impaired motor skills can be ironed out through repeated practice. A sport emphasizing marksmanship and distance throws with hand held projectiles seemed to be the perfect answer to this conundrum.

After having read Larry Dean Olson's book, I spent nearly every weekend canvassing beaches and small urban forests, field guide in hand, teaching myself how to identify useful native plants, trees,

---

[7] This is essentially flaccid baseline muscle tone (not low volume or diminished strength), as a potential manifestation of brain disorders that affect motor nerve control, or muscular strength. It is often manifest in conditions such as developmental dyspraxia, and sensory integration dysfunction, where impairments in the cerebral cortex impact both fine and gross motor development.

shrubs, and stones within Western Washington's south Puget Sound trough. Plant ID drills emphasized the identification of species with potential use as constructive materials. Before long, I learned that crabapple, madrona, and vine maple are reasonably good timbers from which to make archery bows, stinging nettle yields a fine, strong fiber which can readily be woven into twine and rope, and that many common basalts fracture with sharp enough edges to serve effectively for cutting tools, and projectile points. One of my first completed projects, made just months after reading Olson's book, was a full grooved hafted ground basalt axe. The hafting was made by wrapping a pliable willow sapling around the circumference of the groove and securing both halves of the sapling in the middle, with a leather thong. I even managed to chop down several small hardwood timbers with that axe. These timbers were usually hazel, vine maple, and crabapple saplings no larger than two inches diameter. The severed ends of the timbers betrayed an appearance more reminiscent of those tree limbs gnawed by beavers, than any cut with a manufactured cutting tool. But I was abundantly proud of that axe. After procuring about five or six miniscule timbers with it, the handle eventually broke and needed replacement. This was my first introduction to the nature of Stone Age technological systems. Months later, I attempted to make a small bow from one of the crabapple timbers harvested. However the bow broke during the manufacturing process, before an arrow could even be passed through it. I even managed to chip some basalt flakes into crude stemmed projectile points. The points I made, might pass as originals to a novice archaeologist, and might even inflict a lethal wound on a deer, if affixed to the end of an arrow shot from reasonably stout bow.

To supplement my often sporadic trial and error learning of primitive technologies, I read voraciously on the subject. I became a regular patron at both my high school campus library and the local Federal Way regional public library. I would typically check out and read books on native flora, fauna, rocks, and minerals. Books on Pacific Northwest ethnobotany and pre industrial technologies also became a preferred source of mental fodder. Reading was a considerable challenge at this stage of my life but was one that I was more than willing to deal with, for the sake of nourishing the germinating seed of a latent intellectual curiosity. Olson's book managed to spark something in me that the public schools never could.

After figuring out which natural resources in my geographic locale were useful for given purposes, I eventually, with persistent trial and error, taught myself multitudes of Stone Age technologies. My specialties were stone tool manufacture and the use of stone tools for various tasks, namely the working of wood, bone, and antler. This has been a lifelong pursuit, one which not only lead to my earning of an MA in experimental archeology but one that has held a variety of meanings for me throughout my life. It was this dedication to craft and the enrichment that follows, which has saved me from a life of "true despair'.

Toward the end of my junior year in high school I first became aware of various learning disabilities and realized that I most likely suffer from such a condition. As far back as I can remember, I always knew something was something different about me. Yet, I was virtually an adult before discovering any plausible explanations as to just what that "something" was. I remember the initial moment of recognition like it were yesterday.

While walking to school one morning, I ran into a friend of mine named Martin. Martin always hung out in the library as I did. To this day, I can't remember how we actually met, but somehow we did. Like myself, Martin also displayed a slow strained pattern of speech and awkward bodily postures. In fact, he basically spoke "just like I did". I always wanted to ask if he had any clinical history pertaining to his symptoms, but never knew how appropriate it would be to do so. Nonetheless, the issue came up in our conversation that one morning in which both crossed paths on our way to school. We began talking about our grades and school work, perhaps a frequent topic of conversation among high school students. Both of us were in a precarious situation in terms of our prospects for graduating on time. He expressed frustration over a letter sent home, from school, to his parents. The letter recommended his placement in an IEP (Individualized Education Program) or "special ed" English. He was failing the subject, even though he had been in mainstream English classes throughout high school. He did not want to go back to taking IEP English again. He then mentioned having a "learning disability" which caused some difficulties with retaining the content of reading material, despite having excellent comprehension abilities. Like me, he scored at college level reading comprehension during the 9th grade. Noting the commonality in both of our difficulties, I asked, "What do you mean by learning disability?" "I'm dyslexic," Martin replied. "I also have ADD, on top of it". "Damn, you know, I think I might have either one or both of those myself!"

30

"You mean you haven't been diagnosed yet?"asked Martin

"No but I can see what you're saying about reading difficulties, despite doing well on the placement tests"

"Dude, I'd get that checked out if I were you".

Our conversation continued and I asked the general question as to the symptoms of dyslexia. It was a term I had heard before but knew little about. He gave me an earful. The symptoms he described included classic word and letter reversal problems, confusion with directional orientation, etc. He began to describe his speaking and communication difficulties as an aspect of his condition. For the remainder of our walk to school, I simply let him monologue about all of his symptoms and difficulties. This was very informative and somewhat liberating for me.

By the time we got to campus, I tried to see if I could find a book on learning disabilities in the library. No such luck. There was only a limited amount of time to do so before the start of my first class. During my first three classes, I eagerly awaited the lunch hour, so I could search for more literature on this matter. My first three classes dragged on longer than normal and my focus was not on the classes. However this was nothing new for me. When the lunch hour arrived I went to the campus library to see what offerings they had on learning disabilities. After the conversation with Martin, that morning, I now had some keywords and subjects to use in my research. I asked the librarian for assistance and she pointed me in the right direction. I encountered a plethora of dated but useful literature-much of it dating back to the 1970s and 80s. One in particular, though I can't remember the title, described multiple symptoms of dyslexia I could relate to, including all of the characteristics Martin described. It all fit me to a T-the speaking and communication difficulties, word/letter reversals while reading, etc. This was like a Eureka moment for me, and very liberating at first. However, it later became a point of sadness and bitterness.

Immediately, I began to reflect and ponder upon occurrences throughout my childhood, and on things I was told by my parents regarding feedback from guidance counselors and teachers. While in the third grade, my mom disclosed to me that one of my first grade teachers thought I might be dyslexic. However, neither my mom nor dad agreed and they never bothered to follow through with investigating the matter any further. This was in spite of having been held back in the first grade, due to academic problems.

Grade school was marked by frequent occurrences of being called out of class by school psychiatrists to undergo exhaustive batteries of psychometric tests. I never understood why I had to take them. Nobody ever explained this to me. Such instances contributed greatly to the sense of confusion and alienation that plagued my childhood and adolescence. The testing sessions were always conducted in a wing of the school reserved for the education of pupils who were noticeably different. Floors and walls were draped with blue Naugahyde^tm tumbling mats. This was a safety precaution to prevent the children from injuring themselves, should they bump into a wall or fall down. There were pupils afflicted with cerebral palsy, ambulating in electric wheelchairs, barely able to speak or even move their limbs. There were kids my same age with a speech capacity commensurate with children not even old enough to attend public school. Many of these pupils regularly wore helmets, elbow, and knee pads to prevent accidental injuries. "I do not belong here", I always thought."Why am I here?" Why is this strange lady asking me to assemble these different puzzles, and walk across this balance beam?" I recall being summoned for sessions like this in the first grade, as well as the 4th and 6th grade respectively. At least these are the years for which I most vividly recall them. As I grew older, I felt increased shame, knowing that this is what was done with kids who were "different". In both the fourth and fifth grades, I was required to attend occupational therapy (or OT) sessions on a weekly basis. The OT regimen was an ineffectual attempt to remediate my identified motor deficits through a wide variety of specifically targeted exercises. But it did no good and only served as an unnecessary form of public humiliation. I was always so indiscreetly summoned from class to attend these sessions.

In the fourth or fifth grade my attitude became increasingly argumentative and I would more frequently challenge and question the occupational therapist. One in particular, Paul Hill, was a tall, lanky very modern and urbane looking young Caucasian man with wire rimmed glasses, who seemingly always wore Khaki trousers and pin-striped shirts. With his frequent and easy smile, and demonstrable humor, he betrayed a kind, infinitely patient temperament, which I attempted to exploit to my advantage. My hope was to at least get some answers to alleviate some of my confusion. Based on my Gestalt impression of his character, he seemed to be one who would tolerate my interrogations, more so than the actual staff or faculty members so commonplace in the conservative North Carolina public school system. While never indolent with Mr. Hill, I frequently spoke to him in a manner that I never dared to with any of the other more stern and harshly reactive authority figures at the elementary school I attended. I would constantly grill him by asking questions to the effect of; "what are these tests for?" "Why must I see you every week?" In response to my questions, he would only volunteer condescendingly simple and unsatisfactory answers. He would just make statements to the effect of "your body is not working right". Continually pressing him for more specific information only yielded more of the same evasive, non-specific answers that meant nothing. It was like trying to draw blood from a stone. Was he simply withholding further information, for reasons only he understood? His evasiveness further heightened my suspicions. I wanted a diagnosis and its full meaning and implications. Yet Mr. Hill's unwillingness or perhaps inability to convey this information only left me wondering if there was something so severely wrong with me that he withheld a diagnosis for fear that such knowledge could be psychologically damaging. Memories of these interactions contributed to my later apprehensions as a young adult, toward securing an official diagnosis. Even as a "self diagnosed" young adult, I still feared that a neuropsychological exam would reveal a condition much more frightening and severe than either dyslexia, ADD, or some combination thereof.

On one fairly recent weekend visit with my mom and dad, I was rummaging through school documents and projects that my mom had saved from my childhood. Among them were letters sent home following the testing sessions with various school psychologists. Most of these letters were dated to the early 1980s, when I was in the first grade. The tests were administered by a school psychologist with the sole intent of determining eligibility for the IEP (Individualized Education Program). None of these were conducted by a clinical psychologist with any authority to render a legal diagnosis. Though no actual diagnosis resulted from these sessions, numerous comments alluded to a specific learning difficulty, featuring psychomotor and sensory integration dysfunction. The reports also endorsed the embryonic formation of major social functioning difficulties. Some of the comments were as follows:

33

"Severe disorder of vestibular and tactile systems, poor ocular-motor control"

"distractibility".

"Excellent imagination"

"Does not initiate play with classmates"

"Individual testing by teacher shows [performance] much better on individual than group functioning."

There were two major outcomes of these tests. One of which was being required to take IEP math classes, from the first grade until my freshman year of high school. The second outcome was being relegated to undergo occupational therapy during my 1st, 4th, and 5th grade years. Other than that, I was deemed to be entirely competent for mainstream placement in other classes.

But why did my parents opt to sweep it all under the rug, refusing to give this matter the attention it deserved? Did they not understand the contents of the letters sent home? Were they ashamed to acknowledge my special needs? Or were they only interested in their immediate ease and convenience? Perhaps it was a combination of all three factors. Though nothing can be done about it now, these are still questions that still sometimes haunt me to this day.

When that initial moment of discovery occurred at the age of 17, I could connect all of the dots from my past-repeating the first grade, frequent calls home from teachers and guidance counselors regarding both academic difficulties and conduct problems, being summoned from class to take myriads of psycho-educational tests, OT during the first, fourth, and fifth grades. It all added up and made sense. Yes, I do in fact likely suffer from a specific learning difficulty. It was a tremendous relief to have arrived at the most plausible explanation for all of my past difficulties, and present struggles. Moreover, this random moment of self-recognition could not have occurred at a more auspicious time. It was the second semester of my junior year in high school, and I was mired in a mess of scholastic failure, barely passing most of my classes, flunking the rest. By this point, I was beside myself, trying to figure out how to most expediently undo all damage to my academic track record. Repeating another year of high school was the last thing I wanted to do. During my previous two years of high school, I would cut classes, refuse to turn in assignments, and engage in frequent social conflicts. These behaviors all stemmed from the confusion, frustration, alienation, and insecurity I felt from knowing I was different but never understanding why. Moreover, at the heart of it all was an underlying sense of inadequacy, stemming from my inability to keep up academically. Being a chronic troublemaker seemed the only way that I could ever be taken seriously. Sometimes it seems much cheaper and easier to gain recognition for negative behaviors than positive ones.

Stumbling across some basic knowledge of learning disabilities also proved a major godsend for another reason. In late adolescence my speaking difficulties seemed to have reached an utmost severity and I did not understand why.

From the age of 15 to around 19 or 20 my lexical access[8] was very impaired, resulting in a very slow and labored rate of speech. After about the age of 21, the problem began to steadily improve. Yet in mid to late adolescence, I remained in total bewilderment as to the cause of this particular symptom, and was frantically desperate for answers. Scouring through any medical textbook I could get my hands on, yielded no satisfactory explanations. This was before the days of widespread internet use, so I couldn't just type in some choice keywords on Google, hit "search" and find useful information. When I would ask my parents about it, suggesting that I should see a professional, they would always respond in their usual, evasive manner with statements such as "there's nothing wrong with the way you talk". Did they really think I was so stupid as to not detect such

---

[8] Lexical access in speech generation refers to the ability to select, from a mental lexicon (mental vocabulary database or "dictionary") of available words. This occurs after the first stage of speech generation, known as conceptual preparation, and involves a "competition phase" of selecting between closely related lexical alternatives. For most persons speaking their customary language, this process occurs with little conscious effort. However, an number of organic brain differences can significantly impede this process, including dyslexia, aphasia, or deficits in concentration or memory. Lexical, from the Greek root; *Lexis*, meaning "language".

transparent efforts at dodging their responsibility towards any genuine involvement, in this matter, thinly veiled as an attempt to improve my self esteem?

When speaking, I knew what I needed to say, but words would not flow. It was as though the words were buried deep down in some "mental basement", stored in a box with no particular order, leaving me to climb down into the basement and dig out the correct word(s) and put them in the correct order. But often I couldn't even find the right crate and would have to search among several. As far back as I can remember many of my peers would point out such peculiarities in my speech patterns-sometimes just out of curiosity, other times out of sheer malice. Either way, it hurt just the same. Curiously enough, from mid adolescence to early adulthood, it seemed as though my speech anomalies trans-mutated into an especially perplexing and troublesome form of impeded lexical access. Prior to about the age of 14, my speech had always been described as slow and monotonic but still well connected and fluid enough. Even today, my speech is often described in this manner.

After the age of 21, I became a frequent reader, developing many scholarly interests, and subsequently improvements in my verbal fluency followed. I believe that more frequent mental processing of the printed word may have improved my lexical access somehow. Today, however, I experience residual problems with tangentiality and impaired organization of verbal thought content. The analogy I use today is one where the words/ideas are randomly scattered about before me, and it's my job to assemble them in a way that makes sense. At times I have been accused of speaking in lengthy monologues, which is a big no-no in our short attention span, front and left brain oriented culture. I believe that my tendency towards monologue could also simply be the result of a more concrete and holistic thought process, making it difficult to identify "key ideas" that need to be expressed. When combined with an impaired capacity to effectively organize thought content to the concise point by point sequence, it becomes very difficult to express one's thoughts concisely and economically.

Upon becoming aware of various learning disabilities, I constantly craved more and more knowledge on the subject. Months would pass before another significant random moment of discovery would occur, shedding more light on my condition. In the summer of 1992, following my junior year of high school, we had moved to the town of

Auburn, Washington approximately 15 miles SE. of Federal Way. Federal Way was where we had been living during the past six years, after having moved to Washington State from North Carolina in August of 1986. After, fully transferring all of our belongings to our new Auburn residence, I was shelving boxes of books in the living room, and found one of my dad's books, entitled; *The Cambridge Encyclopedia of Language* (1987). With my summer school English class having just been successfully completed, I had some extra time on my hands, to browse through the book. In it, I came across chapters on American Indian and Australian aboriginal languages that appealed to me. I summarily read both chapters, and rummaged the book's contents further. Fortuitously, I found a chapter on language handicap in the book. Needless to say, I was compelled to read the chapter, hoping to glean more info on my lifelong speech difficulties. The chapter described dyslexia in some detail, including some notable characteristics not commonly associated with the condition by most clinicians today. Part of the descriptive criteria listed in the chapter included the symptoms of slow and labored speech, motor clumsiness, impaired short term memory and, general visual perceptual impairments. With those later non-psycholinguistic features listed among the descriptive criteria of dyslexia, I was sure that this had to be my problem. The book was published in 1987 and the diagnostic criteria for dyslexia, and other learning difficulties has changed a lot since then. Dyslexia is now considered strictly a psycholinguistic learning disorder, with other once associated features now falling under rubrics of separate, more recently recognized organic mental disorders.

From that point on, I found myself in an ongoing process of frequently checking out library books on various learning disabilities in an effort to acquire as much knowledge as possible to better understand my condition and what I was going through. Exemplary titles that I often read included; *Smart but Feeling Dumb* (1985), by Dr. Harold Levinson, *Total Concentration* (1990), by Dr. Harold Levinson, and *You Mean I'm Not Lazy, Stupid, or Crazy* (1993), by Kate Kelley and Peggy Ramundo. Most of my readings only focused on the more widely known conditions of ADD or dyslexia. However, many of my symptoms, most notably the motor clumsiness, perceptual impairment, and sensory sensitivities did not seem adequately accounted for by the commonly known criteria of either dyslexia or AD/HD.

Moving from Federal Way to Auburn prior to my senior year proved highly beneficial with regard to the change in school systems. At Auburn high school, students had the opportunity to take both "O period" and 7th period classes. For various reasons students took these classes to abbreviate their high school career. Many were Running Start students, motivated by a desire to quickly get on with high school to begin their college career. Others like myself, needed the opportunity to make amends for egregious wrongdoings in their academic history. In addition to "O and 7th period classes", there was a credit generating study skills class, as opposed to no credit study hall sessions. In the study skills class students were intended to use it as an opportunity to work on homework and to develop effective study skills and time management tactics. I took full advantage of the study skills classes, making my homework load (from eight classes) far more manageable. My new understanding of my condition and its symptoms also afforded a newfound resolve and work ethic to push forward with utmost effort towards repairing my academic track record. The attitude of the faculty and staff of AHS seemed much more personable and helpful too. I could readily approach them with questions as to how to best improve my odds for success in the class. I even came to know many of my teachers on a personal level. This never occurred at the previous high school I attended.

My two favorite instructors were Mr. Stanley and Mrs. Randall. Mr. Stanley was a long time science teacher, who had taught at Auburn High School since 1970. He and I connected because coincidently he, at middle age, was going through a similar predicament I was, with recent self recognition of suspected undiagnosed LD. He was 52 at the time and speculated, based on news reports and reflective observation that he was suffering from adult attention deficit disorder. Students and colleagues dubbed him "the absent-minded professor", due to his distractibility and chronic forgetfulness. Short-term memory lapses were especially frequent for him. For example, after taking role, he might have to spend some time to "jar his memory" of the day's lesson plan. I still recall one occasion where he started lecturing the prior day's lesson material for the first five or so minutes of class before a student asked him if that was the same material from yesterday.

During the first semester, he announced in class that he read a magazine article about ADD which described numerous symptoms he could positively identify in himself, and that this may very well explain his oft noted lapses in short-term memory. Impaired short-term memory was certainly a problem I was able to relate to. Yet for me, this became less problematic with age. On the day of his announcement, Mr. Stanley and I conversed at the end of class about what each of us was going through. He wasn't at all distraught about his situation. At least this was not indicated in his demeanor. He was 52, had established a rewarding career, enjoyed a successful happy marriage, and betrayed no hint of actual suffering. He was even debating as to whether or not medical intervention was necessary, for him, expressing concern that such treatment might eliminate his trademark quirk of absent mindedness which he became so fondly noted for.

Mrs. Randall was my study skills teacher. To this day, I still remember her infinite willingness to go the extra mile to help students. I informed her of the situation and she was instrumental in directing me to the resources I needed to get back on track. To this day, I credit her support and encouragement to enabling me to pull through my predicament. She had the perfect solution to every problem. In progress reports, she always wrote such glowing remarks about my academic performance and integrity of character - an experience hitherto unknown to me.

I proceeded through my final year of high school with a newfound resolve, a more positive attitude, and the support of helpful and dedicated teachers. I managed to earn 3.5 overall GPA during both semesters of my senior year. I had not seen a GPA so high since the eighth grade. This was the first time in all of my public school years that I didn't completely dread school. By this point, I felt obligated to at least put forth the effort make my final year of public school the best year. By June of that year, I was still short a half credit of US history. I thus arranged to remedy the problem by taking a summer quarter 5 credit history class at Green River Community College, in Auburn, Washington. The last thing I wanted was to repeat an entire semester. How humiliating this would be; attending a public high school campus at 19 and 20 years of age. Had it not been for taking a summer school English class and taking extracurricular "0" period classes during my senior year, this may have been the only option. My entire senior year of high school was largely a matter of playing "catch up".

After having saved sufficient funds from my allowance, I was able to pay tuition for the remedial history class at GRCC. For some inexplicable reason, I found this class much more engaging than other academic classes I had taken. Perhaps a seed of erudition, planted by Larry Dean Olson's book, beginning to germinate. Yet, I was battling two contradictory impulses-one to satisfy an incipient intellectual curiosity, the other to resort to somewhat anti-intellectual attitudes, manifest as technophobia and the shunning of rationality, and worldly, scholarly pursuits. These were domains which had always disenfranchised me. Paradoxically my former impulse had arisen from a need to justify the latter impulse. I would knapp stone tools, read and watch documentaries about postcolonial indigenous cultures, idealizing their life-ways as being the most noble and ideal state for humanity. I once romantically envisioned such cultures as living in a virtual Garden of Eden where all live cooperatively among themselves in total harmony with nature. If only I were a Yanomami in South America, I wouldn't have to learn how to drive a car, or use a computer, and there would be no need to read, write, or do complex mathematical calculations. My neurodiversity would be no object, living in such a society. I could spend my days hunting, fishing, making tools and implements, playing games, and performing rituals with other villagers. Survival would not depend on devoting tireless hours to an incessantly demanding, degrading and dehumanizing job. Moreover, it is a mode of living that is less taxing of the earth and less degrading of human dignity. That was my thought. However, I have long since learned that it is not wise to make value judgments, either positive or negative about any cultural practices different from one's own. Cultures, of all sorts, simply adapt to their circumstances and environment to the best that their resources will allow. But at an unconscious level, my philosophical retreat to technophobia and anarcho-primitivist thought was merely a means of validating myself as a person whose learning disabilities militate against technical competence.

While I found the GRCC class to be more engaging than I normally found academic classes, the desire to fulfill my high school graduation was still by far, a prime motivator to take a serious interest in the class. While I thoroughly enjoyed the class, writing essays and studying for tests was extremely taxing. Also, I did have a good rapport with the instructor which meant a lot to me. The instructor, Mr. Gundersen was very postmodern, liberal, and approachable. His character completely contradicted my long held, pre-conceived notion of the typical college instructor persona. He was a far cry from the high school teachers I dealt with in the Federal Way school district. Mr. Gundersen was a tall, lanky, 2nd generation Norwegian American, who passionately embraced his

40

old country heritage. At the time he taught the class, he had spent time in Norway and had done historical and sociological research related to Scandinavian culture and society.

He would often teach the class wearing very casual attire, sporting a day or two of beard growth. Classmates would remark behind his back as to how unusual his attire seemed for someone in his profession. I never recall him brusquely haranguing students for discussion input that may have been only obliquely relevant or unsatisfactory. He had a knack for effectively integrating all students input in some way or another.

At the time, post secondary school was the last option I considered for my future. However, I remember thinking that if I were to pursue a college degree, I should hope that all of my teachers would be like Mr. Gundersen. Yet any time I even considered pursuing a college degree, I would immediately tell myself to "perish the thought". Such an endeavor would only be a fruitless one, ridden with academic failure, scorn and ridicule from haughty, arrogant instructors, marked by virtually indelible emotional scarring. I would never be so fortunate as to have an instructor like Mr. Gundersen. I harbored much residual mistrust towards educators, resulting from my public school years in childhood and adolescence.

The level of effort required for me to succeed in that one class further convinced me that college would not be worthwhile. Just taking that single 5 credit class, necessitated an effort above and beyond holding a full-time job. At that point, I hadn't even developed the study skills that I acquired while pursuing a post secondary degree, seven years later. During late adolescence, my attentional deficits were such that even reading an entire Field & Stream magazine article in one setting this was a major feat of concentration. Then to describe the articles contents, beyond a few trivial facts, obliquely related to the main thesis, this was a major feat of memory and comprehension. I also dealt with the technological limitation of lacking access to electronic word processing technologies. In the early 1990s home PCs were growing in popularity, but certainly not as widespread as today. There were no such devices in my home. I also knew of no campus computer lab, I could go to. I did not even know how to use a computer anyways. My mom and dad had a Panasonic electronic typewriter but I could never learn to properly type. Hunt/peck typing my way through an essay, would involve frequent corrections of typographical errors and misspellings, using those crappy whiteout ribbons, which may/may not work properly. The other option was messy whiteout ink. Not only is it messy but it necessitates rolling the page up to make the correction, waiting for the fluid to dry, then rolling the page back to position, trying to resume perfect alignment. Mr. Gundersen was very understanding of my predicament and willingly allowed me to pen-write the final essay, provided that my handwriting is legible. Though penmanship has always been slightly problematic, legible handwriting is generally not such a tall of an order to fulfill.

Proceeding through the class was something of an ambiguous experience. I was very out of step with the world around me and any exposure to social situations only reminded me of this. Yet I accepted it. Most of my classmates had aspirations of furthering post secondary education, many of whom were already quite accomplished both academically and professionally. Some were older students pursuing a second degree, to make a career shift. To me, they all seemingly spoke another language. They would converse about their academic studies, their computers, their careers, trends in pop culture, and it was all completely unintelligible to me. My life focus was very constrained. I never felt any overt scorn or hostility from my classmates as was often the case in junior high and high school. It was just simply a case where I couldn't gel with them, as I was practically from another world.

On the first day of class, Mr. Gundersen began by taking role, allowing each of the students to introduce themselves, stating their name and purpose for being there. When it came to my turn, I specified my reason for taking the class then added a comical remark, stating that they don't award academic credit in high school for ditching school to go fishing. Such a remark seemed consistent with the stereotypical nonchalant, if somewhat underachieving adolescent. In this way, I hoped to "conceal' the dysfunction behind my situation.   My remark drew numerous chuckles from fellow classmates. Moreover, I knew that their laughter was attributable to the remark and not the speaker. This seemingly insignificant occurrence held a personal significance that few would understand. For, it was an instance of interactive spoken communication, of a kind that had been hitherto alien to me. I made a remark with a humorous intent and others, responded accordingly. All too often, my customary experience, in spoken communication, had been such that I might say something and get no response from the party of whom I was speaking with. Either they did not understand, or the contents of my speech were not particularly meaningful to them. Likewise, verbal input from others would usually elicit similar responses on my part; I either didn't understand, wasn't interested, or a combination of both factors. This was a frequent reality for me. This is why any brief occurrence of truly interactive spoken communication felt like something of a breakthrough. Most people think little of occurrences such as these. They surely would feel satisfied that their intentionally humorous remark served its purpose, eliciting laughter from others. However, most people don't feel as though some major breakthrough had been achieved, just in being able to connect with others.

As the class proceeded, I seldom interacted with anybody and worked diligently to sustain high academic performance in the class. I was unemployed and only enrolled in that three credit history class. This left me free to work at my own pace and in my own unusual way. The college campus was an alien province to me, and I had no concept of available academic resources and how to utilize them. It never even occurred to me that the campus might have library that could be used in a similar way as any public school library, or municipal public library. I would come home from class, and attempt to read material from the textbook in my bedroom. The problem: I would easily get distracted by the TV or radio. The solution: do my reading/writing in the garage. It was weird but it worked. The lighting inside our garage was grossly inadequate for reading, so I often left the garage door open. All while reclining on a dingy mustard yellow 1970s sofa, surrounded by a lawn mower, a weight bench, a weed eater, and dusty oil saturated fir-wood shelves containing hand held power tools, old coffee cans filled with various hardware and fasteners, and an 18 cubic ft. deep freezer. Our neighbors must have thought I was one strange character just sitting there in the garage, doing something so completely out of context, given the setting, but it worked for me. There were three days of the week, which class didn't meet. Such days typically saw me planted on the banks of the nearby Green River, from dusk to dawn, with textbooks in my backpack and fishing tackle in hand. I would sit for hours on my favorite large granite boulder reading and writing for class during the better part of the day, my concentration aided by the monotonic rambling of the river. At dusk, my books, pencil and paper were retired to my daypack, my rod and reel summoned to duty, and 2-3 hours of fishing would conclude my study session at dawn. Typically, I would catch rainbow trout and once even caught a prize steelhead that summer.

There were about three tests in class and a final essay. Mr. Gundersen was always keen on informing the students, days in advance as to which topics to focus upon, in relation to studying for tests. I found this aspect of his teaching approach very helpful. Despite always staying abreast of readings, I seldom contributed to class discussions and Mr. Gundersen seemed okay with this. Aside from reading to obtain rote knowledge to pass exams, I really was not moved or impacted by the readings in a way that would enable me to discuss the subject matters in depth. Mr. Gundersen may have been aware of this so he really didn't hold me, accountable to any real class participation. Or perhaps class participation simply wasn't part of any grading criteria. At any rate, class discussions always reminded me that I was out of my league academically, so I it was best to keep my mouth shut, rather than risk making a fool of myself. Just passing all tests and assignments with high marks was good enough for me.

The campus was located approximately 3 miles from our house and I walked there every day as I walked just about everywhere I needed to go. I couldn't, and still don't drive, and did not know how to use the city bus service. Dysfunctions in equilibrium, sensory integration and depth perception, also preclude the use of any conventional upright (non-recumbent) bicycle. I didn't fully understand that these were the exact causes of my inability to ride conventional bicycles. I just sensed that it would not be a very safe transportation option for me. Besides, walking gave me a chance to ruminate and sort things out in my head while traveling to various destinations. It was somewhat therapeutic for me. This was a time in my life where I really had so much to sort out.

While walking to campus one morning, I was simultaneously scanning the roadside for knappable stones, stinging nettles (for cordage), or other natural materials from which to fashion Stone Age implements. I always built time in my morning walk to campus to allow for material procurement. My scanning and browsing were interrupted by the presence of an early 1980s black Toyota pickup truck which slowed down alongside me as I was walking. I turned toward the vehicle to see if the driver needed help with anything, perhaps to ask for directions. Driving the vehicle was a comely older woman, perhaps in her early 30s, with long brown hair, a slender build, and a gracious smile. She stopped by and offered me a ride."

44

Wow, she's hot and I really wouldn't mind talking to her", I thought. I paused for a second, debating as to whether to take her up on her offer." No thank you", I politely said to her." Oh damn, why did I do that?" I pondered as she drove away. I knew why, but still regretted the decision. I had dire social anxiety over the most innocuous situations. If I saw no practical need to communicate with others, I never would, unless I felt reasonably assured that we could immediately establish a positive rapport. This was particularly so with women of whom I would have wanted to make a favorable impression with. If a total stranger offered me a ride, I never accepted, even if it seemed perfectly safe to do so. I had no way of knowing how the person might react to some of my differences, such as my odd speech pattern or even if there may be some risk of the person harming me are making an attempt thereof. At any rate, I walked to campus that morning proceeding through class as normal.

The opportunity eventually came for the class to hold a discussion in which I would become one of the most active and perhaps somewhat dazzling participants. My participation was surely a far cry from my normal lack of participation in the class. I completely bewildering and amused the class with my input. During about the third or fourth week of the quarter, Mr. Gundersen scheduled a discussion in which we were to debate the best solution(s) to pressing global issues discussed in class (e.g. environmental degradation, large-scale warfare, etc.). My take on the matter was that those problems are inherent to large-scale industrial and postindustrial societies and that it is simply best that humans subsist as small-scale egalitarian hunter gatherer bands. I opined that this was the most healthy and natural way for humans to live, with less competition for resources, social stratification, and interpersonal strife. Furthermore, the low pressure on natural resources translates to less environmental degradation and because there is no monetary currency there is no opportunity for inflation and corruption. I then argued that our current level of culture was unsustainable, that civilization would collapse and that we would be rendered back to the level of Stone Age hunter gatherers. Such consequences would be part of a natural system of checks and balances for keeping us in our proper place. Needless to say nobody actually agreed with the entirety of my arguments. However many people found my speech highly amusing and many even considered that I had mentioned some worthwhile ideas to ponder. I even managed to have the last word, when debating another student on the matter. Yet, I got the last word, not through

45

employing actual logic and reason, it was simply a matter of me conjuring up something to say in response to all of her statements. However, my counter arguments did not actually address the points of her arguments. The speech I gave in this class was essentially the same philosophizing I did on a regular basis, regarding my view of technology. Thus it was only natural for me to get up there and speak on the matter, in the way that I did. It became one of my favored topics and this was why I made such a special effort at "wedging it in" to our discussion as best I could.

Mr. Gundersen might have been aware of the fact that I had some special issues and tended to be very accommodating to the manner in which I proceeded through his class. Having no clinical diagnosis, I never officially disclosed my disability, to request formal academic adjustments. I did not even realize that college campuses would provide such accommodations for learning disorders.

After our classroom debate, I had an opportunity to converse with Mr. Gundersen and few students, regarding my interest in primitive technologies. Although considered somewhat outlandish in my world view, those who came to know me, tended to regard me as an interesting person and a serious discussion partner. It was the first time I had ever known what it was like to be taken seriously in that way. As the class proceeded, I continued to plod forward, working steadily, though inefficiently, and studying religiously for each test. Eventually time for the final exam and final essay came and I passed both with flying colors. On both my term paper and final exam, the instructor had written a number of very positive remarks, including; *"Excellent essay. You have strong convictions and an eloquent way of expressing them"*, and *"Well conceived paper. A personal perspective as well. You put out a good argument and support it well* through *using NA [Native American] lifestyle comparisons for modern ways"*.

Receiving positive feedback on the basis of demonstrated academic merit was still something of a rare occurrence for me. This was precisely why it was always quite exhilarating when it happened. Still, I did not foresee myself furthering my education any time soon. But Mr. Gundersen felt I had strong academic potential. At the end of the quarter, I called him on his home phone to ask where I could collect my graded final exam and essay. He told me where to collect these and preemptively informed me that I had earned an A on both assignments. This was a tremendous relief. We then had something of a brief philosophical discussion on technology in general and it's effect, positive or negative on human culture. We even talked about whether or not humans were becoming more like machines or vice versa. I would only realize years later as a graduate student, what a sophisticated discussion this was. He then asked me what I planned on doing now that my high school graduation was final. I described to him my life plan of dropping out of society to live as a retreatist, making money by selling stone tool replicas as a handicraft. To which he responded' "well don't forget to further your schooling, you're a very promising student". I felt proud that he so seriously believed in my academic potential. Yet it would be another seven years before I would actually follow his advice.

I passed the class with a solid, well earned A, so it was now time for me to collect my high school diploma. Shortly after the final day of class I marched about 4 miles on a balmy late summer afternoon to the Auburn Sr. High campus, entering the records office, with sweat saturation forming a triangular pattern from the neckline of my snug, form fitting fishing T-shirt. My long, wavy wind-blown chestnut colored locks tangled in every which direction. Upon my entry into the office, I was greeted by the registrar, a short stout gray-haired bespectacled matron, who enquired "How may I help you, son?" "I'm here to pick up my high school diploma, my name is Allan White" I responded, handing her my progress report from Green River Community College. She collected the progress report to be filed away. The registrar then reached into a charcoal gray aluminum filing cabinet, from which she rendered a forest green, metallic gold embossed vinyl wallet, encasing my diploma. "Congratulations" she said, while transferring the sacred bound parchment to my ownership. I gazed at it long and hard, clasping it in my sweaty hands, visually fixating on my name "Allan Lee White" inscribed in black Old English lettering on bone white paper, with the date reading "June 13, nineteen-thousand, nine hundred and ninety three". While gazing upon the diploma, I reflected on all the blood, sweat, and tears that culminated to its very existence. I worked ever so feverishly just to prevent it from reading "June 13, one thousand, nine hundred and ninety-four". The days of awakening at 4 O'clock each morning, hours upon hours spent in the school library, homework occupying my weekends, and two summer vacations sacrificed, all to squeeze in as much extra credit as humanly possible within a year's time; it all finally paid off. It's as though I fully undid the academic damage incurred from dithering around in a fog for the vast majority of my high school years. With the burden of

47

high school graduation off my back, I had yet another challenge to overcome; finding my niche as an adult.

••••

My introduction to the craft of primitive technologies was an auspicious life event for me. It was particularly auspicious given that it concurrently materialized with discovering my disability. In my dedication to this craft, I created a space of intellectual and academic inquiry, where my learning and enrichment could thrive. From the initial seed, planted by reading Larry Dean Olsen's *Outdoor Survival Skills*, I developed not only a dedication to craft but an intellectual curiosity on many subjects relevant to the human condition, as they relate to early technological adaptations. The intellectual inquiry resulting from the craft of primitive technologies is still very much a part of my life today. My learning still continues to develop from this initial seed planted years ago.

But the awakening of this dormant intellectual curiosity was more than a case of finding subject matter(s) I could take interest in. Essentially, I found a space for inquiry absent of the marginalizing structures and symbolic violence which had always marked my experience, within formal learning institutions. These were the very power structures relegated and solidified my status as a substandard learner. Consequently, much of my public school years were spent alienated from intellectual inquiry, aspiring only for minimal performance standards, required to pass on to the next grade level.

Merely months after my introduction to primitive technologies and prehistory, my intellectual transition was such that I could easily hold conversations with professional academics. Bruce Gundersen, my community college instructor opined that I showed promise as a post-secondary student. As I reflect upon my personal transformation, I cannot help but wonder as to what effect symbolic violence in traditional academia has toward further entrenching the "learning difficulties" and marginalization of labeled youth. Moreover, how does this process of marginalization impact our development into adulthood? Perhaps this could be a subject of inquiry in the field of disability studies.

So how do we formally institutionalize an inclusive and libratory educational system that promotes the best in all learners, despite

48

individual differences in natural ability? This could be the topic of another book. It could also be an important project to grapple with for the 21st century.

In Neurodiversity, Dr. Thomas Armstrong describes innovative programs around the country which largely avoid the negative aspects of both regular and special education and incorporate rich learning experiences for both labeled and non-labeled kids in a single classroom. For example, Dr. Armstrong describes Patrick O' Hearn Elementary School in Dorchester Massachusetts, which practices full inclusion of its special education students which constitute about 25% of the student body. This school emphasizes strengths and staff are trained to encourage each child to shine. There is no segregation, based on ability and students of all levels of ability learn in the same classroom. Each student is encouraged to achieve to their utmost potential at their own pace. Communitarian benchmarks are rejected. Unlike traditional educational assessment which is *normative*, thus comparing a learner to groups of students who took standardized tests sometime in the past, assessment in a neurodiverse classroom is based on *ipsative* progress which is based on a child's own past performance. The goal is for students to continually enhance themselves as part of an open-ended development process. This model of education promotes a more inclusive way of thinking, which is a critical component to developing a more inclusive society.

Research also suggests that students who learn in more inclusive classrooms construct a more positive image of themselves, compared with students who learn in "segregated" classrooms. And in many cases, it is the non-labled students who benefit greatly from the experience. For example, the autistic daughter of anthropologist Roy Richard Grinker was fully included in the Smithsonian Early Enrichment Center, which uses experientially rich collections of the Smithsonian Museum Complex to build a diverse curriculum. According to her teachers, Sharen Shaffer and Jill Mankowitz, Jill's presence in the program was a positive influence on the other students. Both educators noted that Isabel made the other children less selfish. When Isabel was absent, from the school, the other students seemed different.

"They were more competitive with each other, they snapped at each other. They didn't fall apart but it was like they lost

49

their center. Then when Isabel came back to the classroom, they got back to normal".

The scenario described by Isabel's teachers is a perfect example of how inclusion, when practiced in the truest sense of the word, benefits not only the differently abled learner, but other students as well. Moreover, it is a perfect example of how such inclusion, which enables all to express their own individuality, can create an environment where the neurodiverse are not a problem to be dealt with, but an asset to their community, *because of*, not *despite* their uniqueness. As a crucial aspect of creating a neurodiverse friendly society, the question remains, how do we make inclusive neurodiverse friendly classrooms, like those described above, mainstream rather than alternative? How do we formally institutionalize them as such, so that they are the norm and thus available to learners coming from all socio-economic backgrounds? Questions such as this should be a critical aspect to the larger discussion of creating an inclusive, neurodiverse friendly culture and society. Such could be the topic of a new book entirely. Yet no discussion of neurodiversity in society would be complete without asking not just how to reform special education, but the very institution of education, as it presently stands.

CHAPTER 2-CRAFTING A NEW REALITY:

"The plight of the outcast may soon stretch to embrace a whole generation"

-Zygmut Bauman

It's now late summer 1993. At 19, I am officially an adult, freed from the throes of America's notoriously inept public school system. By convention, this is the time to make ones way in the world. For me, however, reality could not have been a starker contradiction. I didn't stand a chance. The neoliberal social Darwinian world inherited first by my generation could not be a worse place to come of age as a young, recently self – recognized, and imbalanced neurodiverse adult.

It took years for the full concientization of the concrete circumstances behind oppression to occur. However, I knew even during my nascent late teenage stage of adulthood, that the national economy and mainstream of society held no place for me. I sensed this tacitly but nonetheless all too powerfully. Like a canary entering a coalmine, I first detected society's toxicity while in high school, hearing my classmates' second hand accounts of acerbic workplace abuse on their first jobs. More disturbing was the prevailing attitude that this was all part and parcel to doing business – an opprobrium one should just accept. Having already been dealt too many harsh wounds of disrespect and marginalization, from the time of entering school, I knew the morally bankrupt neoliberal world was no place for me at all. Thus, I felt the best course of action was a retreat from the world which denied me a valorized social niche before I was even born.

Anesthetized to a painful reality by the powerful opiate of imagination, I concocted what seemed an infallible blueprint for a retreat from society. It was a life plan conceived of since my senior year of high school. One whereby I would utilize my then still rudimentary skills in primitive technologies to develop my own cottage industry, making and selling replicas and reproductions of ancient stone implements. Through these efforts, I firmly believed it

51

possible to earn enough to save sufficient funds to purchase rural property and live inexpensively off the grid in a remote location. Though perceptuo-motor deficits impeded my ability to master flintknapping to an artistic level, I was convinced that with practice, I could soon develop sufficient mastery of stone tool making to develop such a business. Today, I can produce a fairly wide range of different stone implements with relative ease. However, this was certainly not the case then. For I had only 18 months of semi-regular flintknapping practice to account for. No flintknapper can produce very spectacular work with only that level of practice.

I never imagined becoming wealthy from this endeavor. However, I felt that surely I could easily save money while living with my parents to purchase cheap rural property and other material resources to drop out and live off the grid. With all necessary resources in order, I could live a fairly insular and self sustaining manner, away from the rest of the world. I began to read as much as I could about off the grid sources of electricity and running water. I was also gathering information on vegetable gardening, and raising livestock. Additionally, many remote locations will be close to sources of wild game, fish, and edible plants. With no rent, utility bills, and minimal grocery expenses, it should be feasible to live comfortably on a modest income. In essence I wanted to create my own reality by replicating a preindustrial existence in the midst of the postindustrial era. Moreover, I sincerely believed it possible to enjoy what I perceived to be the merits of living in the preindustrial era. Developing my own cottage industry seemed to be a portal to a leading a simple, slow-paced, low stress life. Moreover, such a life would afford me the freedom to choose my interpersonal involvements. In this way, it becomes possible to minimize contact with toxic trolls who make me feel inadequate.

With no other life options in store, I just had to make this work. It seemed the perfect plan though a part of me knew it wasn't realistic. Yet whenever reality beckoned, my imagination would take me to an illusion of my future. This was the mirage of my future life; inhabiting an idyllic setting, making tools and implements in a backyard workshop. Occasionally, I might travel to town to sell my works at a public marketplace, or to purchase a few supplies for the homestead. From these excursions, I would return to a modest rustic abode to pull weeds in my garden, feed livestock, and enjoy venison stew that had been cooking in a Dutch oven all day. There are no rents, nor utility bills to pay, and my taxes are so simple and minimal as to be easily calculated and paid with no emotional or financial hardship.

What a sharp contrast to the mainstream of society and the normal working world. Day in and day out one slogs through bumper-to-bumper traffic, street signs and lights dictating your next move. Your work place is a shark tank, where you must constantly watch your back professionally, worried that one slight *faux pas* could completely jeopardize your career. Then to top it off, there is the ever present stress of how you are going to pay exorbitantly priced rent, or mortgage, utilities, and taxes which are disproportionally high in relation to your income. All the while, you are bombarded by constant noise and chaos, incessantly worried about falling victim to street crime. It's bad enough you're already being victimized by actions that should be criminal-actions perpetrated by the two pillars of global capitalism; large multinational corporate oligarchs, and a mismanaged underfunded public sector, that caters only to corporate interests. Both are the pillars upholding a social order in which overwork, poverty, and inequality are rampant and social chaos abounds. These social conditions are miserable enough for many "normal" people to endure. For many neurodiverse persons, it's a fate worse than death. So the alternative life plan I attempted to bring to fruition was more than a mere romantic vision of "escaping the rat race". Rather it was a desperate though misguided attempt to escape a reality I knew I simply could not adjust to.

Before putting any life plan into motion, I begrudgingly accepted the need to learn how to drive a motor vehicle. From the beginning, I was rather ambivalent about learning how to drive, yet had not quite understood why. I certainly felt I could do without the stress and complexity that went with owning a car. But I only scantly understood how I might struggle inordinately with grasping the basic operation of a motor vehicle. I had some insight as to the motor and perceptual aspects of my disability. However, I had not fully understood the severity of these difficulties, nor the consequences in relation to driving. I negated the need to recognize these issues, by philosophizing about the moral ills of automobiles. I would tout the degradation to the environment cars incur, the culture of waste, greed and over consumption surrounding them, the corrupt oil industry, etc. etc. etc. In this way, my reluctance to adopt automotive transport was not a function of any defect on my part, but an ethical choice of striving for a higher existential morality. This made it a positive thing, and a way of internally whitewashing what I considered the ugly truth of my disability. Acknowledging my inability to drive due to neurological deficit placed me in the world of extreme disability. I did not belong there. Likewise, I did not belong in with those severely handicapped kids in the wing of the elementary school where I took OT sessions. Surely none of those pupils would ever grow up to obtain a driver's license. Recognizing my inability to drive due to neurological deficit also validated the labels of "slow" and "retarded" that I was oft referred to by peers. I mean, all I really have is a specific learning difficulty. This should pose no hindrance to operating a motor vehicle. It's not as though I have severe cerebral palsy or a severe intellectual disability, defined by a WAIS (Weschler Adult Intelligence Scale) IQ score below 70. Like so many issues, surrounding my disability and its ramifications, I had a very confused interpersonal awareness, and confusion as to my place in society. This, most likely was a legacy of the lack of earlier recognition, intervention and education on my disability. My parents, for the sake of their own short term convenience, simply swept it all under the rug, raising me as if I were perfectly normal, yet my peers reminded me on a daily basis that I was not.

In my internal tug of war between wanting and not wanting to drive, the desire to drive won out. At least temporarily, anyways. After all, how could I collect materials needed to make handicrafts, and haul the completed products to the town market, without effective means of transport. I considered many alternatives. Such options included; a bike with a cart, or a hand pulled cart similar to a rickshaw, etc. But a motor vehicle was certainly the more practical option. While taking the history class at Green River Community College, I had also been simultaneously preparing for the written test, to obtain my learner's permit. I read the Washington state driver's manual religiously. What is more, I must have taken the sample quizzes at least five or six times before I felt prepared to take the written test.

Going to the DMV office for the written test seemed like taking a step into another world. By this time I grew so enmeshed in my own fantasy world, that the external material one seemed increasingly foreign, confusing, and completely disenfranchising. The DMV reeked an institutional ambiance, and an aura of discontentment and misery that pervaded the entire building. My senses went numb and I wanted the ordeal done and over with as quickly as possible. The overall unhappiness in the air validated my then firmly held anarcho-primitivist view that people are not supposed to live in large scale industrialized urban societies. At the DMV office nobody was smiling, and they all seemed in a state of misery for some reason or another. This was my perception, anyways. It all seemed a far cry from contentment and inherent freedom enjoyed by many of the remote South American Indians I only knew about through books or televised documentaries. They always seemed to find joy and merriment from many occurrences in their daily lives. Men return from a hunting expedition with a tortoise or tapir on the pole and the entire village celebrates. They hold communal rituals with everybody dancing, singing, drinking cassava beer, and having a great time. Nobody has any more or any less than one another and they all seem so content. While surely their lives are much shorter than ours, they seem to be much happier lives. My puerile musings were soon interrupted by the mechanical beckoning of my number being called. "Number 43, window 2 please, number 43, please step up to window 2".

I stepped up to take the visual and hearing exam, followed by the written test. I passed the basic sensory function exams, but failed miserably with the written test. To my recollection, I must have answered less than 50% of all items correctly, requiring me to retake the test. Over the following week or so, I spent my days reading the state driver's manual, and flintknapping on the front carport. This time, I was knapping not merely for fun, but with the intent of making items to sell at the local flea market or similar venue. I was also reading my dog-eared and dilapidated state driver's manual repetitively. My daily readings were followed by quizzing myself on the sample questions at the end of each section. I set a standard of being able to answer all items correctly before making another attempt at the written test. Before long, I was able to satisfy this standard. Subsequently, I set out to retake the test. The second attempt at taking the written test proved to be a success. I scored significantly better, answering 90% of items correctly - more than adequate to obtain the learners permit. I left the DMV, feeling as though I had cleared another major hurdle, towards achieving my goals.

I managed to produce two obsidian bifaces; one 3' inches in length, the other 4 inches long. These were bifaces I wanted to haft and sell somewhere but I had no idea where. I thought that they represented some of my best work to date and was quite reluctant to sell them. The work was of a quality that certainly does not come easy for a person with psychomotor and visuo-perceptual impairments. Even many people without such impairments, who take up flintknapping, abandon it out of frustration. It can be a very difficult skill to master. I was happier to just keep them for display and bask in the admiration others expressed for my work. But I needed the money, and thus begrudgingly sold them.

My small victory, of becoming legally authorized to partake of driving instruction, along with producing paltry startup inventory, towards my business felt empowering. Even such minor advancements made me feel well on my way to creating a workable alternative lifestyle, where I could thrive. I had to take solace in whatever I could. What else was there for me?

With my learner's permit in hand, the time was right for my first driving lesson. On our way home from the DMV, my dad pulled into an empty elementary school parking lot, where I took the wheel to practice maneuvering the vehicle. It was a hair-raising experience for us both. I attempted to drive the vehicle around the circumference of a circular planting strip within the parking lot. It seemed simple enough. However, I was not even able to drive a full quarter turn around the circle, before veering off course, losing control of the vehicle and driving over the sidewalk surrounding the school campus. "The brake!, the brake!", my dad exclaimed "hit the brake!" In my state of panic, alarm and confusion, I confused the brake pedal for the gas pedal, and drove over the sidewalk, towards the school building, almost colliding into it before stopping. We both breathed a sigh of relief when the car stopped, just in the nick of time. My dad was obviously shaken, but did his best to be strong and not let it show. "We won't let mom know about this", my dad said, attempting to alleviate the tension of the situation.

> "Do you want to continue driving?"
> "No, you can take over from here." I replied,

Our next driving lessons took place in a larger, more spacious empty Fred Meyer parking lot, before the store opened for business. After about three of these sessions my driving ability improved to the point, where I could easily maneuver around each parking cluster, and usually park into each individual stall. On most occasions, I could keep the vehicle comfortably within the lines of each stall, permitting someone to park next to me with adequate space for the driver and all passengers to exit the vehicle. Yet even after numerous practice sessions, there were still frequent occasions where I would either park too close to one line, or take up two parking spaces altogether. The effects of my psychomotor and perceptual dysfunction remained apparent all throughout my attempts at learning to drive. After repetitively driving the car around the Fred Meyer parking lot, my dad and I felt that I could safely drive the car home. Eventually I achieved a level of competence that permitted me to drive to and from the parking lot to further practice maneuvering the vehicle. The town of Auburn, where we lived, was a relatively small town, containing less than 20,000 people. Because of the small town setting with its low traffic and uncomplicated two way streets, I was able to drive to and from the Fred Meyer parking lot without difficulty. However I could never manage to park the car into the curved, sloped driveway of our house. I would always simply opt to park alongside the cul-de-sac in front of our house. Eventually I was driving the car throughout town with my dad in the passenger's seat. But again this is usually within lightly traveled rural or semi rural roads with minimal visual stimuli to process.

Through selling some of my stone implements, I was able to generate sufficient funds to afford the $230 tuition for driving lessons held by a certified "mom and pop" driver's ed class in Kent. After about a month of practice, using the family vehicle, I enrolled in formal driver's education, for professional instruction, under more rigorous driving conditions. On my first day of the program, I sat in the small wood grain paneled lobby waiting to meet the instructor. The receptionist then lead me to a small study room. It was the room where students watch supplemental instructional videos and take written quizzes. She invited me to take a seat in the room, and I did so. The receptionist then exited the room, closing the door behind her. While waiting to meet the driving instructor, I overheard the instructor and receptionist conversing with each other. Though in the next room, I overheard their conversation well enough to discern that they were talking about me. Though the receptionist made no firm judgments, I knew she was basically telling the instructor not to expect much from me. She started out by disclosing what I told her over the phone about having minimal driving experience. Then she made a statement to the effect of "he seems a little slow" based on my then marked speaking difficulties. Their conversation ended and shortly afterward the receptionist invited me back into the lobby to meet the instructor. The instructor walked into the lobby and the receptionist introduced us to each other. From the start, I knew that driving instruction would be hell. "Allan this is Rick, Rick this is Allan", the receptionist and registrar stated, introducing us to each other. I said hello to him, and he said nothing without even offering to shake my hand for a more formal introduction. I immediately detected a rather surly demeanor on his part. Owing to the prior feedback from the receptionist, he most likely knew I would be a difficult student and was not eager to work with me. At any rate, I wanted my license more than anything and was willing to go through hell and high water to get it. Following our rather icy introduction, we both exited the office and entered the instructional vehicle.

Upon starting the ignition, utterances of dialogue from a conservative radio talk show emanated from the stereo system." Oh no, he listens to this crap?" I thought."No wonder why he seems like such an asshole! I bet he will be a really hard-nosed, high strung bastard!" He shut off the radio and we begin to discuss some preliminary issues relating to my skill level and prior experience with driving. In our conversation, I volunteered only that I had limited driving experience a level of anxiety about driving, above and beyond the norm. I wanted to reveal that I also have some learning disabilities, manifest primarily as motor impairments and difficulty with following verbal instructions, but I failed to do this for two reasons. For one, I had no clinical diagnosis at the time, so I felt it inappropriate to disclose the issue. Also I perceived the instructor's personality to be such that he would only treat such information with skepticism. Thus disclosing such information may not have made a difference anyways. I had a very strange way of reacting to and perceiving the world around me that I feel has improved considerably with maturity and education. Now I am a better self advocate about my condition than when I was younger. This is attributable to both a better understanding of my condition and a new view on disability. Because of my involvement in disability studies, I do not view disability as inherently negative. Over the years, I have also developed the attitude that you can't always fix ignorance, but it never hurts to try.

After disclosing to the instructor what I did, he did his best to assure me that he had a brake pedal on his side of the vehicle, to minimize the prospects of a collision. He also stated that he had experience with highly anxious students. Therefore he knew to have them pull off to the side of the road and calm them down when it seemed that their anxiety was getting the best of them. His words did nothing to allay my fears, but I just wanted to get this thing done and over with. Our conversation ended and we drove out of the parking lot. Immediately at that point, he expressed alarm over my driving habits."Stay in a straight line towards the right-hand side of the exit" he exclaimed as we drove out of the parking lot. We approached the

58

first intersection and I applied the brake "not so hard!" he blurted out. Our first driving lesson together went by reasonably well without too many angry words expressed. When we returned to the office, I pulled into the parking lot, making one of my typical errors of parking too close to one side. He pointed that out is an area where I need towards improvement, and of course I didn't argue. Because he needed to get on with his next client, he didn't have me take the time to correct my parking error, but insisted that we emphasize parking in future lessons. Other problematic issues he noted included; braking too abruptly, general inattentiveness, and responding accordingly to directions of left/right. At that point, I debated on disclosing my "suspected" learning disability but still felt that it wouldn't be entirely worthwhile.

I returned home from that first formal driving lesson feeling lackluster and agitated. Still, I yearned for my driver's license and the freedom it afforded. I did what I would normally do after these situations. I sat out in the carport, knapping obsidian, with the intent of producing an artifact to sell. Flintknapping represented something of a netherworld that I typically retreated to. It was a craft I had gained a useful level of proficiency in, and thus represented an endeavor that made me feel competent and talented when the outside world seemingly dismissed me as incapable and worthless. In my mind, it was a connection to a more inclusive civilization. Just the mere ability to strike a stone flake from a larger core was a valuable skill in most stone tool using cultures. I could do this. Among hunter-gatherers, anyone who could produce useful sharp cutting edges was valued card carrying member of society. Simple sharp stone flakes were the mainstay of most Stone Age toolkits. These unassuming Stone Age multi-tools served many functions; skinning and butchering game, working wood, bone, and antler, cutting cordage, and hides, etc. So for me, my flintknapping represented a bastion of dignity and self-worth in a world that accorded no positive place for me.

At least 2 to 3 times a week, I attended my driver's ed. sessions, with Evergreen Driving School in Kent. I supplemented this formal instruction by driving to different locations with my dad in the family car. Most of the driving school lessons took place in the larger, more heavily populated nearby towns of Kent and Federal Way. This is where my driving difficulties became especially pronounced. To this day, I wonder how I drove through the larger towns without being involved in a major collision.

59

Typical problems for me included; overlooking street signs and road markings, impaired ability to control my speed, typically driving below the speed limit, poor timing of my actions, complete inability to parallel park, or back around corners, and persistent difficulties with accurately parking into allotted stalls. After nearly two solid months of repetitive driving practice, I reached a plateau in my learning curve, where no amount of practice, lead to any improvement in my driving ability. My sessions with the driving instructor left me feeling very belittled and discouraged. At times the instructor would become so angry and say very insulting things towards me about my driving ability." Pay attention to what you're doing!"," Watch the road"," listen to what I'm saying"," you have to get aggressive with the car!" Typically I would come home from each session seething with a rage for which I had no other recourse but to keep bottled up. I was completely cut off from all of my friends from school, with no clinical intervention available and my family didn't understand what I was going through. It was around this time that I would attempt to share with my parents, everything I was discovering about learning disabilities. Yet they would hear nothing of it. This is despite all that I went through in public school. In their mind, I just had low self esteem simply because I thought that I had LD/psycho-motor impairment. I knew that I could not rely on them for support. As usual, I was left to my own devices emotionally.

On my last day of instruction with the driving school, the registrar informed me that the instructor did not think I was sufficiently competent to obtain pass the DMV driving test. Thus no certification was awarded to me. They simply recommended that I continue practice driving on my own time, with the family vehicle. Perhaps my skill may eventually improve sufficiently to pass the driving test at the DMV. After having gone through what I did with the driver's ed. course, however I soon lost interest in driving and opted to pursue the automobile free lifestyle that I maintain to this day. A pivotal occurrence, solidifying this decision happened a few days after exiting the driver's ed program. Basically, I came close to striking a young girl approximately seven or eight years old, on her bicycle while driving with my dad. It was a bright, clear autumn day, the girl suddenly darted in front of me while she was crossing the street. The sun was blaring in my face, making my depth perception more impaired than normal and I was just narrowly able to apply the brakes in time. I must have come within less than 3 feet of hitting the girl, yet she seemed completely oblivious to her near encounter with possible death. She just darted off in her own merry way. I couldn't get over how careless she seemed, even relative to her apparent age. Did her parents not teach her any better? Surely I knew better than to do such foolish things at her age. Angry and bewildered as I was, I couldn't properly blame the girl for the near mishap. I really had no business operating a motor vehicle at all. Motor and perceptual impairments simply make masterful maneuvering of a motor vehicle highly problematic for me. Compounding these difficulties are sensory sensitivities, including light sensitivity in the eyes. Thus I am especially susceptible to sunlight blindness. I even wear shades when it is overcast. This incident was the proverbial straw that broke the camel's back. My driving days had all but effectively ended at that point.

Despite failing to obtain my driver's license, I remained convinced that I had the means to build a respectable alternative lifestyle where my disability poses no hindrance. I just needed to figure out alternatives to using a car. Perhaps a sturdy pack frame can serve to haul large loads, as could a bicycle with a cart. Despite my myriad limitations with regard to crafting ability, organization, and time management, I tried my hardest, to make my retreatist lifestyle work. There was simply no place for someone like myself in our national economy. Yet public assistance was not an option. With no dependent children under my care, I couldn't apply for state welfare benefits. Besides, congress was trying to chip even further away at these. Perhaps with extensive clinical documentation of my disability, and a good lawyer, I could have applied for and eventually won GAU (General Assistance Unemployable), or SSI (Supplemental Security Income). But I didn't know that. I had absolutely no awareness of these particular programs. Even if I did, it didn't seem appropriate to apply for that level of assistance. A part of me somehow internalized everything I had been taught at home about public assistance. According to my dad, the only people who had legitimate reason for receiving such assistance were those with the most severe disabilities. Examples might include; those with severe intellectual disability, delusional psychosis, severe cerebral palsy, severe autism, multiple amputees, the blind, aged or quadriplegic. Basically, these are "classic disabilities", commonly acknowledged as such by the general public. After all, I only have a specific learning difficulty with psychosocial problems. There should be a way of working around that to achieve full self sufficiency, right? As I would only find out several years later, it's not that simple.

I would literally spend the better part of each day on the carport of my mom and dad's house in Auburn, working on various projects that I intended to market. Often, I would start work at the break of dawn, and work well into the night, aided by an electric carport light in the garage. By this point I had accumulated an ample horde of raw materials, in the form of basalts, granite, obsidian, and Jasper, seasoned tree limbs, goose tail and wing feathers, elk and deer antlers, vegetable fibers, animal skins, pine resin and hide glue mastics, etc. Every day, I would flintknapp regularly and diligently. But with my minimal level of knapping experience, I could seldom produce implements with any market value as handicrafts. But it had to work. During most knapping sessions, I failed to produce anything more than a handful of small "arrowhead-sized" bifaces. This was on a good day.

Longer bifaces, around 4 inches or longer, by about two or more inches wide, and relatively thin are much more sought after as handicrafts but are more difficult to produce. During the bifacial reduction process, longer, thinner, and wider bifaces are much more susceptible to breakage from end shock. There is a larger proportion of unsupported mass which is subjected to repeated shocks from the energy of each blow executed to dislodge flakes from each side of the biface. It is a process highly prone to failure. Flaked stone tool production places an utmost premium on concentration, manual dexterity and eye to hand co-ordination to accurately apply force to properly prepared platforms. Good lateral bodily integration is critical for this process. It often takes several years of practice for a non-impaired knapper to reach the point of craftsmanship of being able to consistently produce sizable well proportioned bifaces. Many who attempt to learn flintknapping, give up on it before achieving this milestone. Yet I never did. After all, flintknapping is not like driving where any mishap could so easily result in a life changing injury or death.

In my diligent but ineffectual efforts at producing stone implements for sale, there were many days in which I produced nothing at all, save for random flakes and debitage[9], or waste flakes. However, among stone tool using cultures, simple sharp stone flakes were

---

[9] In flintknapping/lithics jargon, debitage is essentially waste material produced while flintknapping. debitage usually consists of flakes that are too thin, too small, chunks, or just any piece that cannot effectively serve as a sharp flake tool or modifiable stock from which to produce bifaces or unifaces.

imminently useful. Needless to say, though, these simple, expediently produced Stone Age multi-tools have no market value as a contemporary handicraft. They appear to the untrained eye as mere random fragments of stone. After a little more than a year flintknapping, I was at a skill level in which I could produce mundane implements that would serve most practical day to day uses among any given stone tool using culture. I could knap core struck flake tools with useful cutting edges, and make myriads of different scrapers, suitable for hide working and plant fiber preparation. I could also make projectile points suitable for most archery arrows or atlatl darts. Yet the ability to make really impressive stuff took years to achieve. Ironically development of my flintknapping skill would be further impeded through later years spent in the prison of conventional higher education, supposedly studying anthropology and archaeology.

During those numerous occasions where I worked so feverishly yet unsuccessfully at producing something for sale, I justified these occurrences by writing them off as skill development sessions. The more I practiced, I reasoned, the more efficient I would eventually become at producing marketable implements as handicrafts. I had a sense that my impaired dexterity and bodily co-ordination were impeding my learning process. Yet I was convinced that more practice would eventually enable me to produce dagger sized bifaces. In the early 1990s, such implements could be sold for $120-$400 each if hafted into a decorative wooden, antler, or bone handle.

In the 1990s, primitive technology practitioners were becoming somewhat more numerous. Clubs and organizations devoted to such enthusiasts were cropping up across the nation. New publications on the subject were cropping up and existing newsletters and magazines saw an uptick in subscribers. Examples included; Chips, The Bulletin of Primitive Technologies, Primitive Archer, etc. Those typically served as venues for primitive technologists to market their work. For most, this was not their full-time occupation. It was merely a means as a means to obtain funds to offset the expenses of their hobby (e.g. exotic tool stones, and other materials). I was aware of this. Yet I firmly believed that learning how to directly exploit various natural resources within my environment would make it possible to subsist comfortably on a relatively low income.

Frequently, I would call/write to many of the guys who ran their primitive technology based home businesses and pick their brains for information on what they do and how they do it. This was akin to a pen-pal type correspondence. It was also my primary connection to the outside world. I had such correspondents all across the country and even some in Canada, England, and Australia. To this day, I am amazed at the tremendous patience these men had with me, doing nothing more than calling to chat about primitive technologies for up to an hour or so. Maybe they dismissed me as a young kid who had not quite developed a sense as to the value of time, particularly in business. One of my most frequent correspondents was a man down in Lufkin Texas who was then the editor of *Primitive Archer* magazine. *Primitive Archer* was a burgeoning publication at the time. The magazine is still in circulation and can be found in many newsstands throughout the country. Approximately 2 months after earning my high school diploma, I published my first article in *Primitive Archer* magazine. The article was about making cordage (i.e. twine/rope) from stinging nettle fiber and was simply titled: *Cordage from a Stinging Nettle Plant*. It appeared in issue 2 of the second volume (Spring 1994) of the magazine. In writing the article, I was essentially attempting to emulate the literary style of the renowned Tom Brown wilderness survival guides. It is a mystical style that emphasizes the values of spiritual reverence for nature, and earth stewardship. Tom Brown was a major hero of mine at the time and I was positive that I would be just like him and about 10 years. Of course I didn't even come close to emulating the style of Tom Brown, in my article. Furthermore, my article described only very crude and inefficient method of making stinging nettle cordage and I have since learned other methods.

Nonetheless, having the article published not only served as a boost to my self-esteem, but represented a step in the right direction with regard to the lifestyle I sought to establish. In lieu of cash payment, I accepted a Sweet Gum (*Liquidambar styraciflura*) bow stave[10], as compensation for the article. I really felt like I was on my way to creating a pre-industrial reality in a post industrial world.

It was pure elation to see my name in print. I spoke to the editor afterward and he informed me that he received a lot of very positive

---

[10] A length of wood, from which an archery bow is fashioned, usually through hewing, whittling scraping, sanding and tillering

feedback in relation to the article. He was interested in featuring more articles authored by me. It was the greatest honor I had ever known and convinced me that I was on the right path in life. Further solidifying this notion was the fact that around the same time that my article was accepted for publication, I also managed to sell three obsidian daggers, and an obsidian tipped atlatl dart set. I sold these at a booth which I rented at the nearby Green River Community College. The daggers I sold consisted of three that were 3 inches long and two that were between 4 1/2 and 5 1/2 inches long. The atlatl set that included three obsidian tipped darts constructed from wild rose, and oso-berry, fletched with goose tail feathers. After paying my booth fee, the sale netted me a total of $750.00. This seemed like a substantial sum to me at the time. It was definitely a nice supplement to the $40 per month allowance I was getting from my mom and dad. I practically spent nothing on a daily basis. Hence small sums of money easily solidified into larger sums. I was confident that before long I would eventually save enough to finance my goals. I put the money earned from the sale into a savings account where it virtually remained untouched for a year. I always added about $10 per month to this account.

I voraciously read books obtained via alternative mail-order book distributors, about largely unknown means of land acquisition, in which it is possible to purchase land at rock-bottom prices. A text that I frequently referred to was, *How to Buy Land Cheap* by Edward Preston. In it, Preston describes avenues such as purchasing tracts of" surplus" land from government agencies such as the Bureau of Land Management, the Department of Motor Vehicles, etc. According to the author, government agencies are primarily interested in auctioning off and ridding themselves of such costly and unproductive property. However, in some instances they may only sell these properties to those with a specific plan to use it in a particular, usually charitable manner. According to Preston, government auctioned properties can be purchased for unheard of prices often as low as a few hundred dollars per acre. The author described well documented and recent occurrences where individuals have found incredible bargains. For example, tracts of land have been sold for as little as $50 an acre or entire houses and surrounding property have been purchased for as little as $700. The prospects were enthralling.

Immediately after reading the book, I contacted various state agencies and requested that my name be placed on their mailing list for their land auction program. If the individuals, described by the author were able to purchase homes and property for such unheard of prices, there's is no reason why I can't do the same. I could easily generate around $500 to purchase some bargain-basement priced property.

After having figured out an avenue to obtain property, given my modest means, my other concern was learning how to build an inexpensive home/dwelling. Minimally, I could build some type of "primitive dwelling" on the property, using on site natural materials. At least this should sustain me until I could build a more permanent and sturdy home equipped with an off the grid electricity source, and water supply. A well pump or rainwater collection system should be fairly easy to construct. One highly influential book was; *The $50 and up Underground House Book*, by Mike Oehler. Armed with such rare and seemingly empowering knowledge, an alternate reality seemed well within reach. I had to make it work. No other life options existed for me.

Cast adrift from the rest of society, I occupied myself in one of two ways. Either I was working at making something to sell or studying remote off the grid living. Often, I would venture into the woods surrounding our house and study the native flora, (field guide in hand), as potential sources of wild edibles. Additionally, I practiced, often successfully, means of procuring fish and game animals using inexpensive wilderness expedient methods. The usual technologies I worked with, included snares, trotlines, throwing sticks, and lances. This was my "training phase".

Just shortly after submitting my first article, for publication, I went on a few outings, in which I managed to successfully procure game animals, using essentially Stone Age weaponry. The first of such occasions was the harvesting of a non-migratory Canadian goose with a flat cross sectioned and curved throwing stick. Essentially this is the same weapon as the Australian aboriginal non-returning boomerang or the ancient Hopi rabbit stick. My throwing stick was nothing more than a blunt lens shaped cross sectioned curved wooden throwing stick about 3 feet long with a 40° curve situated at 2/3 of its length away from the handle. This was the first fully serviceable primitive weapon that I made while a senior in high school. It was hewn, whittled, and scraped from a seasoned naturally curved section of a madrona (*Arbutus menziesii)* tree trunk.

I procured the goose off the bank of The Green River and it was

66

more or less an opportunistic harvest than the outcome of a preconceived hunting strategy. I just happened to have the boomerang with me one autumn afternoon, while scouring for natural constructive materials. I was also checking some rabbit snares that I set in a nearby forest clearing the night before. None of my snares had yet been set off at that point. After collecting about ten wild nootka rose (Rosa *nuutkana*) shoots and a handful of dead stinging nettle (*Urtica dioica*) stalks, I decided to scour some outcroppings on the river in search of tabular and oblong water worn basalt pebbles. These serve ideally as raw material blanks for the manufacture of axe-heads, adz blades or mace-heads. While approaching the outcropping, I spotted a flock of geese sunning themselves on the riverbank. I withdrew my boomerang from my belt, approaching the flock gradually, and incrementally, maintaining a low profile so as not to frighten them. I was within 15 to 20 feet of the entire flock before my presence was detected and they all simultaneously took flight. On a whim, I hurled my throwing stick at one of the last geese to leave the ground, while it flew directly overhead of where I stood. In a blinding flash of time, the boomerang collided with the upper chest of the bird, virtually knocking it end over end in mid air, before it fell to the ground. The bird remained on the ground, wildly flailing about, perhaps in a frantic attempt to resume flight and escape. Was it just injured or were its erratic gyrations simply a nerve reaction, the last remaining vestiges of all neuromuscular activity exiting its body, prior to death? The movement of its jaws and beak resembled attempts at a distress call, but no sound emanated from its mouth. It was a solid hit. The main frontal mass of the throwing stick apparently made contact with the goose's upper thoracic region. But I was still unsure as to whether the goose was dead or just stunned. The bird's reaction was surely very different from that of grouse and rabbits that I had shot with either a high powered air rifle, or .22 rim-fire rifle. With the goose flopping about on the ground I grabbed it by the feet and recovered my boomerang. The goose was still flailing erratically. I then placed its head and neck over a large nearby driftwood log, and issued the *coup de grace,* by using my boomerang to deliver a sharp blow to the animal's upper neck. The animal's bodily twitches then became shorter and more rapid, before finally going completely limp. So there I was, standing at the edge of a ravine, with ample poultry to feed a family, harvested with a simple hand propelled hunting device-a weapon made with my own two hands, nonetheless. My feeling of ineptitude, stemming from my then recent failure with driving, faded into thin air. While thrilled and

67

excited, it was a brand of excitement I could not quite describe. There was no urge to jump for joy, and shout in victory. This was an excitement coupled with a lot of introspective Zen-like contemplation. I pondered on my place in the world and how I might have thrived in a hunter-gatherer cultural context, given my functional anomaly. Would I have been considered abnormal or different then? After mentally ruminating on this question for a moment, my focus shifted to the issue at hand. The goose needed to be plucked while the carcass was still warm and it needed to be brought home for butchering. Hopefully, I could get the bird home without encountering any game wardens. Not only did I lack the necessary non-migratory waterfowl stamp, but I also used a hunting method that is strictly prohibited by law.

After getting my bearing back, I withdrew some cotton clothesline from my fanny pack and hung the goose by its neck, on a nearby black willow tree. While the carcass was still reasonably warm, I began plucking it. The feathers are removed much more easily this way. Gripping the deceased bird firmly by its feet, I began tearing off handfuls of the outer feathers. I soon realized that they detach much more easily if one pulls upward toward the head. In a similar way, scaling a fish is done by scraping towards the head with a sharp knife. Then came the inner down feathers. Removing these was not too strenuous but it was surely a mess. They went everywhere. Before long, the entire riverbank was littered with the snowy white down. I had no idea that so much down could come from one goose. It looked like a pillow had exploded. When all the smaller feathers were completely removed, I rinsed the bird off in the river. Having only my Swiss Army knife and no gut hook to properly eviscerate the animal, I opted to execute that detail at home. Given that I was only within a 40 minute walk to my place of residence, there was no harm in waiting so long to gut the bird. I packed the carcass with some wet moss placed in a burlap sack, and secured it to my pack frame and began to trek home with it. I have long since learned a more efficient method of processing geese and similar game birds, but the method I used adequately served its purpose at the time.

I walked home from my outing that day, energized with an intoxicating sense of liberation. It was a successful outing. I procured some premium quality constructive materials, and enough poultry to feed a family. It were as though I had mastered a completely different economic domain, one forgotten by most of us, in Western civilization. Another world had opened up for me. It were as though I were no longer connected to any other person. This was my safety net and no longer did I fear going hungry or without shelter. Nor would I have to lower myself to the indignity of handouts from either the government or food-banks. I was my own man.

Upon arriving home, I unloaded my natural bounty in the garage. I placed the nettle stalks and wild rose saplings across the wooden trusses to dry. I had to inform my mom and dad about the goose that I harvested, before gutting and butchering it. It was late October of that year and perfect timing to have the goose for Thanksgiving dinner. Yet, I was uncertain of how my parents would react, knowing that I essentially poached the goose. However, they couldn't really do too much about it. After all, I am an adult, and I don't think they would turn their own son into the authorities over such a relatively benign offense. It wasn't as though I physically harmed anybody, stolen valuable property, or defrauded anybody. So I can't see what they would be too upset. Still wrapped in burlap, I left the goose on top of the chest freezer in the garage. I then went inside the house to check on my parents and see what they were up to. They were both seated at the dining room table, looking for houses in the paper, hoping to actually purchase a house in the near future. I interrupted their browsing to announce to them about the goose I harvested.

"Mom, Dad, I got a goose, it's in the garage!"

"A goose?" my mom asked, Where did you get a goose at?"

"Down at the Green River. I used my boomerang".

My mom and dad followed me to the garage, where I opened the burlap sack, pulling the deceased bird out by its neck.

"How did you learn how to pluck it?" my mom asked
.

"From one of my game preparation guides".

"Did it die right away? ", asked my dad.

"It didn't suffer too much. It seemed well stunned and incapacitated after being struck in flight with a thrown boomerang. Afterward, I used the boomerang again to quickly dispatch it with a sharp blow to the upper neck".

My mom and dad really seemed more shocked than angry. I later found out that my maternal grandpa could be quite an adept poacher himself. But he only resorted to such measures when money was tight and he needed to provide meat for the family larder. This could have been why my mom and dad didn't seem to think too much about my illegal procurement of the bird. Before I set out to eviscerate and decapitate it as well as remove the feet and wings, my dad suggested that I singe the remaining hairs with a Burnz-o-Matic™ butane torch. I agreed and my dad lit up the torch and singed all remaining hairs, while I held the carcass. I then took it to the kitchen sink where, under my mom's supervision, I rinsed it again, gutted it out, and severed the wings, feet tail and head. As I finished processing the bird, my mom noted that it smelled very fresh. I knew I had done everything right. My grandparents raised geese for poultry so my mom knew about processing the meat and detecting signs of spoilage. We all agreed to have the goose as the main course of our Thanksgiving meal for that year. I saved the wing and tail feathers for fletching material for primitive archery arrows or atlatl darts. It was a happy occasion for us all.

I walked down to a nearby forest clearing where I had set some rabbit traps. I needed to check if there were any rabbits ensnared or if I needed to reset any of them. I had set quite an extensive line of spring loaded snare traps, at least for that small clearing anyways. There must have been about 20-25 of them within an area no bigger than an American football field. Most of them were completely untouched, and left in the same state as when I had set them the night before. Two had been set. One of which a coyote had managed to get to the rabbit before I did. The broken splintered out vine maple spring pole and tufts of rabbit fur littering the adjacent area were obvious signs of what had happened. Protection from other predators was a factor that I needed to address in my future trapping strategies. At least the trap worked. What is more, another animal was able to derive nourishment from my successfully set trap in exchange for a valuable lesson in snare setting strategies. The other snare had a barely breathing rabbit dangling from the noose. It was an adult male snowshoe hare (*Lepus cascadensis*), about 2 lbs at most. I grabbed it by the feet and whacked it over the head with the same boomerang that I killed the goose with earlier that day. I eviscerated the rabbit in the field and took it home to skin,

70

decapitate and quarter. The meat was highly laden with tendon matter, making it less suitable for table fare. The flesh on these creatures is nothing like that of the cotton tail rabbits, or Belgian hare I was more accustomed to hunting. Snowshoe hare is definitely an animal only to be eaten in a survival situation, with no better quality protein available. I ultimately decided to boil the portions whole and feed them to my beloved Maine Coon cat, Sage. Sage was so named because he liked to roll around in my mom's sage plants in our front patio area. The cat eagerly devoured the rabbit meat. Months later, I snared several more rabbits just to feed this cat. I liked to use the rawhide from the rabbits as a primitive lashing material and cordage.

The next day, I spent much of the day flintknapping on the carport. I made about three corner notched obsidian arrowheads to tip some arrows that I wanted to make for a bow that I had been building. I also made a nice hand held hide scraper to de-flesh and shave more rabbit hides. There were also a number of decent core struck flakes that I had produced, which would make excellent scraping and whittling implements for working green wood with. This was a typical flintknapping session for me. Nothing was produced that could readily be sold for adequate profit. However, I did well as far as my personal projects are concerned. Oh well, I learn more with each session. Eventually I will master the full circle of primitive technologies and become a pro. I cleaned up all of my debitage, and disposed it into a large plastic paint bucket. My dad always hauled off my full debitage buckets to a nearby municipal dump with other household garbage. With the lithic debitage interspersed with the plastics, metals, and glass of modern garbage, there is virtually no chance that it could be taken to be part of a prehistoric trash midden by future archaeologists.

After cleaning up my mess, and putting away my flintknapping tools, I went into my bedroom to secure all of the trappings of a bow making project I had been working on for a number of weeks. The bow, made from vine maple bow needed to be tillered. Tillering is a process by which the limbs of a wooden bow are slowly planed to their final dimensions. During the tillering process, the bow is rendered to its final draw weight, and both limbs are made to bend evenly.

While walking down the hall towards my bedroom, I could hear my mom conversing over the phone with my grandmother. She was boasting to my grandma about the goose I harvested and about my upcoming article in *Primitive Archer Magazine*. My parents always knew how to superficially play the role of the supportive doting parent to the extent that it bolstered their self image to do so.

 "Oh yes, dad (my grandpa) would be proud if he were still alive to see it. He did such a nice job at plucking and cleaning out that goose, the meat smelled so fresh, it will make such a nice Thanksgiving dinner this year. Yeah, he's really getting into that stuff".

My mom then handed the phone over to me and asked; "want to talk to your grandma?" I agreed to do so. I put the phone to my ear and said "hello".

>"Hi Al" my grandma replied. "I heard you got a goose".

>"Yep" I proudly said."It's a big one to!"."That's great, she said". "You're a pretty good hunter"."Too bad grandpa isn't still alive"." I'm sure that you and he would have so much fun together".

>"That would be nice".

>"I hear that you're also going to have an article published".

>"Yep, it will be in *Primitive Archer Magazine*."I'm hoping to write more for them, and I'm hoping to sell some of my tools that I make".

>"Yes certainly, don't let your talent go to waste".

The conversation terminated shortly after that point and I went out to the front carport to work on planing and tillering a Vine Maple (*Acer circinatum*) wooden bow. While traversing back from my bedroom, tools and wooden stave in hand, I could hear the conversation between my mom and grandmother. My mom was commenting on how I managed to learn many primitive skills and wood lore simply through self teaching. For me this was achieved largely through reading books, magazines and conducting a lot of trial and error experimentation. "When that boy puts his mind to learning something, there's just no stopping him", my mom would say.

72

Her statements were in the context of lamenting that I seem to underestimate my abilities, hence my giving up on learning to drive, and not seeking conventional employment. In the conversation, she was also bemoaning that I never had anyone in my life to teach me anything. I always had to learn everything on my own. Such was the case in the disconnected home and family life I grew up in. It was literally like a group of strangers living together. To this day, I remain unsure as to what impact, this aspect of my upbringing may have played in my current inability to relate to others and interface with my outer world.

I returned to my makeshift carport workshop to commence with tillering a primitive wooden bow I had been laboriously coaxing into shape for weeks. I sought to achieve a 50 pound pull for this bow and intended to use it for deer hunting in the following year.

Methodically, I would scrape fine shavings of wood from the belly [11]o f the embyonic bow using a steel cabinet scraper. Every so often, I would check it's bend on a tillering board, bolted to the side of a weathered plywood woodshed on our front carport. While tillering the bow, I was basking in the warm autumn ambience of our Green River Valley home. The colorful canopy of orange yellow big leaf maple trees, dotted with fire engine red vine maples, accented the backdrop of Cedars, Douglas firs, and still green but fading alders, and yellow cottonwoods. It's this type of atmosphere that fuels the soul. As gentle breezes swept away fine shavings of wood, peeling from the seasoned stave, with each stroke of my cabinet scraper, I reflected upon my recent victories and pondered my future. "Well I sold an article, and a small quantity of primitive implements. I also bagged a goose with a throwing stick. If only I can step up production for my stone tool making, and publish more articles, as my knowledge improves. I should be well on my way to breaking free from it all, to live a simple, low stress, but dignified and self-sufficient life. Yet this is a difficult goal to achieve in an era of unbridled global capitalism. Well I think I've got it all figured out and am well on my way there. The remainder of the afternoon was spent shaving down my bow stave while slowly and gently coaxing it to an even bend throughout. Eventually, I shaved the bow to the dimensions required to sustain a 48 lb pull, and both limbs bent in

[11] This is essentially the underside of an archery bow. In cross-sectional view, the belly of a bow, is the side of a bow's limbs that face toward the archer as the bow is drawn.

an even D shaped arc. An elated feeling of self satisfaction came over me as a fully functional bow came to life. "The basic mechanism is now complete. It now only needs is a string, a wood finish, and some arrows". I'll be good to go on a primitive archery deer hunt next year. I already have some thin rabbit rawhide, from which to make a string for this bow".

While gathering my tools and materials to put them all away, our downstairs neighbor Abby came up to check her mail and we began to talk. I showed her the bow that I essentially just made and told her about the goose I harvested, and my upcoming article in *Primitive Archer Magazine*."That's amazing!" She replied." You have every reason to be proud of yourself", she said. Abby was a divorced single mother of a son and daughter, about my age. She was a junior high teacher, who had moved into the unit down below us to cut costs while paying for her daughter's through college education. She was a scarce spot of sunshine and warmth, in the cold depressing world I came to inhabit. Always so upbeat and quick to smile, she could always put me in such a positive mood any time I spoke with her. She always tolerated my never-ending ramblings about primitive skills and indigenous tribal cultures. Abby was a rare and shining example of one who at least seemed to genuinely enjoy conversing with me. This felt like a rare treat, when most other people only expressed boredom and disinterest in me. I use to imagine that I would have been so much better turned out if my parents were more like her; positive upbeat, extroverted and energetic. She showed me genuine warmth, whereas my actual parents would only show mechanical, ultimately self-serving gestures of interest, love and approval. Yet such superficial gestures were always so easily contradicted by their more usual state of disinterest, and verbally abusive tirades over my slightest mistake or mishap. From an early age, I felt like nothing more than an unwanted pet to them.

I put all my stuff away to retire for the evening to have some coffee, watch the news, and catch a weather report. My bedroom grew redolent with aromas from the woodlands. In one corner of my room were stacks of raw stinging nettle and fireweed stocks drying. Pegs on my walls held the combed and rolled fibers of various plants, waiting to be woven into cordage. My bookcase had shelves designated for mastic materials such as dried fish skins, bladders, and bones. There were also shelves for stone flakes, and pebble blanks, and bifaces worked to various stages of completion. It was

74

the quintessential Stone Age man's workshop.

As I watched the news, drinking my coffee I would hear so much negativity; political scandals, gang-related shootings, armed robberies. "I'm simply too good to live in such a morally bankrupt society", I mused. Perhaps this is my true disability; I'm not a sociopath, yet I'm sure that any clinician would readily point out many gross abnormalities on my part. Yet I would never do half the shit people hear about on the news. But I'm considered abnormal and disturbed? What is wrong with this culture that we live in? After watching the news that evening, I retired for bed with the intent of getting up early in the morning to do some salmon fishing on the Green River. The river was only a block or two from our home. I decided to listen to the radio before going to bed and found a talk show that grabbed my interest. It was the Dr. Laura Lee show and Dr. Laura was interviewing a man who had learned didgeridoo music from aboriginal musicians in Australia. It was a topic that held major fascination with me. I missed most of the program, but the one that followed was equally amusing, but for different reasons. It was atypical conservative radio talk show. The right wing discourse of this sort was becoming so extreme that it sounded virtually satirical and highly amusing. I listened to it partially for that reason. I also relished the intellectual exercise of analyzing the flaws in their reasoning. This grew easier and easier to do, the more I did it.

Before long, I fell asleep and woke up in time for my fishing trip. It was a success, having caught two chum salmon-one 8 lbs the other a bit smaller at 6 lbs. I gutted out both fish, and walked home with my catch in hand. As I walked home, there were a few friendly honks of the horn from passing motorists who would then give the thumbs-up sign as a way of congratulating me for my catch. When I brought the fish home, I scaled and filleted them, and subsequently stored them in the freezer. After processing and storing the fish, I returned to my room to work on writing a letter to one of my pen pals at the time Nate Waller. Nate lived in Mistassini Québec, Canada and enjoyed the very lifestyle that I dreamed of pursuing. He spent much of the year living in a wilderness cabin with his wife and three children. I myself never envisioned starting a family, but the idea of living remotely and off the grid was my long term goal. I corresponded with Nate frequently, to pick his brain for insights on how to pursue that lifestyle.

I sat in my room, composing the letter then mailed it off. My

75

correspondence with Nate Waller opened the door to many other contacts and mail order suppliers of goods for off the grid living. This was how I became aware of mail order retailers such as the Whole Earth Catalog, Lehman Brothers, and book distributors such as Eureka Resource and Loompanics Unlimited. Nate also connected me with a young man, about my same age at the time, living in Battleground Washington, who felt the same way about the world as I did. His name was Todd Youngblood. Todd was about 18 at the time and just completed high school. Like myself, Todd lived with his parents, but aspired to live remotely, and off the grid. Unlike me though, Todd held odd jobs, but often did not get along with bosses, supervisors or other authority figures. His employment was typically short lived, ending on unfavorable terms. Todd obviously had similar social adjustment issues that I had, and sought a similar solution based on his involvement in woodsmanship, outdoor sports and rural lifestyles. Mostly when Todd and I corresponded, we would discus survival skills and primitive technologies. Yet, we would also discussed politics, social issues and problems with culture and society. In particular, we both decreed the needlessly competitive "dog eat dog" nature of modern culture. By this time I grew quite connected, via postal correspondence, to a network of people and resources throughout the country, involved with off the grid living.

My handicraft production was a largely unprofitable endeavor for me. It was only on rare occasions that I can produce any marketable items. However, the few occurrences in which I did succeed at producing marketable goods really kept me going. Not only was I earning funds towards my goals, but it boosted my self esteem. I received many kudos on the quality of my craftsmanship. In my state of denial, I was convinced that with continued practice, I can more frequently produce profitable implements. This would only earn me more money towards my goals. Every slight improvement in my battery of primitive skills I was a monumental occurrence for me. For it was an improvement upon my means to break free from mainstream society and escape its toxicity. Never would anyone impose unreasonable demands upon me and mercilessly harangue me for failing to meet them. Certainly nobody would ever make fun of my manner of speech, or my inability to pay attention and follow instructions. I was following a mirage in a very real desert of suitable opportunities.

I rather enjoyed life in Auburn. I felt certain that all I needed was another year of living at home to develop my skills and attain the resources to pursue my goals. I could then strike out on my own and create my own virtual Eden.

In May/June of 1994 my parents announced that they were looking to purchase a house, through the VA loan program. My dad spent 16 years in the US Marine Corps and served in the Lebanon conflict during the early 1980s. This made him eligible for a VA home loan. Cost was their primary consideration in purchasing their home. I hoped that they could find an inexpensive place and another fairly small town, close to some woodland with good fishing opportunities. Yet such homes too often are highly costly, and I knew that most of these properties would be out of their budget. So I had to brace myself for the prospects of living in a more urbanized setting. This did not appeal to me in the slightest. Where would I collect natural materials to make my implements? How could I fish and practice wilderness survival skills? These were especially vexatious issues for me. Given my neurologically based inability to drive, how would I even escape such a nightmare? I knew that there was nothing in store for me with regard to job prospects. I knew that I would just not do well in the normal workaday world and there were also no social services available for me. I had no financial means to move out on my own, lest I live as a homeless vagabond. But such a life is all too often very short-lived, incurring frequent arrests for urban squatting, and dying of ailments that you don't have the resources to treat. I knew that I didn't have what it takes to lead that life either. All I could do was hope that my mom and dad could find a rural place to live, similar to our Auburn residence. However, our place in Auburn was a unit in a rental duplex, and this was why we were able to afford to live in such a setting. Buying a home was a different matter altogether. There tends to be a major price differential between most urban houses and those closer to the country, in favor of the latter option.

At any rate, I was confident that I would only be living at home for another year, so I just thought that I would make the best of whatever situation were to materialize. I had $700 total to my name. This is undoubtedly a paltry sum but a good start, in my mind. I knew of highly exceptional, but well documented cases, of private individuals purchasing acreage is low was $50 per acre. With the ability to construct a sturdy home from on site natural or recycled materials, it should be entirely doable. All I had to do was find a cheap piece of property and build a crude shelter on it until I had the resources to build a more permanent dwelling.

I began this chapter with a quote from Zygmut Bauman. The quote originates from the opening paragraph of an article in the on-line version of the UK based *Guardian* newspaper, published on May 31, 2012, authored by Bauman, entitled *Downward Mobility is Now a Reality.* In its original context, the quote reads;

> *"Every generation has it's measure of outcasts. However, it doesn't happen often that the plight of the outcast may embrace to a whole generation. Yet this is precisely what is happening in Europe now."*

And it is likely happening in America too. Bauman's quote, I feel sums up what can be observed in the transition from my generation (generation X) to the millennial generation to come of age. As a member of generation X, mine was the first to come of age, during the full onset of the neoliberal economy. Mine was also the first post-WWII generation for which a trend towards downward mobility was predicted. Yet, among my peers, I was still the oddity, in that I had graduated from high school and was still living at home for a number of years afterward. Most of my peers moved away their parents soon after leaving high school. Either they had gone on to college or into comfortably paying employment. Though I would hear all the laments and doom among radio talk show hosts and social commentators about my generation and their unwillingness to grow up and get out in the world, I seemed to be among the few that such commentary was descriptive of. Yet I was still representative of the out-casts among my generation.

As I wrote this chapter, reflecting upon my coming of age during the early 1990s, I was constantly reminded of many of my millennial friends, who now are in the same boat I was at their age. Yet many such persons have no functional limitations as I do. They simply inherited a harsher, less inclusive and more competitive economy and society that the one I grew up in. For their generation has been saddled with; more outsourcing of work, more cuts to public spending to fund wars, greater transfer of wealth from labor to capital, and no child left behind, with its emphasis on putative high stakes testing. Thus it is little wonder that many millennials, thus far have proven ill-prepared for the world, unable to establish any footing. However, the basic underlying cause of my lamented coming of age related primarily to the work intensification inherent to the global capitalist economy. Whereas with today's youth the trend towards pronounced downward mobility is more a function of outsourcing and a jobless recovery of the great recession. Yet all facets of the problem are rooted in the same underlying cause; 40 years of free market fundamentalism as Americas guiding economic policy.   As a neurodiverse person, I have been among many canaries in the coalmine of toxic neoliberal economic and social policy. How bad must it get, before society at large seeks to exit the mine?

CHAPTER 3-A NEW ECOLOGY:

"No one is born fully formed: It is through our self-experience in the world that we become what we are"
-Paulo Friere

In late July of 1994, my mom and dad settled on purchasing a house in Tacoma, Washington. It was a 2 story, 2,100 square foot, slate blue composite home with teal trim. Originally built during the turn of the 20th century, the house had been remodeled at least twice that I know of. Situated on a 1/3 acre parcel, there were multiple fruit trees on the property, including two cherry trees, two apple trees, and two pear trees. Other trees and shrubbery included yew, willow, lilac, and rhododendron shrubs. Located in a middle working class, neighborhood in south Tacoma, the area was rather rough around the edges, but the house was much nicer than any we ever lived in, as I was growing up.

Days prior to finalizing our move, I bought a $100.00 Huffy mountain bike, hoping to enhance my mobility and independence in the bigger city. Perhaps I could use the bike to get away from Tacoma every so often, maybe to ride up to Gig Harbor, just across the Tacoma Narrows bridge. I was not comfortable taking the bus, but knew that relying entirely on walking, would lead to severely restricted access and mobility in a larger city like Tacoma. On the day of purchasing the bike, I walked it out of the store, and across the parking lot to my dad's pickup truck. While doing so, input from my kinesthetic senses cautioned me that a mountain bike may not be a workable solution to my mobility conundrum. I could not see myself maintaining equilibrium, while peddling at any effective pace. It was a major point of confusion for me. I rode bikes as a young child, form the ages of 5-10 years without difficulty. As a kid, I could keep up with, and often lead my playmates while we were all out and about on our bikes. So were my vestibular dysfunctions becoming worse as an adult? Could it be that growth in height and subsequent elevation of one's center of gravity exacerbates the effect of equilibrium impairment in adulthood? I could not understand why the bicycle seemed so awkward, just from walking it. Perhaps if I just practice a

81

little by peddling through an empty parking lot, I can re-habituate myself to the use of a bicycle. There were numerous occasions in which I attempted to do so, with no success. My efforts were completely futile and I never regained the ability to ride a conventional bicycle. Traversing downhill at an effective speed was impossible.

The bike remained in the garage at my mom and dad's house collecting dust for a number of years-that is until a friend and college roommate would buy it and put it to good use. About five years after purchasing that bike, I discovered the relative merits of recumbent cycling. In my college years, I found that using a recumbent bicycle, with it's lower center of gravity, makes it possible to enjoy a level of physical mobility I could never have imagined. But such mobility is contingent on residing in a well connected town with wider roads and abundant bicycle lane mileage.

Tacoma was the last place on earth I wanted to live. This is the most drastic understatement I could ever have made. In the early to mid-1990s, the town had a well deserved reputation as being a major violent crime hotbed in Washington State. In 1995, the town made headlines throughout the state due to a major bust of the Tacoma hilltop Crips street gang. I was terrified of the prospect of living there. But what else could I do? I wanted to be gainfully employed, living on my own, with the freedom to choose my residence. I wanted these things just as much as any other young man. But my disability completely relegated these life options to nothing more than idle hopes. I felt trapped. Hope for deliverance resided entirely in placing my name on the land auction mailing list for five different Washington state agencies. I clung firmly to hope that a parcel of land would turn up for auction that was within my meager purchasing power. Yet I knew that such occurrences were exceedingly rare.

Among my more immediate concerns however was staying safe from crime while living in Tacoma. Given my relegation to walking everywhere I go, I am without the protection afforded by the faster moving metal, polymer, and Plexiglas capsule of a motor vehicle. Thus, I am much more vulnerable to encountering violence on the streets. Not yet old enough to buy a handgun and obtain a concealed pistol license, how would I defend myself in such an event? How can I survive physically? How can I survive psychologically?

I begrudgingly moved with my mom, dad and sister to the city of Tacoma. In the mid summer of 1994, the move was complete. Once settled into Tacoma, much of my time was spent figuring out ways to adapt my primitive technology activities to my new urban environment. Though largely urbanized and industrial, a few vestiges of Tacoma's natural history remained undeveloped by the hand of man.

There were a few small urban forests, within blocks of our new residence where I could collect timbers, cordage materials, and igneous stones. Igneous stones are readily shaped into multitudes of implements through the process of pecking and grinding. My favorite urban greenbelt was an 80 acre area known as Wapato Hills. It had an easy access point at 56th and Tacoma Mall Boulevard. At this location was an open field at the base of the forested moraine. A cleared trail, radiating from this field led up a steep slope and on to the plateau of the wooded moraine. It was an oasis of rugged natural terrain in the middle of a gritty chaotic city. This urban forest was a mixed conifer and broadleaf zone, situated on top of a glacial moraine which formed a large plateau on top of a steep hill. There were ample quantities of hazel, bigleaf maple, oso-berry, oceanspray, cottonwood, fireweed, and stinging nettle, all of which would yield timber or fiber for many of my projects. In addition there was a plethora of small woodland fauna, namely rabbits and squirrels to either snare, or shoot with a slingshot or blowgun. At the base of the moraine was an outcrop, containing large quantities of basalt, quartzite, and granite pebbles. These will serve nicely as lithic materials for flintknapping. If I could figure out a bus route to Jerry's Rock and Gem, I could purchase my obsidian there, just as when I lived in Auburn. A Tandy Leather also existed just a few blocks away from our new Tacoma residence. Here, I can purchase buckskins, rawhide and beeswax. At least I now know that I have many potential sources of constructive materials for my primitive technology projects. I also had plenty of natural materials, brought over from Auburn to continue working with. Finding resolution to that issue went a long way to putting me at greater ease about living in Tacoma. Thus I knew I could hold out until I was able to obtain at least a half an acre of property and the freedom it afforded.

Immediately after unpacking and storing all of my belongings, I was out in the backyard doing exactly what I did while living in Auburn-knapping obsidian, intent on producing 3 inch or longer, thin, well proportioned symmetrical bifaces to sell. I scoped out all possible places where I could rent table space to sell any wares that I produce. There was a flea market off of 72nd and South Tacoma way, about 4 or 5 blocks south our residence. I also found the Tacoma Community College and Pierce College campuses and knew that I could rent table space there as well. That base was covered. By this time, I had nearly a solid year of *concentrated* flintknapping practice under my belt, and over two years' flintknapping experience in general. Yet, consequent to lifelong motor and perceptual deficits, my knapping skill remained stagnated, to a point at which producing any aesthetically desirable, marketable, implement was nothing short of a monumental achievement.

My attention and focus started turning more towards ground stone This particular technology is much more approachable than flaked stone knapping. Ground stone tools appear relatively recent in prehistory, becoming commonplace throughout the globe after the Pleistocene. Examples of such implements are the ground stone axes, mauls, and fishing weights that one might see on display in an anthropology museum. Essentially, ground stone tool manufacture necessitates a slow, repetitive chiseling and grinding processes (i.e. "pecking and grinding"). Pecking is merely the process of using a hard hammerstone to slowly crumbling away the surface of lithic material, by repeatedly striking the surface with a series of short rapid strokes. The final shaping is typically done by grinding the implement on a coarse stone, often with a slurry of sand and water as an additional abrasive. In a nutshell, that is the essence of ground stone tool manufacture. Many different applications of these techniques have been used in prehistory as well as by modern knappers to produce really fine and often elaborate ground stone objects. Though rather monotonous, the outcomes of the process are far less chaotic than those of flaked stone technology. By this point, it seemingly behooved me to concentrate on ground stone technology, as my progress in mastering flaked stone technology was hitting a major plateau.

I also relished the meditative state that ground stone tool production seemed to induce. The process was nothing short of completely surreal to me. Through nothing more than the application of repetitive working processes, merely amounting to a human induced hastening of natural geologic processes, iron hard pebbles could be transformed into shapes unknown in nature. It seemed that only a Stone Age or at least pre-industrial man would have the patience and tenacity or protracted concept of time to regularly practice this particular technology. I virtually knew of no other practitioners of primitive technologies who were as passionate about ground stone tool manufacture as I am.

That following autumn, after having moved to Tacoma, I worked largely on a few axes, a mace head, a mortar and pestle set, intending to sell these items in the following year. I would spend the entire day out in the backyard pecking and hammering and grinding away these implements, then retire for the evening by watching the news or writing a letter to one of my many pen pals throughout the country.

I wrote frequently to Todd in Battleground Washington. Being stuck in Tacoma, I envied his place of residence. Battleground is a small town of less than 2000 people and boundless opportunities for wilderness activities in the surrounding countryside. Any letter that I received from Todd was like a portal to the life I aspired for.

Todd just returned from a trip to Misstasini Québec, where he visited our mutual correspondent Nate Waller and his family. Upon his arrival home, I called to ask how his trip went. He reported a very disappointing experience, finding out that Nate Waller was something of a charlatan, not nearly as adept with primitive technologies as he lauded himself to be. Contrary to his claims, Nate did not actually make most of the products that he sold through his home based business. The items that he did make, such as his primitive archery sets were frequently returned for poor workmanship. The more I corresponded with Nate, the more I began to suspect this was the case. His lack of expertise was at times betrayed in the rather evasive manner in which he answered specific technical questions I posed to him, regarding primitive technologies. However, I always gave him the benefit of the doubt. Needless to say, neither Todd nor I had any more to do with Nate after that occurrence.

I spent so much time in the backyard working on my various projects and my activities often elicited the curiosities of neighborhood children. After all it's not every day that a person sees somebody chipping or crumbling away at one stone with another stone or hewing away a section of tree trunk into some discernible shape. I enjoyed sharing my knowledge with them and sometimes would hand them a piece of material to work with, enabling them to try their hand at it.

I once had a nine-year-old boy produce a coal with a bow drill[12] and he acted as if it were among the happiest moments in his entire life. My dad suggested that I become a teacher, because I could always elicit such rapt attention and enthusiasm on the part of young children when I spoke on subjects relating to my research and interests. Was this a spark of something that had been lost to the ravages of growing up with and undiagnosed learning disorder, bad schools, and a dysfunctional home and family life?

Once I figured out how to obtain usable constructive materials from my new environment, my mom and dad's backyard became my own sanctuary. I seldom left home, except to browse the local Borders Books and Music, to procure materials at Wapato Hills park, or to mail off something to one of my correspondents. I was very socially withdrawn but could sometimes really connect with others depending on the context and circumstances of the interaction. For example I could often evoke strong enthusiasm when I conversed about primitive technologies and human prehistory. Even those who had no prior interest in the subject seemed to listen intently to one of my monologues. On one of my first visits to the Tacoma Borders Books and Music, myself and a total stranger were able to draw an entire audience, when discussing flintknapping, fire making and cordage manufacture. The conversation, started from our browsing of the same wood lore guides in the nature section of the store.

1995 started out like any other year. My plan of making ground stone implements for profit had not come to fruition. Ground stone tool manufacture does indeed place less of a premium on acute fine motor coordination and perceptual ability. However, problems arose from my very short attention span that made it nearly impossible to work on such a monotonous task for longer than 30 to 40 minutes at a time. But because ground stone tool manufacture is such a slow and inefficient process, it is impossible to accomplish significant

---

[12] A bow drill is an ancient device usually for firemaking. The device consists of 4 major components-a spindle, a hearth (fireboard), a bow, and a socket. The thicker end of the spindle is placed inside a notched pit in the heart and the top smaller end is held in place with the socket. The spindle is then rotated clockwise and counter-clockwise with the thong of the bow. Friction between the thick end of the spindle and the hearth generates heat, producing charred wood dust that becomes compacted in the notch of the board, forming a coal. This hot coal is then used to ignite a bundle of tinder, from which the fire is built upon.

progress toward a finished product in only 30 to 40 minutes of working time. I managed to complete one of the axes, I set out to make. As for the other products, they remained at various stages of completion, only to be finished a year or two later.

I did, however feel that by that point, I had acquired sufficient knowledge and experience with ground stone tool manufacturing processes to write an article for Steve Hulsey's then burgeoning *Wilderness Way* magazine. I contacted Mr. Hulsey, and inquired as to his interests in such an article. I felt that the level of attention devoted to ground stone implements by contemporary primitive technologists was rather sparse and that his magazine would be the perfect place for such an article. Steve Hulsey agreed, and I set out to write the piece. I initiated the writing of the article in February of that year but did not complete it until April. Organizational and concentration deficits, poor time management, and the inability to touch type really slowed down my progress. Yet Steve was always so infinitely patient in working with me. I don't recall ever explaining to him that I have specific neurological impairments attributable to my slow pace of writing. But he never seemed all that perturbed about my particular habits as an author. Perhaps he simply operated on the basis of working with whatever he received in terms of freelance submissions from authors. He may have been receiving more than ample material to keep them busy and just simply incorporated whatever he could use into each periodical issue of the magazine. At any rate, I eventually completed the article which was about 3000 words in length and mostly hand drafted illustrations. I only had a handful of completed implements to photograph, but had a good understanding of the processes and how to apply them. This is why I felt confident to write and publish the article.

On the day of submitting the article an uncustomary level of terror was bestowed upon me. It was a day I will never forget. After sending the article off through the local post office, I visited the south Tacoma public library just across the street. On my way back, I was walking home and encountered a somewhat vagrant looking individual who requested a dollar for bus fare. He bore many physical traits of a chronic drug user, casting suspicion as to why he was actually requesting the dollar. His bloodshot eyes, ashen, pasty white freckled complexion greasy red hair and beard, and incoherent speech left no doubt that he was likely a meth fiend. Despite my suspicions, I was in a good mood and had no problem parting with a dollar, trusting that he will use it for what he says.

Certain that I had a one dollar bill, I retrieved my wallet from my hip pocket, only to discover that the smallest denomination I had was a $20 bill. I had just spent my smaller denominations to send my manuscript down to Lufkin Texas. It was probably the first time I spent anything since my most recent purchase of Obsidian at Jerry's Rock and Gem, at least three weeks prior. I spent money so rarely that I could seldom maintain a working memory as to the amount of money and constituent denominations in my possession. I apologetically told the man that I had nothing smaller than a $20 bill and could not help him after all. He then insisted that I give him a $20 bill so that he could make change at a nearby store, only to take the one dollar he needed. I told him that I couldn't allow him to do that and that most stores do not allow customers to make change without purchasing something. I started to walk away and he kept following me insisting that I give him the $20 bill. I was equally insistent and my refusal to do so. He then bolted forward and stood squarely in front of me and demanded the money. Feeling threatened, I pulled out my Asp telescopic baton and in one fell swoop, lashed out and pelted the man across the side of the face, striking with sufficient force as to cause blood to spurt out and throw him off-balance. I then kicked him sharply behind the knees, knocking him off his feet. While he was on the ground, I delivered multiple lashes across his back and shoulders until he was completely incapacitated, begging me to stop hitting him. Within minutes, my frenzied attack was interrupted by the sound of angry shouting from across the street. I looked over my shoulder and saw two husky rough hewn men, one of whom was armed with a baseball bat. Both were both shouting at me demanding that I stop hitting the man. Were the friends of his? Were they good Samaritans who didn't see the entire sequence of events, and thought I was the initial aggressor? I didn't know. I just saw that it was going to be three against one with one of my antagonist being armed. I began running as fast as I could before the situation materialized as I feared. As I ran the two men chased me for a short distance before giving up. After about 100 yards, I looked back and saw that they were assisting the man that I just defeated. Thankfully, I was able to escape unharmed.

Upon returning home, my heart was still racing, and my head spinning, and I felt like I was walking on air. I thoroughly washed and sanitized the baton I used in the attack. I then sat in my room to get my bearings emotionally. I knew Tacoma was a chaotic madhouse. But could I convince my stupid parents of this? Certainly not! This was the first physical confrontation that I been involved in since I was a sixth grade schoolboy and I came out on top. Moreover, I came out on top, against individuals who in all likelihood were more seasoned street fighters. Something told me I should have felt at least a modicum of remorse for having inflicted such pain on the man that I defensively assaulted, but I felt none. Yet, I was concerned about the fact that I had such a stark lack of remorse. This seemed abnormal for my character. The last fight I was involved in, as a preteen left me feeling utterly miserable about having inflicted pain upon my adversary. I learned afterward that this is one reason why it's best not to solve personal conflicts with physical aggression. But this was different. It was much more than a mere personal conflict, it was a case of me acting defensively in response to a perceived threat. It was a matter of survival, where it was either me or him. Sociologically, it was a case of an informal sanction meted out against an individual behaving in a socially deviant manner. In that way, he arguably got his just desserts. This is especially so, given my counter-attack was delivered in a way most likely to merely incapacitate with no potentially lethal consequences. Thus the greater sin was on his end. He set the entire situation in motion in his attempt to forcibly extract money from me-an act which he had no legal or moral right to do. Ideally, I felt that I may have taught him a lesson about randomly harassing and intimidating people for his own illegitimate gain. Perhaps my defensive assault may have prompted him to at least think about the way he conducts his life and to consider another way of being. Or perhaps I was only being idealistic and further justifying my actions.

My feelings of triumph undoubtedly were a product of the intense anger and contempt that I always felt for criminals and miscreants of all sorts. As far back as I can remember, I always felt and still do feel that we live in a world of moral chaos where anything goes, and that there are too seldom adequate consequences to infringing upon the well-being of others. This holds true in business, on the streets, and in our personal lives. As an unapologetic socialist, my contention has long been that our culture and society are too libertarian, and that moral integrity and social responsibility are shunned while the unscrupulous and self-serving rewarded. From corporate welfare to the systematic coddling of both street thugs and white collar criminals, there is simply no accountability in our culture. Therefore, I saw this incident is one where the tables were turned and it was a miniscule but symbolic victory of good over evil in a world where evil generally prevails.

After the initial philosophizing and mental perseveration passed, fear of retaliation set in, and I grew highly agoraphobic. I worried that either the man I attacked or one of his cohorts would recognize me in another setting and seek to retaliate. Worse yet, they might be armed with more formidable means than what I had. Subject to turn 21 in the following month, I was soon legally old enough to purchase a handgun and to obtain a concealed pistol license. To my recollection, I had slightly over $800 to my name that I had been saving up to purchase property to live on. After that incident, however, I could easily justify the expense of a handgun and a concealed pistol license. Several weeks later, my check came in the mail for the article I submitted. The total was $50. This would go some way towards helping to pay for a new handgun.

In late May of 1995, I turned 21 and shortly thereafter, hit the streets, shopping for a handgun that was within my budget. Not wanting to deplete my "back to the land fund" too much, I was hoping to spend less than $200 for a serviceable used handgun. For $175, I purchased a serviceable used Charter Arms Bulldog .357 snub-nosed revolver. I just dare some lowlife street thug to try harassing or intimidating me, now. I'll show them the business end of this bad boy and they'll have one hell of a reality check! Should they choose not to defer, I will simply wipe them off the face of the earth with a squeeze of the trigger and there will be one less criminal deviant for society to deal with.

Standing in the gun shop, examining the weapon felt like something of a rite of passage, akin to attending the voting polls for the first time when at age 18. As I held the weapon, I fantasized about carrying it, relishing the feeling of invulnerability from knowing that I can potentially annihilate anyone who wishes to either harm to me or any other innocent victim. In a sense, I became a citizen soldier, joining a battle, fought from within. My actions were symptomatic of a society where law enforcement and legal sanctions are inadequate to protect the general public from those who wish to harm others. The body politic of larger society is fundamentally ailing.

Seven days after purchasing the revolver, the gun shop called to inform me that I passed the background check and cleared to finalize the purchase. The next day, my dad drove me to the gun shop so that I could pick up the weapon. We were both uncertain of the laws pertaining to the transport of a firearm on foot from a place of purchase.

My dad was rather curious as to why I bought the gun. It was of a make not generally intended for sporting purposes like hunting or competitive target shooting. The Charter Arms Bulldog is a gun for which its only legitimate use is personal defense. I knew that my dad suspected my intent of carrying the gun for personal protection, and he didn't fully approve. Thus I saw no reason to lie when he asked me why I bought it. I told the truth, revealing my intent of carrying the gun for personal defense. Detecting his unease over my choice, I mitigated the proclamation, saying that I would only carry it while traversing the more crime ridden districts of south and central Tacoma. I further stated that I would most likely be using the gun for informal target practice like shooting heavy bowling pins, where a lighter handgun cartridge such as a .22 rimfire wouldn't suffice. We had a slight disagreement over my carrying a handgun for defensive use. It wasn't a very heated argument, though. Despite his strong pro-gun stance, my dad didn't seem to like the idea of me carrying a loaded revolver. Yet I think that his disapproval was rooted in other sources, irrelevant to his personal political and philosophical views on guns. My dad grew up in the largely rural Midwest during the 1960s where people commonly owned shotguns and rifles for hunting, or target shooting. Yet hardly a soul could fathom the prospects of using a firearm defensively against a fellow person. Nobody even locked their doors, in the small town my dad grew up in. His was a different world than the one I had always known. I think he was mostly perturbed about the prospects of me facing legal troubles and/or great personal anguish in the event of using the gun defensively. On our way back from the gun shop he sternly cautioned me that were I to pull the trigger on somebody, I must bear in mind that whether the person dies or not, there's no way of recalling the bullet. Struck by the conviction and gravity with which he delivered his advice, I couldn't help but wonder about possible experiences he may have had while serving in the US Armed Forces. Yet something told me not to ask. He was seemingly trying to reconcile the parental desire to forbid me from arming myself in that manner, with the understanding that I was an adult responsible for making my own decisions. I wanted to request that he to take me to the County City building to apply for a concealed pistol license. However, I felt that this would be too disturbing for him. I thus opted to take care of that detail on another day.

I returned home with my dad, now in possession of a new handgun, ammo and holster. I immediately went to my room where I was admiring my new gun, holding it and sighting down the barrel. I eagerly awaited the first time I would fire it on a shooting range.

The seemingly innocuous event of owning a handgun for the first time was one of numerous events that elicited much confusion as to my station in life and place in society. I'm old enough to legally purchase such a weapon but am still living at home with my mom and dad, as when I was a juvenile schoolboy. I have been legally deemed psychologically sound enough to purchase a high powered handgun, but would be crippled by my impairments in typical workplace settings. And what about all of those psychometric tests I had to take in grade school and junior high? Surely nobody found out about those during the required background check to purchase the weapon. Would a background check, implemented through the National Investigative Center (NICS) even reveal such a history? Well if they did come across this information, the tests probably didn't reveal any condition too severe or I wouldn't have been approved to buy the weapon. I must be basically okay. I mean, they wouldn't approve someone too severely impaired to purchase a handgun would they? Probably not even in the USA.

Well now that I bought these goodies, I needed to make more money to replenish what I just paid out. I also needed something of a financial buffer that would enable me to comfortably purchase my concealed pistol license. I gathered my flintknapping tools and set out make something to sell for profit. I sat in the backyard for a flintknapping session, but did not produce anything marketable. Oh well, I thought, I'll try again tomorrow.

The next day, I took a cab to the County City building to purchase my concealed pistol license. I wanted so badly just to ride my mountain bike there. It was only a three mile distance from my abode. But riding a bicycle just seemed impossible to do. Public transit wasn't an option. I was simply too afraid to take the city bus for fear of encountering random violence. With all things considered, I felt justified in paying the $10 cab fare, including the tip, to travel only 3 miles each way to and from my place of residence. I went to the County city building, filled out the application, and paid the $60 fee, to have my fingerprints taken.

I returned home and went straight to work on some wooden hafts for two ground basalt axe heads I recently made. One was a basic triangular round poll celt type. The other was a typical North

92

American ¾ grooved axe. To haft the celt, I had a young growth branch of Oregon White Oak. For the ¾ grooved axe, a pliable hazel sapling would be wrapped through the groove and secured with buckskin lashings. My plan was to set up a table at Tacoma Community College to sell both of these axes, along with other implements I previously made.

My sister Laurel was home along with Irene, a long-term friend of hers from high school. While sitting outside whittling away on the Oregon White Oak, Laurel and Irene presented me with a 20 ounce can of Foster's, knowing that this is my favorite beer."Happy 21st", they both said in unison, handing the beer down to me, as I sat on the back porch, whittling away. "Why thank you" I replied. I laid down my crooked knife to grasp the offering of lager. Being a lightweight that I am, I devoured a little over half the beer before growing too inebriated to safely handle a sharp woodworking tool. The stopping point was when I almost sliced myself across the left shoulder, when the edge of my knife abruptly dislodged from the wood I was carving. I then put aside the timber and my knife then went inside the house to join Laurel, Irene, and another friend of ours, Phil. After all, it is my birthday. They were amused that little more than half of beer was enough to inebriate me to the extent that it did. I polished off the Foster's and we all had rum and coke while watching movies. All of a sudden, I went into a major drunken stupor and began orating a satirical philosophizing redneck monologue. Assuming the stereotypical back hollow southern accent, I attempted to debate the merits of having an IQ lower than 80. As I recall my oratory was something like this:

> "Ya don't need an IQ any highern' 80. Once thet IQ be getin' highern' 80, yer dang brainhousin' group jest goes all screwy an catty-wompus sideways on ya cuz ya gets mer thinkin' smarts goin' on up inside yer brainhousin' group then yer common sense knows hai ta handle, an ya sturt gettin' all them fancy thinkin' communist ideas in yer head bout' yer inner child an hai we all comes from little green monkeys thet dun lived in da African rainforest some 8 million years go. I tell ya, them folks wit 80+ IQs aint got a lick a common sense thet the good lord done gave a piss ant an thems the folks thet be screwin' up this great country of ours. An I done figured thet out wit jest ma trusty ol' 65 IQ. It's jest common sense. Ya see thets

93

why I be right proud of ma 65 IQ-keeps ma brain on da straight an narrow path wit-out bein' led astray by a bunch a useless thinkin' smarts!

Laughter emanated from the others.

"What in turnations so dang funny, I retorted. It's jest plain ol' common sense!"

"What an authentic accent" Laurel replied.

Do they have flush toilets where you come from? Irene jokingly added.

Wut in turnations' a durn flush toilet? Sounds like you be speakin' French or Russian or somethin'. Don't tell me you one of them uppity edumacated city folks thet thinks you all high'n mighty cuz you speaks mor'n one language!"

"No....I don't speak more than one language and toilet is an English word. City folk use them to well .... you know.... do their business!"

"English? So them things comes from England then? You aint from England are you? Nai I be cornfused, you says you only speaks one language and you be speakin' a'marcan. Do you speaks both English an a'marican? You probably gots an IQ highern' 80, no wonder why you be talkin' so much stuff thet don't make a spit lick a sense ta me. An jest what kinda business do city folks do with them thar toilets?"

"Well.....you know....crap and pee..number 1 and number 2.....you know".

"Why cain't they jest use an outhouse?"

"Because, there are sanitation codes against it".

"Dang, big brother always be tryin' ta tell everyone how ta live they durn lives! Its worse than the old Soviet Union, I tell ya!"

"You sound just like some of the people who call in

94

on republican talk radio programs" Phil replied.

It was my Reverend Earl (aka Rev. Earl Fajen Lee) personae that I was acting out. This "Reverend Earl" personae, developed that night, became an alter ego that I would use for calling conservative talk radio programs and orating satirical commentary that ridicules simplistic short sighted conservative beliefs and the low intellectual capacity they betray. This often proved to be highly cathartic.

After hours of drinking and watching movies I went to my room in an attempt to sober up and get to sleep. I turned on the radio and tuned into a conservative talk radio program. I found great amusement with the veritable idiots calling up to chime in with their thoughts and opinions on political hot topics of the day. The topic for discussion on that evening's episode was corporal punishment. I had the perfect Reverend Earl monologue for the topic. Still heavily under the influence of many alcoholic libations and inspired by Phil's comment that my redneck oratory sounded reminiscent of conservative talk radio discourse, I decided to do just that-call the talk show host and spout off satirical conservative commentary using my Reverend Earl personae. Being too drunk to properly dial the number, I dialed the same wrong number twice, before finally dialing the correct one. I reached the screener initially, who asked me whether or not I agreed with the host (who shall remain nameless).

"Hell yeah, I agree!" I exclaimed in my falsetto voice.

"Thet's what's wrong wit dis durn country. Ya caint even take a good ol' hickory switch to the backside of some tyrannical spoiled rotten brat without havin' CPS on yer durn case! They be worried ya might bring down they self esteem, or damage they inner child!"

"How true", the greeter replied. "I'll put you on the air".

So here I was, heavily intoxicated and managed to fool the screener to let me on the air.

"Hello, you're on the air."

"It's the Reverend Earl Fajen Lee, here and I gots a story ta tell."

"A-a-a-and what is your story, sir?" the host replied with nervous suspicion.

"The story begins in the German speaking province of Braunau, in the former Austro-Hungarian Empire on April 20, 1889. For on that day a baby boy was born. And he was born to a couple overeducated beyond they natural common sense and brainwashed by the satanic secular humanistic venom of the day, espoused by one Sigmund Freud, who hath led many a parent astray from the Lord's Divine axiom that if you spare the rod, you'll dag'um spoil the child. And these folks weren't nary an exception. So when their son was five, he would put on his mother's apron, stand on a chair and pretend to preach like a reverend conducting a holy sermon. And rather than whip the boy's backside for his irreverent acts against the church, they spared the rod and spoiled the child! Well when the boy was 10, he took a liking to drawing artwork! So not wanting to stifle the boy's self-expression they indulged his frivolous pastime, and they spared the rod and spoil the child! And when he would rather idly sit around, drawing his pictures, they spared the rod and spoil the child, and praised the boy lavishly for every single drawing he did regardless of its true merit. Now when the boy was 18, he applied for admission to the Vienna Art Academy. He was rejected. And rather than look within himself to what he could have done to be accepted to the Academy, he reacted with an infantile rage, the wrath of which would cause death and destruction of biblical proportions! The boy's name was Adolf Hitler!"

"Okay, Mr. Reverend have a good night!" the host said with total scorn and disbelief, before brusquely hanging up. When listening to a rerun of that episode, the host was clearly not happy with the fact that I managed to get on the air with this fallacious commentary. "Who the hell is that joker, and how did he get on the air?" He grumbled after my call.

"Hitler grew up to be a ruthless dictator just because he was spoiled rotten and not spanked enough as a child; nobody believes that! It was probably some smartass liberal college kid trying to play some stupid gag to get a laugh from his dorm buddies!"."Oh but what the hell, I guess a little bit of comic relief every now and again isn't going to hurt us. But my God what a silly kid!"

In June of 1995, I was afforded an opportunity to take a brief, albeit strikingly authentic and moving glimpse into the life that I had so long dreamed of. Todd invited me for a wilderness survival outing with his uncle and cousin down in Cougar, Washington. This would be the occasion where our woodsmanship skills would be put to the truest test that either of us had yet to experience. Todd's aunt and uncle lived in a travel trailer, essentially as vagabonds. They lived off the land, surviving by hunting, trapping, fishing, foraging and selling natural resources such as animal pelts and different types of mushrooms.

On one early summer day, I took a train down to Vancouver, Washington. There, Todd's sister Kathy and his brother in law Jacob picked me up at the Amtrak station. On our way to Todd's residence, we talked about many things. We talked about previous correspondence between Todd and I, as well as the novelty of Todd and my endeavors in primitive technologies. Multiple other topics came up that I only vaguely recall.

It was the first time, Todd and I actually met in person but it felt like we had known each other for years. In a way we did, though our only means of communication consisted mostly of either pen letters or sound waves transmitted through miles of copper wire. Arcane as they now may be, the power of such communication modes can never be underestimated.

Within minutes of our initial meet and greet, Todd and I gathered our meager belongings, and loaded them up in his red Subaru station wagon. We then set out for an abandoned trapper's cabin near Georges Creek, just out of Cougar, Washington. Later that day, we would meet with his uncle, aunt, and younger cousins. Todd spent many of his summers there. This was also where he did a good deal of his autumn hunting. Our plan was to construct some simple but sturdy wikiup shelters and catch some trout, perhaps some whitefish and collect some wild edibles. On our arrival, we unloaded our belongings in the cabin and grabbed our fishing tackle to secure our main course for dinner. We used typical commercially manufactured angling gear-basically five and a half foot spinning rods and reels with 6 lb. test monofilament line, along with metal hooks, lead weights and Styrofoam floats. In addition, we supplemented our gear by making some monofilament trot lines with small 16 oz plastic pop bottles as the floatation rig. Todd caught the first rainbow trout, then I caught the next two and he caught a whitefish. By that point, we felt that we each surely had enough protein for the next few days. We kept our catch live in 10 gallon paint buckets filled with water, while I sought to secure some edible vegetal matters and Todd worked on building a large wikiup shelter. Using a digging stick made from a hazel sapling with a heat hardened sharpened tip, I collected about 3 lbs of cat-tail roots and about a pound of tiger lily bulbs. Both of which are a great source of carbohydrates and the tiger lily bulbs providing many essential nutrients and minerals to enhance energy utilization. Now that we had our sustenance, we needed a means to cook it all. To that order, I answered by collecting some small alder saplings from which to weave into a grill to place over a low alder wood flame. The use of alder for both the grill grate and fuel induces an aromatic smoke that imparts a nice smoky flavor onto our rustic natural repast.

While walking back to our campsite, I dropped my folding saw into a tuft of Oregon grape shrubs. I then knelt down to pick up my tool from the forest floor. While doing so, I felt a sharp sting on the heel of my right hand. The sting felt not unlike that resulting from contact with a young nettle shoot. Yet no nettles could be seen covering the adjacent ground where I reached down with my hand. After picking up my saw, I examined the site of the sting and it was already noticeably swollen and inflamed. Yet there was no stinger or visible point of injury. A number of wasps flew from beneath the fern and Oregon grape I was just rummaging through. It had to be a wasp sting. Though I never had an allergic reaction to insect stings, I felt compelled to monitor the wound for signs of a more serious reaction. My hyper-vigilance was surely motivated by an occurrence years prior at the age of 15, in which I sustained a bee sting that led to blood poisoning. Luckily, I recognized the symptoms of blood poisoning and had it treated with antibiotics in a timely manner. So I knew to watch out for increased swelling, fever, chills, and red streaks radiating from the site of this wound. My increased diligence with this wound was also motivated by the fact that we were in a more remote location with compromised sanitary conditions. Being aware of the tannic acid content and hence anti-microbial properties contained within many tree barks, I stripped off some bark from a big-leaf maple sapling and wrapped it around the site of the wound before heading back to camp. I arrived at the base camp with the edible tubers, alder wands, and bandaged hand.

"What's with the hand wrap?" Todd asked.

"I think it's an insect sting. The cambium layer of this big-leaf maple bark has some mild antibacterial properties to help stave off infection."

"Oh I didn't know that. You learn something new every day."

"If you don't mind, I'm gonna find some plaintain leaves to make a more effective antiseptic poultice for this wound before I commence with cleaning the cat-tail and tiger-lily roots. Also, if you don't mind, it would probably be best if you cleaned all the fish that we caught to minimize the risk of this sting getting infected. Once we have all of the food prepared for cooking, I'll show you how I fashion a cooking grill from these alder saplings to cook everything with."

"No problem" Todd replied. While Todd was busy cleaning all of the fish, I hiked out of the ravine and onto higher, drier ground with more abundant plantain weeds. I collected several handfuls of these-enough to make multiple dressings. I applied the first poultice dressing, by pulverizing some of the plantain leaves and applying them directly to the wound-especially around what seemed to be the entry of the sting. I then placed two whole plantain leaves over the applied poultice and secured them all in place with several lashings of the big leaf maple bark. The pain and discomfort subsided very quickly and before long, the swelling was slowly starting to ameliorate. As to whether the plantain dressing had any effect, or it was just normal healing of the insect sting, I was uncertain. But at least by that point, I was assured to have been out of the woods for any prospect of infection. After dressing my wound, I went back to our campsite and helped Todd complete the preparation of our meal. Upon our arrival, Todd had completely cleaned all fish and washed all of the root vegetables.

"Wow! all done?" I asked. "That was fast."

"Yep, I got er all done".

"Well I've got a good dressing on this hand and can get our fire going and cook everything."

"Fair enough. Oh also there's some firewood stacked up in the cabin", Todd informed me.

"Good, I'll go fetch some."

"I'll get it", Todd replied. "You were just up in that direction."

Todd then darted up the hill to get some firewood. In the meantime I gathered some suitable stones to make a good hearth. After constructing the fire pit and hearth, I started a small fire started in the pit. I used dried moss, and scotch broom twigs for kindling and ignited the entire bundle with two wooden matches. In the ultimate act of fortuitous timing, Todd came down with a sizable bundle of firewood from the cabin. "Perfect timing" I said as Todd, descended down slope with the firewood. "Looks like well seasoned alder and maple too!" "That will work perfectly." I wove the small alder saplings in a crisscross weft and warp pattern forming a coarse grate. I placed the grate over the stone hearth which kept it suspended about 10 inches above the flame-perfect for slow roasting our fish, stuffed with watercress leaves. The cat tail and tiger lily bulbs were placed directly on flat tabular stones set alongside the fire. Knowing that they would take longer to cook, I started cooking those prior to the fish. In less than a half hour, we had the perfect meal, very nourishing and tasting not unlike anything that would be prepared in a backyard barbecue.

While we were finishing up the consumption of our meal, Todd's uncle Tim, aunt Nell, and two preteen cousins Troy and Crystal, stopped by to park their trailer and join us for a visit. My fire pit contraption and the meal that Todd and I cooked on it readily became to topic of conversation among us all. "What do you have wrapped around your hand?" Tim asked me.

"It's just a dressing I made for a wasp sting-basically some plantain leaves pulverized and held in place with a plantain leaf bandage and some bark wrapping."

"This guy is really handy with plants" Todd added.

How's that dressing working?" Tim asked.

100

"Seems to be working okay. The swelling is going down, and I don't feel the sting at all."

"Good deal" Tim added. "I'll have to remember that, next time one of us gets stung by something out here."

Todd's aunt Nell soon emerged from the RV approached with a bag of potatoes and a few cans of soup that she obtained from a food pantry in Battle Ground. That was her family's evening meal. Tim got started preparing a separate campfire on to cook their family's meal.

Todd and I departed for a brief show and tell session, sharing each of our tools and implements we each had made. I presented Todd with a 3" long mahogany obsidian dagger that I hafted in a hazel wood handle, secured in place with deer gut lashings. We then did some informal archery shooting, aiming at a 1 gallon milk jug target with a primitive vine maple bow that Todd made. We discussed our plans for the week including the snaring of a deer and dispatching it with a lance. Afterward, Todd and I would preserve the meat through drying and smoking. "How is the shelter coming along?" I asked. "We'll have to finish it up tomorrow" Todd replied, but we can sleep in the cabin for tonight. Once we were done shooting the bow, we went up onto the plateau to check on Todd's aunt uncle and cousins. They were all enjoying their dinner. We sat around the campfire bantering on various subjects of interest.

I was captivated and moved by some of the stories that Tim and Nell told about the way they lived. But it was also enough to make me "re-conceptualize" my romantic notions of living as a rural vagrant. Tim had limited use of his left hand, due to some broken bones that had not set properly. He had no insurance to effectively treat the injury. Both he and his wife were missing teeth and showed many obvious signs of poor physical health. Neither of them even graduated from high school. Nell only had a fifth grade education and Tim quit school in the ninth grade. It were as though they had few other life options but to live the manner that they were. It struck me as very sad, but Todd really seemed to look up to his uncle and greatly romanticized the way he and his family lived. Though not explicitly stated, I got the impression that neither of Todd's cousins Troy or Crystal were even attending school regularly. After our visit with the family, Todd, Troy and I retreated to the old Trapper's cabin where we went to sleep for the evening. We discussed various topics-mostly political ones, involving Ruby Ridge, Waco, and Timothy McVeigh. Todd harbored allot of anti-government sentiments and wanted to join a local militia. I too expressed equal dismay over the ATF's handling of Ruby Ridge and Waco. However, being of a more leftist orientation, I did not consider overthrowing the government as a workable or viable solution. Yet I too was just as discontented with the mainstream norm of society as Todd was.

By this point, I had seen and heard enough. I got what I came for and then some. I needed to get back home, rethink my life and figure out a more realistic plan. The next day, I woke up, and my wasp sting was nothing more than a mere memory. The inflammation completely subsided. No longer did I need the dressing. I showed Todd how expediently the wound healed and he was impressed. We set out to work on the shelter and planned on spending the day fishing and collecting wild edibles just like the day before.

I was compelled to create some type of excuse to cut this trip short and return home as soon as possible. The day was still young, and Todd and I completed the shelter. I went back up to the cabin, stating that I was going to fetch our fishing tackle and root harvesting equipment. I did just that. While in the cabin, I also found my day planner and wrote "Grandma/Aunt Joyce visit" for the next day. With all of my gear in hand I jotted down the ravine, where we built our shelter. I then rendered to Todd my fabricated reason for cutting the trip short.

"Damn, I'm so absent minded" I exclaimed aloud.

"Why" Todd asked.

"Well I forgot that my Grandma and Aunt Joyce are visiting this week. In fact they will be at our place tomorrow. I can't stay down here this entire week. I'll have to leave either today or tomorrow."

"I understand" Todd replied. "We'll have to take this up another time". "My sister Kathy is off today and can drive you down to the train station in Vancouver."

"Yeah, I might have to do that, if she wouldn't mind". At any rate, I think we have had a good time so far, and hopefully we can do this again some time."

102

"Definitely", Todd replied.

Todd drove me back to his home in Battle Ground where his sister arrived to pick me up to take to the train station. Todd and I shook hands, said our goodbyes and promised to take our projects up at another time. I waited nearly all day at the Amtrak terminal, nearly numb of all emotion, and still trying to take in all that I observed in Cougar.

It wasn't just Todd's Aunt and Uncle who were living this way, I also briefly met another vagabond survivalist in the area who was suffering tremendously. He was a Vietnam vet and citizen militia member. He was afflicted with severe PTSD. His story was heart wrenching. By that point I was realizing that I had far better options in life than what I witnessed down in Cougar.

Within a few months after that trip, Todd and I were no longer corresponding. I sent the final letter to which he never replied. Perhaps he was aware that I concocted a fallacious reason to abort our trip early and was disappointed that I did not embrace the wilderness living experience as passionately as he did. Such is life. I just had to accept that loss.

After my trip to Cougar, reality was steadily weighing on me with greater frequency. Increasingly, I was coming to terms with the fact that my life aspirations were exceedingly unrealistic to say the least. It was time for a new game plan. I harbored thoughts along these lines before. It was only my trip to the remote wilderness of southwest Washington that caused me to pay serious heed to them. My psychic anesthesia was wearing off and the pain was growing unbearable. Yet I felt caught between a rock and a hard place. Surely my parents will not be alive forever to continue supporting me and I am never going to get my business off the ground. Yet is there any occupation available that I can do? There has to be. But maybe it will just require additional training. But how do I obtain that additional training?

At the behest of reality's beckon, I would submit applications for employment in which I at least thought the work to be feasible in relation to my capabilities. Yet, I was operating on only a sketchy understanding of my limitations, and an incomplete understanding as to performance demands of various occupations. Basically there were a few select retail jobs I wrongly assessed to be fairly slow in pace. These were jobs I would apply for. Service sector jobs, being

103

the most prominent occupations on the post-industrial urban landscape, seemed the only natural choice. Typical examples of jobs I applied to included bookstore jobs, sporting goods store employment, and warehouse employment. It is something of a blessing that none of these employers ever even called me in for an interview. I would only find out years later, that my concept of retail employment was completely fallacious and I would not likely succeed in this line of work.

My cloistered existence made me very naïve as to the ways of the "outside world". I later came to realize that this in itself has long constituted an additional layer of disability in my life. Perhaps my isolation has compounded the effects of the organic impairments I was born with.

In the spring of 1995, I applied for federal student aid to enroll in a landscape management program taught at Clover Park technical College in Lakewood Washington. To me, the idea working in horticulture was very appealing. I enjoyed working in my mom and dad's vegetable garden and maintaining the trees and shrubs in our backyard. I could do that type of work all day. Yet unbeknownst to me, working for a private enterprise or government agency is worlds apart from home production work. When you work for an employer, standards of timeliness and efficiency rule the game. Moreover, working in most professional settings places a premium on an ability to effectively co-ordinate work with others to maximize efficiency. These were lessons that I would only learn years later, when finally afforded the opportunity to work in the landscaping occupation.

Several months after applying for federal student aid, I received notice from the Department of Education, informing me that I was ineligible for student aid funding. I got the news just shortly after returning home from Cougar. Their rationale was that my parental income was too high. Not yet 24, I was still considered legally dependent on parental funds for my schooling. Yet my mom and dad clearly could not afford my tuition for the program.

Going into the military and having my tuition paid through the GI bill was not an option for me. I could never pass muster for the physical agility requirements of the PT. The general teamwork involved, and the demands of being required to function in a fast-paced environment, and take orders at a fast pace was out of my capabilities. Emotionally, I could not handle military culture either. I was trapped. That's all there is too it. I was not getting anywhere but

I knew I could not integrate into the normal workaday world. My parents will certainly be alive forever to continually support me. But what the hell am I to do? All I can do is hope that my flintknapping and writing skills improve to a point of being able to more frequently profit from these endeavors. For the next twelve months afterward, this was the hope I naïvely and persistently clung to. I would make frequent, yet often ill fated attempts at producing handicrafts for sale. Only on two occasions after my 21st birthday did this materialize in the profit. During the second half of 1995, I managed to publish two other articles in *Wilderness Way* magazine. Both of which netted me $225. This was enough to largely make up for the gun, holster, ammo, and concealed pistol license I bought earlier that year. However, I got a sense that these articles weren't as well received by the readership of this magazine as my very first one was. In a follow up phone conversation with the editor, he said nothing to me regarding feedback from readers.

In late August of 1995 my dad went on strike at Boeing. He didn't support the strike nor did he vote in favor of it. Yet, as stipulated by his mandatory union membership, he had to be on strike. He was getting adequate strike compensation, to manage all household expenses for the duration of the strike. Yet to ensure an adequate financial buffer, he looked for part-time employment elsewhere.

Feeling the pang of urgency, brought on by our family's looming financial hardship, I felt increasingly obligated to make an earnest attempt at securing a real-world job. It was at this moment in which I considered the prospect that a suitable occupation exists somewhere for me within the national economy. My dad and I both applied for the same types of jobs. These were mostly warehouse work for retailers and shipping companies. I must have submitted around 20-30 applications within one month alone and was even called for my first job interview.

I was not all that nervous about the interview. But this was due more to being in a state of naivety, rather than one of confidence. Having no real concept as to what the job interview entailed, it all seemed perfectly straightforward. I came to the interview dressed very casually, in everyday attire wearing a flannel shirt, high top black Converse™ basketball shoes, and blue denim jeans. I did tie my shoulder length chestnut blond hair back into a ponytail and opted not to wear the jeans that I had with torn knee holes. I answered the questions as best I could, in a straightforward unassuming way.

Both my mom and dad were happy that I landed the interview.

Days later, I heard nothing from the employer. This came as no surprise to me given that I was 21 with no prior occupational experience. Who would hire someone like that? By this time, I began to increasingly realize the need to face reality. But I still feared the outside world tremendously. Fear of being physically attacked on the street was part of the fear but only a minor component. I feared the workplace even more. Certainly it was not the work itself that I sought to avoid. It was office politics and work culture that I considered the most prohibitive barrier. The post industrial global capitalist world of work seemed every bit as violent as prison culture-just in different ways. The parallels between the two are striking. Both are equally social Darwinian, but just with different consequences for the misfits and non players. In the former you lose your livelihood and dignity, in the latter you could lose your life.

So strong was my desperation yet so deep was my lingering fear and mistrust of the outside world, I even began to take a serious look at correspondence courses advertised in magazines. Most people in their right minds would knowingly dismiss these as unworthy, perhaps fraudulent. I had slightly over $850 to my name and was receiving $40 per month from my parents. Many of these correspondence schools offer payment plans as low as $25 per month for their course. After months of wrangling, I finally decided upon enrolling in the gun repair course offered by the once extant NRI correspondence school - a division of the McGraw-Hill company. To me, this seemed the perfect solution; learning at my own pace and within my own environment. Moreover, unlike typical pedagogical settings, there is no requirement for interactive communication. In this way, it's possible to avoid situations that could lead to being disparaged or insulted, in the event of miscommunication with another person.

Given my fascination with firearms and other weapons, gunsmithing also seemed a good occupational fit. In high school, I enjoyed reconditioning old firearms. Such reconditioning typically involved removing rust and corrosion from metal parts, refinishing (either browning or bluing) these metal parts, and refinishing the wood in stocks or pistol grips. However, I never even considered my relative inefficiency of working with my hands, and the hindrance this would pose in any skilled occupation. What is more, overall demand for gunsmithing service is quite miniscule. Only later did I realize that most gunsmiths do not pursue this trade as their entire or even primary source of income.

I never had any real accurate guide-map in life, illuminating a productive path to take, given my disabilities. I had so strongly internalized messages from parents, teachers, and counselors that I am basically normal and just need to work harder. But, as I would find out much later in life, there are very finite limits to what that "extra effort" can accomplish, and equally finite limits as to how much one can be expected to put forth.

I enrolled in the correspondence school in February of 1996, and was financing it from my own pocket at a rate of $25 per month. I would receive the course modules and the instructional material, and complete the course modules in a day or two. The modules did not seem all that challenging. In fact, I could usually answer all the lesson quiz items correctly, "off the top of my head", without actually reading the material. I had my suspicions that the program was little more than a degree mill or an outright fraud. However, in my desperation, I failed to heed my suspicions. About four months into the program, I submitted my fifth lesson plan, and monthly payment, but received no new course material for some time afterward. Then another bill arrived. I paid that bill, but again received no course material. By this point, I was convinced that the course was fraudulent. I wrote them a letter asking about the situation, but received no response. Only more bills arrived. After paying the second bill, with no forthcoming course material, I flat out refused to pay any further bills until they sent new course material. I sent them a letter, explaining this. They simply placed my account in their delinquent files, and began to send increasingly more threatening correspondence. My dad called the company to ask them about the situation and they would only hang up on him, never answering his questions. My dad then pointed to me that their refusal to send new course material, was in violation of the terms of their own contract. Accordingly, I should not be obligated to pay and remain enrolled in their program that I was dissatisfied with. My dad helped me write a letter to them explaining that because they were not abiding to the terms of their own contract, that they should honor my request to cancel my account. If they did not, we would file a complaint with the Atty. Gen. of our state. For months afterward I received no bills, and no lesson material. Because this correspondence program turned out to be nothing more than a fraud, I considered other options.

With about $650 total to my name, perhaps I could fund short term technical training at a local community college or tech school. I was evaluating various course offerings through both Bates technical College and Clover Park technical College. In September of 1996, I discovered a free job readiness training program offered at Bates technical College in Tacoma Washington. The program emphasized resume writing, interview skills, basic computer navigation/Internet use, and interpersonal communication skills. Due to my relative isolation from the world, I felt that a free training program, emphasizing such basic occupational skills would be a good place to start. Motivated by advice *vis a vis* postal correspondence with a social worker, residing on the other side of the country, I would took the ultimate leap forward into the world.

•••

Motivated only by tacit understanding as to the proclivities of the modern labor market and society, I spent the first three years of my adult life, enmeshed in a misguided pursuit of an escape. Yet the escape I sought was merely a mirage. Ultimately, reality beckoned and I attempted to secure what I believed to be a tenable niche in the "real world' given my disabilities. Following this decision, my world had changed in the blink of an eye.

During the three years, antedating my high school graduation, my cloistered world consisted of three primary staples; primitive technologies, alternative "drop-out" literature from book dealers such as Eureka Resources or Loompanics Unlimited, and my many pen-pal corresponedents across the country and throughout the globe. It was the early to mid 1990s, prior to widespread internet accessibility. Yet for me letter writing served the same function that the internet serves for many young neurodiverse adults today. It was a mode of social communication I could effectively use, given my inefficiencies in processing visual and auditory information. I formed some of the most intimate social bonds I had ever known through pen pal correspondence. Many such individuals, I became more intimately connected with than with any of my own relatives. Along with my dedication to craft, it was through these correspondences that I also grew intellectually, through the exchange of knowledge and ideas. Previously, I could never participate in such discourse. Yet, postal communication materialized at a pace that I could keep up with. Many of my correspondents found it very intriguing and engaging to communicate with me, as a pen pal. Many were astounded by my insights on human nature and social sciences that I shared with them.

Today, I e mail and send text messages a lot. Like letter writing, it helps me to solidify bonds with others, making these technologies a sort of "social prosthetic"- enabling me to maintain friendships for longer durations of time, than I could during late adolescence or my early 20s.

In September of 1996, my world changed in the blink of an eye. I truly became disabled. This transition did not occur through illness or injury, or even a worsening of my existing symptoms. But rather, I became disabled by both entering a new social niche, and acquiring a clinical diagnosis. Both occurrences solidified my new social role as one who struggles with disability. No longer was I simply a maladjusted youth, or the quintessential generation X slacker, living off his parents, while pursuing a dilettante lifestyle. The trappings of my former netherworld had been shed for good. During the years following my introduction to the world of disability, I would struggle tremendously not just to find a place in society, but to reconcile my new identity as a disabled person.

Chapter 4 - The Blind Leading the Blind:

"For the bureaucrat, the world is a mere object to be manipulated by him."

-Karl Marx

Three months after reality's beckon, late in 1996, I completed both job readiness training and a 720 clock hour cashier/checker training program at Bates Technical College (BTC). Having earned high marks, and strong letters of reference, I became energized with hitherto unknown hope and optimism.

Just prior to registering for my classes at Bates, I received a land auction notice from the Washington Department of Transportation. The notice contained info on an inexpensive 1 acre parcel of remote land in Okanogan County, located in northeastern Washington State. The minimum bid for this small parcel was only $200.00. It was a real life instance right from the pages of the "back to the land" literature I grew immersed in after graduating from high school. I couldn't believe that this had actually happened. Such accounts always seemed every bit as probable as winning the lottery. Was it an omen? Was someone up above trying to tell me something - perhaps that I should still consider dropping out? My parents ultimately volunteered to fund the cashier/checker training at BTC. Thus I still had the means to comfortably bid $400.00 on that parcel. Despite my epiphany following my trip to Battleground/Cougar, it was still very tempting to bid at least $400.00 on the property. Ultimately, I chose to keep my money and continue saving. With my situation being what it was, perhaps this was the wiser decision.

Deciding against bidding on the property was the final severance of any connection to the fantasy I once sought to create. In earnest, my initial desire to buy the property was motivated by the mere fact that I could do so. The sense of dignity and ownership, associated with owning land was very appealing. Even if I never inhabited or used the property, it was mine. But I needed to put that all behind me. It was now the time to move forward. My world was changing.

No longer was I writing to all of my pen pals, in an effort to glean more knowledge on off the grid living. My massive collection of alternative zines and "back to the land" literature sat idly on my bookshelf and closet shelf, remaining untouched for years to come. I needed to put that all behind me. This was the time to move forward.

Armed with new skills and a battery of strong professional endorsements, and a sharp, well-polished resume and cover letter, I dove into my rehabilitation with full gusto. Every day, I submitted resumes and applications for any open retail position. My job search spanned the entirety of Pierce, King, and Thurston Counties. After two months of diligent effort, I had yet to receive so much as single call summoning for an interview. But my reserve of positive energy had yet to be exhausted. Even in the midst of the robust late 1990s bull market economy, landing my first job at 22 would require nothing short of a heroic effort. Unemployment in the Seattle metro area was miniscule, hovering around 4%. And I was painfully aware of my place among that minute percentage. Still this was no time for negativity and self doubt. Or so I had been vigorously indoctrinated to believe through all of the snake oil rehab pep talk at BTC.

Based on advice from the disability resource counselor at BTC, I sat out to augment my job search effort by applying for vocational rehabilitation services with the Tacoma Washington division of vocational rehabilitation (DVR). My intent was to secure a clinical evaluation of my still speculative impairments. I knew that eligibility for rehabilitation assistance was contingent on confirming a *bona fide* disability and that DVR could help towards these ends. My task was to convince them that I had been operating under an undiagnosed disability. Once diagnosed, I could then seek medical interventions to improve my functioning. What is more, an official diagnosis would secure my eligibility for any ADA services I might need on my first job.

Registering with DVR was my first step into the real world of disability, defined by our society. I didn't feel disabled after having constructed fully functional stone tools. Nor did I feel disabled when procuring sustenance with primitive traps and implements, or having some of the most intellectually stimulating discussions, with pen pals who held advanced degrees. But now here I was thrust in the role of disability, defined by the post-industrial west and having to contend with its institutions both public and private. Whereas before; I was just a dropout, misfit, or slacker. Now I am disabled.

In addition to registering with DVR, I called Another Door to Learning to enquire on the status of the fund for financial assistance towards the cost of neuropsychological evaluations. The conversation that ensued quickly and unexpectedly materialized into an impromptu counseling session. The receptionist started by asking questions, pertaining to whom the evaluation was for, age of the individual in question, and for what reason, neuropsychological evaluation was being sought. I explained that the testing was for me and described many of the functional difficulties I deal with. I told her my story and that I was now trying to get my life on track, and become gainfully employed and self sufficient. This following a lengthy period of; "emotionally convalescing", attempting to retreat from normative society. Saddened to tears, she regretfully informed me that they had not received any new grant monies, and could not place my name on their wait list. The topic of discussion gradually shifted to my job search. I asked how I should handle difficult interview questions, pertaining to my disability itself and my nil employment history stemming from it. She passionately and vehemently consoled me to just remain hopeful, and to never give up. She then left me with the recommendation to perform volunteer work to compensate for my lack of formal workplace experience.

Volunteer work – that should certainly give me a leg up in my job search, especially with favorable references from those that I volunteer for. Following her advice, I promptly got involved with numerous volunteer activities throughout Pierce and King Counties. I volunteered initially for the Tacoma Public Library system's, used book sale functions, and for the Growing with Plants program which was part of the Pierce County 4-H program as part of the WSU Cooperative extension in Pierce County. Growing with plants is an educational outreach curriculum taught through the 4-H division of various university cooperative extensions. The programs intent is to disseminate knowledge on horticulture and nutrition to elementary and junior high school students. The volunteer work I did through the Tacoma Public Library and WSU Pierce County co-op extension were short term perennial assignments. By mid Spring of that year, I found steady relevant volunteer work at the Rhododendron Species Botanical Garden in Federal Way. It readily became a favorite place to volunteer at. I volunteered there frequently. The place felt much more warm and welcoming than my actual home. Everybody there was more than appreciative of the many volunteer hours I put into

113

both the garden and the gift shop.

In late February of 1997, DVR contacted me to set an appointment for an intake conference. A conference was scheduled two weeks out. That following week, Dan Sawyer, my vocational rehabilitation counselor called. He had a number of preliminary questions, based on my application materials. In particular he was puzzled that I had no official diagnosis, and the presence of a disability at that point was entirely speculative. At least from his experience, most prospective DVR clients actually have an official diagnosis at the time they apply. After relating to him, my personal history, and explaining my lack of a diagnosis, he still expressed uncertainty about taking me on as a client. He overtly questioned the likelihood of me even being considered disabled by DVR's criteria. His uncertainty was based on my absence of a legal diagnosis, along with having successfully completed vocational training without special accommodations. He essentially stated that whatever impairment I had should pose no hindrance in a typical workplace setting. The phone conversation ended with Dan advising me not to get my hopes up, but he would see what they could do.

The following week, I reported to DVR for my intake interview. The interior décor of the building, was a relic of mid 1980s efforts at designing public buildings with a softer, less "institutional" aesthetic. It very much reminded me of the elementary school I attended, when newly remodeled. There were cobalt blue ceramic floor tiles. And horizontal oak trim midway up the walls, divided one half with a pastel geometric floral print wallpaper, and the bottom half a solid drab pastel blue carpeting. It may have served its purpose at one time, but by then had become the new "institutional look" complete with the patina of age.

As I often do for any such appointment, I arrived several minutes early in advance. This habit results from my need to overcompensate for the use of slower transportation methods, coupled with my impaired sense of timing. I filled out the intake forms and handed them to the receptionist. She looked them over and pointed out a place for a signature that I overlooked and forgot to sign. I signed it and handed it back to her.

"You have very pretty hair, the receptionist commented. What do you do for it?"

"Oh nothing special". "I just wash it and apply a

114

cream rinse afterward."

"Oh you're so lucky, you don't have to perm it or color it or anything."

"Yep, but it can be very laborious to wash and comb, through."

After a brief exchange with the receptionist, I took a seat and began reading an issue of National Geographic that was kept on the waiting room table. The issue featured an article on the tool making capacities of *Homo habilis* which caught my attention. At least I had some worthwhile stimuli to pass the abundant time while waiting on my appointment. With still about a half an hour to spare, I could probably have finished reading the article prior to my appointment. But after less than 10 minutes, my reading and pondering were interrupted by the beckoning of my name "Allan White", summoned by a male voice emanating from across the receptionists desk. It was my counselor Mr. Dan Sawyer. I dropped the magazine to meet my counselor. Mr. Sawyer and I discussed at length, my eligibility for rehabilitation services. In this conversation, he seemed more assured that DVR could actually assist me. He was far more confident of this than during our phone conversation a week earlier. Did he consult with one of his supervisors on my case? Was he able to detect my disability now that he met me in person?

After sharing with Mr. Sawyer, my success in the training program at BTC and my transcripts and letters of reference, he was perplexed that I had not found a job yet. I explained to him what I felt to be the most baneful aspect of my track record. This aspect, being my lack of formal employment history. And of course my lack of employment history was a secondary consequence of grave emotional dysfunctions stemming from an undiagnosed learning disability. He glibly dismissed the matter altogether. Instead, he suggested that a big part of my problem could be as simple as my manner of dress. In particular, he cautioned that my shoulder length hair, usually worn in a ponytail could severely impede my job search. Yet I wasn't buying that. His advice might have carried much more weight in the 1970s or much of the 80s. In my time, however, I had seen far too many pony-tail wearing male employees in varied professional contexts. I simply could not accept his advice. I wondered too, how strongly he actually believed the advice he was dispensing. Was his advice simply a means of negating the realities of the modern labor market and contemporary social relations with regard to life

115

prospects of those with "simple learning disorders"? Perhaps it is a way of maintaining the validity of those in his profession, in a time where the rehabilitation paradigm is now proving obsolete.

Though he was taking the time and effort to conduct an intake interview, he was still acting rather hesitant to assist me. I could not make sense of the apparent contradiction in his actions and mannerisms. Was I not disabled enough? Was I so severely disabled as to be a "lost cause"? Mr. Sawyer seemed a veteran of his line of work, and possibly developed some sense, if not bias, as to which clients would likely succeed and which ones wouldn't. He had a number of certificates and awards in his office dating back to the early 1980s, but none more recent than 1990. He had obviously been around the block for some time. His occasionally sullen demeanor betrayed a diminished enthusiasm for his work. His was a classic example of reaching a point where he was simply going through motions putting one foot in front of the other, stoically drudging towards retirement.

After our conversation, he proceeded to fill out the various intake forms, making note of his observations of me as a client. His observations included some positive attributes such as "good vocabulary", as well as some negative ones such as, "refusal to accept standards of appearance and dress". At least those were among the characteristics he subtly but emphatically enough noted aloud, while filling out the intake forms. Perhaps, this was intended to hint at ways that I should improve my attitude.

After Mr. Sawyer completed the forms, he and I had a meeting with Barb, the director of the office. Barb promptly approved my eligibility for rehabilitation services. Dan then set up an appointment for me to take a gat-b test and the Meyers-Briggs personality and interest inventory. My hunch was that the tests would be little different from those I previously took at BTC. In fact I knew that I had heard the name Meyers Briggs before and could associate it with my time at BTC. Though redundant, I agreed to take the tests.

I came in the following day and took to take the gat-b and personality inventories. Dan and I then scheduled a follow-up appointment to discuss the test results, and their ramifications with regard to vocational goals. The gat-b featured many of the same batteries as the aptitude test given at BTC, through the New Chances program. The version I took featured three separate subtests. The subtests included cognitive, perceptual and psycho-

116

motor batteries. The cognitive subtest included; verbal ability, mathematical ability, as well as verbal reasoning and mathematical reasoning combined. The perceptual battery included; form perception, spatial perception, and clerical speed and accuracy. Finally, the psychomotor battery included; finger dexterity, eye hand coordination, and motor coordination. My results were in some ways shocking, in some ways encouraging, but overall not too surprising. All of my scores within the cognitive battery were average to well above average. Conversely, all but one of the perceptual battery scores were well below average. That one exception being my spatial perception scores which ranked in the 70th percentile. It came as no surprise to me that all of my scores in the psychomotor battery were also well below average. Yet I certainly didn't expect them to be as low as they were. All three subtest scores ranked within the first and second percentiles of the population of test takers. According to the personality and interest inventories, landscape gardening came out as a highly recommended occupation for me. This was most likely due my interest in food cultivation, hence positive response to the survey questions pertaining to horticultural activities.

Despite my well below average motor and perceptual test scores, Dan Sawyer strongly supported the recommendation of landscaping and gardening. I myself would never realize the consequences of these impairments until actually attempting to work in this occupation, several months later. To this day, it baffles me that none of the "experts" at DVR even recognized such motor and sensory perceptual deficits as a prohibitive factor in competitively performing landscaping work.

On the day of getting my Gat-b and Meyers-Brigs results, Dan informed me that I was approved for a neuropsychological evaluation. He and I then scheduled an appointment for me to take the exam. It was an utmost relief to finally have this matter taken care of and dealt with. A major hurdle had been cleared. My evaluation was scheduled for another three weeks. In the meantime, I continually submitted job applications and attended job search workshops held by the DVR. My contract with DVR stipulated that I had to be actively seeking employment, in order to be eligible for DVR services.

On the day of the neuropsychological evaluation, I walked 1.5 miles, from my residence to the Behavioral Medicine Northwest clinic. I arrived nearly an hour early for my 8 am appointment. After filling out a few intake forms, I settled briefly into the waiting room, and began reading an article in an issue of Science magazine on the recent cloning of Dolly the Sheep. Not quite through with the first page of the article, the receptionist led me from the waiting room to the exam room. She handed me what I later found out to be the MMPI 2 (Minnesota Multiphrasiatic Personality Inventory 2). I was given this test to begin working on while waiting for the licensed psychologist to come in and administer the litany of cognitive tests. The MMPI 2 is an exhaustive inventory, consisting of 567 different true/false statements regarding the patient's thoughts and feelings on various selected phenomena. The test is used by trained professionals to help identify personality structure and psychopathology. Some of the questions are rather obvious in their intent, such as; "I have had suicidal thoughts"-true or false, or "I hear voices"-true or false. Some questions, however would seem more innocuous such as "I like cats"-true or false, or "I like tall women" - true or false. MMPI scores are not representative of percentile, rank, or how "well" or how "poorly" one scores in relation to the general population. Rather, analysis of this inventory looks at relative elevation of personality factors in relation to the various norm groups studied.

After completing little over half of the MMPI, the examiner, Marry Wagner walked in and introduced herself. We started with a basic interview where she collected information relating to my educational, family, and vocational background. After the interview, she issued all of neuropsychological tests including; the Wechsler Adult Intelligence Scale, the Seashore Tonal Memory test, the Ravens Progressive Matrices and many others. It was lengthy and very exhaustive session but I persisted through all items. The eight hour testing session was so strongly reminiscent of those I was given at school during my elementary and Jr. High school years. The entire situation evoked strong subterranean emotions that I couldn't describe. I thought I left behind, the need for all of the probing and evaluation when I left school. But perhaps this will always be a part of my experience so long as I am operating within the confines of "the real world". The tests I took were so similar to those I took throughout grade school and Jr. high that I couldn't help but wonder what the results of those tests were and why they were performed. It was yet another piece of the puzzle of my disability that would only remain missing for years to come.

Around 4 o'clock that afternoon, I returned home from the neuropsychological evaluation, imbued with an inexplicable levity. Another hurdle had been cleared and a burden soon to be lifted. Soon I was about to find hard answers and solutions to the learning difficulties which thus far, I could only speculate upon, and try my best to cope, using my own devices. This was a first major stride toward realizing that my disorder was a matter well above and beyond my own ability to manage. The illusion had dispersed.

That following week, I had an appointment to meet with a Dr. Richard Schneider. His duty was to conduct a final evaluative interview and prescribe medications. By contrast to the Dr. Wagner session, Dr. Schneider's appointment was very brief. The main purpose for this appointment was for me to answer questions on the Copeland Checklist of adult Attention Deficit Disorder, and to do a basic clinical interview.

About month after the visit with Dr. Schneider, Dan from DVR called to schedule an appointment to review the results. The test confirmed my suspicions, revealing an official diagnosis of adult attention deficit disorder-mixed predominantly inattentive type. Additionally, I was given the diagnoses of dysthymic disorder, and a mixed avoidant and schizoid personality disorder – all collateral damage. The diagnoses, themselves came as no surprise. Yet reading the detailed description of the results was highly unsettling. The report, based on my exam results essentially seemed to be describing a vegetable. In contrast to the descriptions of severe impairments indicated by the test results, Dr. Warner opined that I was highly employable and had a number of good skills. Dr. Schneider, however seemed more pessimistic. His doubt was based more on his assessment of my psycho-social functioning than any neuro-cognitive features of my disability.

The approximately 18 months proceeding my graduation from BTC proved to be among the most trying times of my entire life. That entire time I was searching diligently but fruitlessly for any job, not just those I was officially trained for. Almost on a daily basis, I was on the street, submitting paper applications, resumes and cover letters to any conceivable employer. After 3 months into my job search, I interviewed frequently. In fact, I recall two months in a row where I had at least two interviews a week. However, no job offers followed. Not even temporary employment agencies would venture the risk of hiring me.

I would augment my job search by performing volunteer work. My intent in doing so was to develop relevant experience, and make contacts. My favorite place to volunteer at was the Rhododendron species botanical Garden in Federal Way, Washington. I worked in both their massive botanical garden and their giftshop. In the garden, I performed basic landscaping maintenance, such as pulling weeds, pruning shrubs, and planting potted plants. In the gift shop, I performed usual retail job functions such as operating the cash register, and stocking merchandise. Perhaps working in both settings would not only provide valuable experience for working retail, but also towards working as a landscaper, should I find a way to get my foot in that door.

Volunteering became more than just a professional development activity. It was also a warm place where I felt welcome, appreciated, and accepted. This was a sharp contrast to my home life at the time which was becoming increasingly hostile and tumultuous. I needed a safe sanctuary as much as I needed gainful employment. At the end of my volunteer sessions, I never wanted to return home.

My dad was in management training at Boeing, hoping to secure a middle management position there. But the job was taking its toll on him, psychologically. He described the professional culture of Boeing management as very cutthroat and harshly competitive. He was working increasingly longer hours and having virtually no weekends off. The long hours, combined with the back biting office politics of at work made him highly short fused and agitated at home. He and my mom argued with increased frequency.

Heightening the stress and tension was the fact that my mom was struggling to manage her type II diabetes. My mom and dad also adopted a Gordon setter puppy for which they lacked the wherewithal to discipline and manage. They succeeded in housebreaking the dog to the extent that it quickly learned not to urinate or defecate in the house. However, the dog constantly tracked dirt and mud in the house, chewed everything in sight, and made constant nerve wracking noise by howling and barking at everything. To this day, I failed to understand why they didn't simply get rid of the dog, so that it could be adopted by a more nurturing and capable owner. Many people are able to deal situations like this without any real hardship, but this was much more than they could manage.

The constant bickering between my mom and dad, the dog making

120

a mess of our home and my mom practically looking for any reason to jump on someone's case made me want to spend as much time out of the home as possible. Our household was becoming completely discordant, and I really did not need that type of stress. In the first place, I was very resentful and ashamed that the income limiting effects of my disabilities necessitated cohabitation with my parents well into adulthood. But the misery of the household environment made things several times worse. My level of discomfort was such that I seriously believed that it more than made up for the rent that I wasn't paying. Even if I had the money to do so, here's no reason why I should have to pay rent to live in the dump that my mom and dad created. Moreover, if I had that kind of money, I surely wouldn't be living there.

Eventually, I resolved to simply stay gone from the house as much as possible. I only really slept and showered at home. I would always pack ample food with me, when out looking for paid work, performing volunteer activities, or spending time in the public library. Maintaining a self contained food source enabled me to stay gone, virtually all day, without having to return home to "re-fuel". If only I could just secure gainful employment that would enable me to move out on my own. Why is this so difficult? Oh, only decades of unbridled global capitalism, that's why.

Volunteering at the Rhododendron Species Foundation was another world for me. It served a duo-function of both occupational development and psychological buttressing. There, I was surrounded by positive, upbeat people who accepted and appreciated me. Alice, the gift shop manager was especially supportive of me. Being surrounded by such positivity is, in all likelihood what kept me going that entire year. There were numerous times in which I simply didn't want to live. The inability to find employment, despite ceaseless diligent efforts, and my own parents showing nothing but contempt and animosity towards me was too much for any person to bear. This is especially so for someone with a disabling condition that makes life difficult enough for them.

Throughout the summer of 1997, Dr. Schneider prescribed four different trial medications to assess which substance would prove most effective towards helping to manage my condition. The medications I took included; Dexadrine(10mg.), Adderall (20mg.) Ritalin (15mg.) and Dexadrine (20mg.) respectively. Neither of them proved beneficial at all, but I would only discover the most probable reason several years later. Both the Dexadrine and Adderall enabled me to focus on reading material for longer durations of time, but they affected my moods in a way that sharply "exaggerated" whatever mood I was in. It was almost like having bi-polar illness. If I was happy, I was "dancing on Saturn", but if I was miserable, I was in the absolute depths of hell. Additionally, both substances adversely affected sleeping patterns. It was virtually impossible for me to sleep at night. I would stay awake all night and drop like a rock in the mid to late afternoon, only to sleep for about three to four hours. Ritalin only had me feeling completely agitated and irritable most of the time, as well as greatly disturbing my sleep.

Compounding the problem, with seeking clinical intervention, were my parent's prejudicial, suspicious, and unsupportive attitude towards it. Neither my mom nor my dad believed me to have any type of learning disability. Even after my first official diagnosis, their own biases caused them to see normal symptoms of my condition as being attributable to the medications I was prescribed. But these were symptoms I had all of my life which they had always overlooked. Instead, they only wanted to regard me as their perfect Wunderkind, - an extension of their own inflated self image. My disability was always an inconvenient truth which they never could acknowledge. And as usual, they blamed and criticized me for my desire to seek treatment for a condition that I knew I always suffered from.

By the late summer of 1997, Dan Sawyer, my DVR counselor, was bewildered that I had not yet landed a job, despite unwavering tireless efforts at doing so. He could not understand why I was having such difficulty given the major economic boom cycle the US economy was in. Western Washington especially enjoyed a robust vibrant economy, attributable to the regional dot com boom of that era. Local businesses publicly lamented that they could not find enough employees to fulfill the demand. This only made my situation all the more disheartening. I would hear about how so many companies were in such a major hiring boom, yet I was certainly not feeling the effects. It was as if I were marked with a scarlet letter and shunned like a pariah. Why can't I get a job? Is it my manner of speech, with it's overall slower rhythm and occasional lack of prosody and affect? Is it my lack of eye contact? Perhaps my prior three years of unemployment was simply an irredeemable bad mark to my professional track record. But why was I so frequently

122

called for interviews in the first place? My absence of any formal employment history is clearly illustrated in all of my application materials. And if this were a factor, why then must the penalty for needing time to emotionally convalesce be such an extreme one?

Mr. Sawyer, in his puzzlement over my situation, proposed that I participate in a community based assessment (CBA), conducted by the Tacoma Goodwill industries. His suggestion seemed reasonable to me. The CBA is a program conducted by Goodwill industries to test the suitability of the disabled job seeker to a particular line of work. DVR often finances these contracts. Goodwill industries pays the employer, the totality of an applicant's wages and places the client in a relevant work setting. Selection of the work setting depends on the client's immediate vocational objective. In no time, Mr. Sawyer and I arranged for me to undergo a community based assessment, working in a retail setting.

On the day of meeting with the community based assessment manager, Kylee Drake, she too was also dumbfounded that I had not yet secured a job in spite of my efforts. Her impression was that I presented as intelligent and articulate, and had already developed a competitive track record. She saw no reason why my three prior years of no formal work experience should count against me. In her view, I had already done enough that year to overshadow my past. Yet, it was as if I were spinning my wheels but accomplishing nothing. And, with all of my letters of reference, Karen clearly saw that I was putting in more than a full hearted effort at finding work. She knew that I had very real disability related barriers to employment but could not quite put a finger on them. During the initial intake, Karen and I developed a plan of action. Papers were signed, agreements were made and we went forward from there. It was the same song and dance over again.

About a week afterward, Ms. Drake called to inform me that she found a business that was willing to conduct my community based assessment. It was the Tacoma Half Price Books and Music, at their old location on 6th avenue. I was ecstatic about the opportunity. I knew that if I could obtain positive references from the manager of a competitive business, this should bolster my credentials considerably. Mr. Sawyer even told me anecdotes about CBA clients who have been hired by the businesses they work at during the assessment period. I knew not to get my hopes up too much in favor of such a scenario. Still, I was willing to do my utmost best and see what becomes of it.

I was on my trial medication of Adderall on the day that I interviewed at Half Price Books. Part of the assessment was to see how well the client interviews. I was so ecstatic over this opportunity and taking Adderall which magnified my merriment. Thus I probably came across as much more upbeat and affable than I normally would have. I remember my speech pattern being more fluid and better connected than usual. I could tell that the store manager, Whitney was intrigued by my intellectual curiosities and involvement in primitive skills. I felt very positive about this situation and felt it could be the ticket, either directly or indirectly to satisfactory employment.

By the time I began the trial work period, I was off the adderall and was not taking any other medications. And the initial two weeks on the job with my CBA, went really well. I walked into the shop, and greeted the assistant manager Alicia with a firm handshake. Alicia showed me around, explaining everything that is done in the store by employees. She walked me through the processes of how used books are purchased from the general public, and how they are catalogued, tagged, and placed on the store shelf. She showed the types of general upkeep and maintenance procedures that are done around the shop, how to use the phone, etc. I then went through the employee training manual, and took all of the quizzes that the end of each chapter. It was exactly as though I were hired on the job. The work itself seemed very easy and within my capabilities.

Immediately from the start, I established a positive rapport with both Whitney and Alicia, the store manager and assistant manager, respectively. We would discuss matters relating to our readings on history and social science. A few of my coworkers were intrigued by my involvement with primitive technologies and by the fact that I had written material published.

That first week, I worked mostly on the sales floor, stocking, and shelving and straightening books. I also answered calls from customers, and assisted customers in the shop. During the second week, I worked the cash register for the first time. From that point knew that I would need additional practice to become proficient in all register functions. This was especially the case with the antiquated less user friendly POS systems at the store. These featured a plethora of different keys of all shapes, sizes and colors with no scanning device. All operations were performed by manual entry. With my severe impairments of motor dexterity, clerical perception, and ocular tracking, I require a great deal of repetitive practice to become proficient with such tasks. I was upfront in disclosing my difficulties with the store managers, and Whitney agreed that they could work with me on that issue. According to what I had been told by vocational experts, ADA statutes stipulate that additional practice time is a reasonable accommodation for employees with cognitive impairments. This is especially the case with a company the size of Half Price Books, which is a national book chain.

Throughout that week and into the next, my manager and supervisor were acting as though they were genuinely willing to work with me, given my unique challenges. Yet during the remaining two weeks of the assessment period, things changed. I gradually noticed being relegated to more of the menial detail. Further, all coworkers including both the manager and assistant manager grew increasingly cold towards me. No longer were they even greeting me in the morning or even talking to me in the break room. It was total exclusion. Naturally I grew suspicious and my agitation mounted. I realize that I did not fit the prominent "hipster" image the store intends to project. Yet this was no justification for the treatment I was receiving.

The "cold shift" seemingly occurred after having revealed less than politically correct aspects of my lifestyle. By this time, a few of my co-workers knew that I fish, hunt, and own firearms. Moreover Whitney and Alicia were both aware that I am legally licensed to carry a concealed handgun in Washington state.

At one point, Alicia overtly castigated my lifestyle and uncharitable views towards criminal deviants. She stated that people like me are of the same ilk as those who were responsible for the Nazi holocaust. For all of her pseudo-Marxian social democratic world views, she obviously failed to muster a more enlightened, charitable analysis, as to why a socially disadvantaged law abiding disabled person would bear such intense animosity towards criminal deviants. Too often the systematic coddling of criminal deviants comes at our expense. At any rate, I knew I struck a raw nerve with Alicia, so I abruptly terminated the offending conversation without further comment. Afterward I resumed to my normal way of being. I remained upbeat, gregarious and avoided conversing on potentially controversial subjects. Nonetheless, it was virtually the day after the heated conversation between Alicia and I, that I was increasingly being excluded and edged out, despite being nothing more than kind and friendly to everyone.

My resentment was mounting and my coworkers and supervisors were well aware of this. By the third week of the assessment period, they had me essentially doing nothing more than taking care of all their back-logged menial duties. This included cleaning the customer restroom which, by Alicia's admission, had not been cleaned in weeks. They also had me shuffling fixtures around, and recycling well over a year's accumulation of cardboard waste. These were mostly "special projects", not characteristic of day-to-day work functions of a retail bookstore. And it was indeed fortuitous that they were getting the work done for free. It was work that their paid employees wouldn't touch.

Feeling used and exploited, on top of feeling excluded, I ultimately grew so angry that I sought to end to the project. I told Alicia that I simply cannot work there anymore as I no longer felt comfortable. She did not argue, or even ask why I felt this way. She readily agreed to terminate the project at my behest. I then called Ms. Drake, the CBA manager and told her that I didn't see myself as suited for this type of employment and wanted to end the project. She was stunned. All of her prior feedback from Whitney revealed that I was doing great, learned quickly and was a pleasure to work with. But when Karen spoke with Whitney, after I terminated the CBA, Whitney outright lied about what happened. Whitney told her that I had a "shift" in behavior and attitude attributable to switching medications from Adderall to Ritalin about midway through the program. I only discovered that this misinformation was conveyed to the CBA manager, after having read the final report and assessment. Yet I was not on any medication during the CBA. It was a complete fabrication, concocted by store management to negate the fact that they were creating a hostile work environment.

Ms. Drake's assessment proclaimed that it was difficult to determine my suitability as a candidate for retail employment. This was allegedly due to my change in medications midway through the assessment. While reportedly taking Adderall, during the first half of the assessment, I was described as friendly, diligent, and detail oriented. But after the purported shift in meds, from adderall to Ritalin, I was described as less communicative, withdrawn, unfocused, and unable to deal effectively with customer interaction. My natural lack of affect and fleeting eye contact were also cited as barriers to effective customer interaction. As such, Karen's report

126

ultimately concluded that I was a completely unsuitable candidate for retail employment and that with stabilization of medication, further occupational assessments should be targeted at determining my suitability for occupations that don't involve a high level of interaction with the public. The report was already written so I saw no point in demanding that Karen revise what was already documented. Nonetheless, I verbally informed Ms. Drake that I was not on any medication throughout the assessment period and my "shift" in behavior, was due to being shunned by my coworkers and supervisor. I had quite a lengthy discussion with Ms. Drake about my experiences, and cautioned strongly against Half-Price Books as a CBA location. There's no telling how well she took my advice though. To this day it strikes me as curious that both the manager and assistant manager virtually acted like they wanted to hire me. Then literally overnight, I became the lowest form of life imaginable to them. It took another three years before I would even set foot in another Half Price Books store as a customer.

It was my first taste of work culture and office politics. I since have learned that discussing potentially controversial matters in any professional setting will most likely jeopardize one's social and subsequently professional standing. This is especially true in the harshly competitive, neoliberal, de-unionized, deregulated global capitalist workplace of the late 20th and early 21st century. Even a trivial infarction as wearing an article of clothing that's five days out of season can jeopardize your career. So much for capitalism being *sine qua non* to individual liberty.

My involvement in the Community Based Assessment only further squelched my hopes. Afterward, it took every fiber of my being to continually push forward, applying for work, and performing volunteer service. Nonetheless, I persevered. Yet by that point, my efforts all seemed in vain. Was I just going through the motions, because there was nothing better to do? I needed some way to stay out of the house. I just couldn't bear living in the toxic cesspool of filth, tension, and chaos, that my parents created. But as far as actually finding a job? Who was I trying to kid? Nobody would hire me. This more "realistic goal" of retail employment was looking just as feasible as my initial post high school aspiration of trying to go off the grid on a sub-shoestring budget. At least I did make some money from writing and selling of stone tool replicas. With retail employment, I couldn't even get my foot in the door.

127

Having performed a Community Based Assessment, with a mixed evaluation, both the Tacoma DVR, and Goodwill industries proclaimed an unwillingness to provide further assistance. They insisted that I find an effective medication, through Dr. Schneider, before proceeding with further rehabilitation goals. They obviously did not listen to what I told them about being completely non-medicated throughout the CBA project.

I was beginning to suspect that the psycho-stimulants, commonly prescribed for ADD would be of no use in my case. My "unique case" of ADD must be quite a freak variation of the condition. I accepted the diagnosis as valid, only because much of the literature on AD/HD, did describe some characteristics I could relate to. However, a lot remained unaccounted for. For example, the motor skill deficits, manipulative limitations, perceptual impairments, and the slowness in completing even very simple low exertion tasks. I simply thought my case had to be an exceedingly "rare variation" of the condition, for which no effective clinical intervention had yet been developed. I tried to explain to my vocational rehabilitation counselor that finding an effective medication would be too time consuming with uncertain outcomes. Moreover, I needed a job ASAP and could not afford the length of time that finding effective treatment would require. My input only infuriated him. He was not keen on the idea of me proceeding with a rehabilitation plan un-medicated. He insisted that I get approval from Dr. Schneider to do so. I knew what was best for me, and was incensed by his patent indifference to my own thoughts and feelings on the matter. For months on end, following the summer of 1997, I had no contact with Mr. Sawyer. I simply did my best to find work on my own, despite my lack of success at it. DVR had no effective solutions. I was at my wits end and time was running out. This was an ultimate no win situation if there ever was one.

By January of 1998, in the midst of the longest, darkest, and most depressing winter I have ever known, Mr. Sawyer contacted me out of the blue. He proposed the idea of placing me in a custodial training program at Clover Park technical College in Lakewood Washington. By that point, I had already applied for, and unsuccessfully interviewed for numerous custodial jobs. Most of these were advertised as requiring no prior experience. I thus seriously doubted that custodial training would make a difference. However, I begrudgingly went along with his idea, thinking it couldn't be any more or less effective, than anything I had previously done.

At that point, it all seemed a matter of going through the motions and hoping for stroke of good luck. With funds allocated from DVR, I enrolled in the program and hopped for the best.

On the first day of the class, it was a snowy late January morning. I rode the city bus to campus, only to find a campus virtually barren and vacated with the exception of office and clerical staff. Nearly 8 inches of ground accumulation of snow that had already fallen. This is more than enough to shut everything down in Western Washington's Puget Sound basin. I enquired with the registrar as to the status of classes that day and she informed that all classes were canceled due to the snow. I took the bus back home. Upon my arrival my dad informed me that Clover Park technical College called and said that the custodial training program was canceled due to lack of enrollment. I wasn't too disappointed. I seriously doubted that taking the program, even passing with stellar marks, would help in any way. Why would it? My stellar reviews from BTC and all of my glowing letters of reference from numerous parties have done no good. Why would things be any different this time around?

Because the program was canceled, Mr. Sawyer made a futile attempt to salvage to situation. He placed me in direct contact with Rhonda Valdez the custodial skills instructor for the program. The intent was for her to help me secure a job in the custodial profession. She had numerous contacts in the industry and provided me with several job leads. I applied for these using Rhonda as a reference and not a single application even led to an interview. After about a month, I realized that this was just another dead lead.

1998 rolled around, and I was subject to turn 24 that year. Federal student aid funding policy now holds new opportunities. At 24, the department of education considers applicants legally independent from parental resources in determining financial aid eligibility. This applies whether or not a prospective student resides with their parents at the time of attending enrollment. I applied for federal student aid as a last ditch effort to steer my life in another direction. By that point I all but abandoned my job search.

Knowing that my chances of approval were far greater than the last time I applied, I filled out and submitted a FAFSA. There is no way in hell they could deny me this time. With the exception of my $480 annual allowance, from my parents the prior year, all other income and assets amounted to zero. $480 was the totality of my entire income for 1997. After submitting my FAFSA, I spent much of the six weeks, waiting for a decision, simply hanging out in the library, reading to pass the time. No longer seeing the point in it, I did very little volunteer work. It was the winter of that year and the RSF had virtually no need for volunteer assistance in the garden. In the library, I would check out and read books on multitudes of different subjects; books on learning disabilities, anthropology, historical weaponry, world geography, etc. My home environment was still a tense and hostile place that I took great pains to avoid. Sometimes I would just walk the streets and browse gun shops and bookstores, anything to be out of the house. I was like a pariah; an outcast with no place to call home and nothing to do that was of importance to anybody. My horde of lithic materials and field gathered timbers remained as motionless heaps collecting dust and waiting to be worked on. Working on these things meant staying at home which, I always sought to avoid. Moreover, I was in such a continual state of agonizing misery and depression that I could not even muster the enthusiasm to participate in activities I normally enjoy. All I could do was stay out of the house and find ways to ease my mind, through any means possible. I even succeeded in losing about 10 pounds through a rudimentary exercise regimen, consisting of body weight exercises and running throughout Wapato Hills Park. This made me happy. At least I managed to do something right, via agency of my own mental and physical effort. By this point, only the mere hope of being approved for federal student aid kept me from taking my own life.

About eight weeks would pass before receiving any feedback from the Department of Education, regarding my FAFSA, and the news was good. The letter informed me that I was eligible for student aid funding, but they needed further verification of income and assets. With my reported income being so unusually low, they needed assurance that I had not made a mistake. I wrote them a letter of explanation, describing my source of income, signed by both my parents and myself.

With approval for federal student aid, I enrolled in the landscape management program offered at Clover Park technical College (CPTC). Another option I debated on was enrolling in a community college to begin a four year degree in anthropology. Of either option, studying anthropology was in fact the most appealing of the two. However, I wanted more than anything to be gainfully employed, self sufficient and living on my own. I could not bear the idea of living

130

with my parents for another four years while attending college. The only way I could afford to live on my own while attending school was to work full-time on top of it. With my learning difficulties and no ability to drive a motor vehicle, successfully juggling work with even part time school is next to impossible. The landscape management program at CPTC lasted only 18 months. Afterwards, I should be more readily employable and able to secure my own place. A career in horticulture had to be the solution. Numerous aptitude tests, personality inventories and interest surveys strongly recommended this occupation for me. I surely couldn't go wrong. Hope again was renewed toward my successful rehabilitation. I began the program at CPTC in June of 1998. During the first two weeks, I remained uncertain of the future. I was incessantly worried that even successful completion of this program would only parallel my experience with BTC. Would this be another scenario where I succeeded in the course, but not in "the real world"? Things only had to get better from this point.

In the first two weeks of the program, I kept to myself and never spoke to anyone, unless spoken to. I was very uncertain as to how I would be socially received by others. By this point, I had heard more than my fair share of verbal abuse at home. When coupled the rejection and exclusion at Half Price Books, I grew increasingly withdrawn and alienated,

Like with the cashier/checker training at BTC, this program was designed in a way that students could work and develop competencies at their own pace. This was especially the case with the first module I took, emphasizing greenhouse horticulture and maintenance. I would come to class, sit through announcements and then either study for upcoming tests, or work in the greenhouse as I saw fit. On the first test, I earned a perfect score- the highest in the class. The instructor, Martha Sales announced this in class, as she returned the graded tests to students. She noted in particular that I scored all items in the plant ID segment correctly. Thus far, Martha had not seen a student score so highly on the plant ID exam. The instructor and many of the students considered this an impressive feat as plant ID was considered very difficult by many.

Though I disclosed my disability to the Disability Resource Center, I never utilized any accommodations (e.g. tutors, note-takers) during my time at CPTC. I received no complaints, regarding my performance in the greenhouse, so I must have been performing

131

satisfactorily. I worked diligently, but probably did not do anything particularly remarkable. After about the third or fourth week into the program, I came to know both the instructor and some of the students on a more personal level. I had established a positive rapport with everyone and I readily became recognized as an excellent student. Others thought I must have a rather prodigious memory.

Once again I was in a setting where I was respected and appreciated and managed to recapture my dignity. After becoming more assured that I was in a safe environment, I began to open up more, and reach out to others. I especially hit it off with one student in particular, named Kirk. Kirk was often called "Kirk the Jerk", because of his spontaneous theatrical tendencies. Kirk was in a similar situation as I was. He was in his mid-20s, living at home, and also suffered learning deficits that made life an inordinate struggle.

My first student aid refund check came shortly after beginning my program at CPTC. $350 was the total sum. To me, this was a sizable amount. It was so much in one lump sum that I really had to think as to how I wanted to spend it. Should I buy a new rifle? Some new clothes? What do I do? DVR paid for my books and supplies. I opted to buy some new clothes with that first refund check, and spent very little else of it thereafter.

It was also during the early summer of 1998, that my sister, who had also been living at home was able to secure a job in Seattle. She then moved to Seattle, sharing a two bedroom apartment with her best friend from Jr. High and High School. My sister and I have both always had our share of social adjustment issues and things were finally working out for the both of us. Though I had yet to acquire sufficient income to move into my own place, I finally had a regular source of income and at least a means of escaping my home life.

By fall quarter of that year, I secured a work-study job in the campus greenhouse. The work involved propagating and maintaining nursery stock, general cleaning, maintenance, and upkeep. The pay was minimum wage, about $7.13 per hour, at the time, and I worked a total of about 15 hours per week. Combined with quarterly refund checks, and my low expense living situation, I was soon able to amass what to me was a large amount of money. By the end of fall quarter, I already had well over $1000 in my checking account. It was as though I came alive for the first time like Pinocchio emerging from his former existence as a wooden puppet to become a "real boy". For once, I felt I had something of a place in society. I would participate in off-campus landscape projects, with other members of the class.

One job site in particular, involved landscaping a 2 acre wooded parcel surrounding a residence, donated to CPTC by its former owner. The former owner-occupant became too aged and enfeebled to manage the upkeep. The 2,300 sq. ft. single story rambler was intended to be reserved for use as a conference building. The landscape management class was contracted to install new landscape and irrigation plumbing and fixtures onto the property.

My involvement with this project, revealed to me, an irreconcilable limitation, with regard to my suitability for landscaping work. As hard as I tried to overcome it, I found myself completely unable to effectively engage in interactive teamwork. If the work had to be done at a competitive pace, my inability to work collaboratively was even more problematic. This is not sat all a personality issue of being unable to cooperate with others. Rather it stems from my inability to follow what others are doing and incorporate my actions accordingly with theirs. This is essentially the same problem I have in playing team sports or following the thread of a larger group conversation. At the risk of crude oversimplification, I compare it to attempting to board a merry go round that is revolving so rapidly and you can't secure an empty space to jump on. Thus you remain left out while the others are able to participate and collectively revel in the exuberance of the moment. There were a number of reasons why I never foresaw this problem.

DVR egregiously misinformed me as to the skills and capacities, demanded by this line of work. My counselor actually told me frequently and emphatically that landscapers and gardeners worked largely in solitude. Even my DVR appointed psychiatrist, Dr. Schneider strongly recommended landscaping as a profession for me, for this very reason. These misnomers, set against my experiential background of happily and solitarily cultivating in a home vegetable garden plot, made the horticulture profession, seem to be a very promising fit. Desperate people will believe anything.

I did well in the program, because I always found things to do, which can be done either autonomously, or with only one other student. This was my approach. I utilized it both on work sites and in the campus greenhouse. Activities I normally did involved weeding, pruning, are planting nursery stock. Nobody complained about my

133

work. In fact I was often commended for being a diligent and steady worker. This was the approach I took which enabled me to succeed at CPTC - find work that can be done largely on my own and stay busy at it. This made a favorable impression with my instructors who saw me as a self starter and a diligent worker. However, it did nothing towards professional advancement. I found it difficult to become directly involved with team decision making and the coordination of projects. Initially I resented the positions I became naturally relegated to. Yet I never fully understood why I so readily became cast to the margins. I eventually reached a point, however where it didn't bother me.

After my first semester, I completed the first module and enrolled in a different one. The next module emphasized design and construction of commercial and residential greenhouse sprinklers and landscape irrigation systems. Not particularly interested in the irrigation module, I wanted to complete it prior to proceeding further.

Throughout my time in the landscape management program, I continued working in the campus greenhouse as a work-study student. I did this regardless of whatever specific module I was taking at the time. It quickly grew apparent that gainful employment in the field of horticulture necessitates both the ability to drive and ownership of a motor vehicle. Why didn't Mr. Sawyer at DVR ever discuss this with me? He knew that I didn't drive. There was no shortage of communication between Mr. Sawyer and I. As a vocational "expert", he is theoretically in a far superior vantage point to assess occupational requirements in relation to a client's abilities and disabilities. His decisions and recommendations never reflected this expertise. I am now trying to fit into an occupational sector where I don't belong, just as I was the year before. DVR is certainly doing nothing to end this cycle, in fact they have only perpetuated it.

I grew highly disenchanted with the landscaping profession. The labor aspect was simply monotonous, and mindless. The business management end did not engage me in the way in which my mind needs to be engaged. It was at this point that I discovered that even at a low level of exertion, I simply cannot do monotonous physically repetitive work. While the work may not be physically demanding, the shear tedium and lack of intellectual stimulation literally exhausts me. After so much as a half hour of a task like raking leaves, I feel tired, but more so mentally than physically. It's as though I mentally fatigue in want of greater intellectual stimulation, but never from the physical exertion. What's more, I shut down and disengage to the point that my work slows down and I can simply no longer do the work.

While near completion of the irrigation module, I attempted one of the related instruction classes required for the technical degree. The technical degree gives graduates the credentials for landscape management, rather than working as a laborer. The related instruction class I attempted was workplace communications. I could not juggle the workload from the related instruction classes along with the core program modules. I really had no use for a technical degree anyways. About 2/3 of the way into the program, my thoughts were running towards doing landscaping only as a part-time job while pursuing my bachelors and eventually master's degree in anthropology. A mere certificate in landscape and horticulture would suffice for what I wanted to do. At least in this way, I would be making some use of the time and effort that I invested at CPTC.

Months prior, I failed all core competencies of the Washington state Nurserymen's Association license. This was following months of diligent and regular study. My heart just was not into it. How on earth could so many people have recommended this line of work for me?

While nearing completion of the irrigation module, I was able to secure, through a temporary staffing agency, a part time grounds maintenance position with the Weyerhaeuser Bonsai Collection in Federal Way. This job did not require working as part of a team. Much of the work was in fact done in solitude. There was also no driving requirement for this job. All of the work was done at a single location, accessible by bus. However, what the job did demand was the ability to work very quickly and efficiently. It was this aspect of the job that made me realize the negative impacts of my motor and perceptual deficits upon this line of work. I could not rake the gravel neatly and quickly enough, nor could I stoop under the guardrails and turn the bonsai pots fast enough. My immediate supervisor frequently became verbally abusive towards me even though I informed him of my disabilities. At times, I literally wanted to drive a sledge hammer into his skull. By this point, it was abundantly clear that landscaping and horticulture were a terrible occupational fit for me after all. I could not satisfy real world standards with regard to work efficiency. Working at the bonsai collection was the ultimate

135

decisive factor with regard to my decision to abandon the landscape and horticulture profession.

After quitting the job, I begrudgingly completed the remainder of my training program at CPTC, though it took every fiber of my being. My main motivation was simply the desire to finish what I started. After terminating my job at the bonsai collection, I had two more quarters remaining at CPTC. It felt like the longest six months of my life.

I spent my final quarter at CPTC, taking a landscape design class and really struggling to complete drawings in a timely manner. I was only able to complete these drawings by their deadline by working on them at least 10 hours per day, including weekends. Putting the drawings together was a torturous experience, sometimes leaving me in tears as I struggled to complete each one. My motor impairments again really hampered my ability to complete the drawings in a smooth sufficient manner. Deficits in visual and form perception further compounded my difficulties. I was constantly erasing, rethinking and redrawing. My decision to finish out with a landscape design module was based on a suggestion by Dan Evans, the landscape design instructor that I could perform landscape design service on a private contract basis, to earn extra money while earning my degree in anthropology. However, after taking the module I doubted seriously that this would be a viable option. I completed the class with a B grade and was satisfied and relieved to have finally completed the training program at CPTC.

In the spring of 1999, I applied for admissions to Pierce College in Fort Steilacoom, Washington, intent on working towards my two year transferable Associates degree. An AAS is key to enabling one to work towards a BA, and ultimately a postgraduate degree. In the fall quarter of that year, I found out that I was accepted for admissions at Pierce College and enrolled in all of my classes in November of 1999. I completed the landscape management program with mostly stellar marks and an occasional B or C here and there. My overall GPA was 3.39 with my lowest marks in both the irrigation equipment and irrigation maintenance courses. I resolved to finish out the program with only my certification rather than a technical degree. Any landscaping work I would do afterward would likely be merely part-time while working through college.

Besides, how would I occupy my time and make money during the interim between terminating my time at CPTC and starting my classes at Pierce College. Terminating the course would once again put me on my mom and dad's bad side. Had I done such a thing, my life at home would likely have been miserable and unbearable.

By December of 1999, my time at CPTC and my dealings with Tacoma DVR were all said and done. I was looking forward to starting a new chapter of my life. This chapter would unfold into an eight year odyssey that ultimately ended with my earning of a Masters in experimental archaeology from the University of Exeter in the United Kingdom.

•••

Registering for services with Tacoma DVR marked my entry into the authentic world of disability defined by our culture. This naturally entailed dealing with society's institutions established for the treatment of persons, considered disabled. The entire experience exacerbated my identity crisis. Walking into the DVR office, there were many individuals with very obvious disabilities. Many of these individuals were in need of assistive devices and were arguably in far worse health than I. It all hearkened to my days in grade school when I would attend OT sessions in a wing of the school reserved for students with very severe disabilities. Outside of those facilities, however, I could interact as equals with many of my "normal" peers and could perform many age appropriate tasks just as competently as any "normal" kid. From an early age, it were as if I had a foot in two separate worlds. This existential contradiction continues to be a recurring theme for me today. It has only been through my understanding of the social model of disability, that I have been able to make sense of this contradiction.

Like the OT sessions I attended as a schoolboy, the institutionalized vocational rehabilitation I went through as an adult, did no good. My story is not at all uncommon among vocational rehabilitation clients. In this way, both scenarios are emblematic of the fundamental fallacy of the medical model of disability, which guides the protocol of many of our society's institutions for dealing with disability.

My dealings with DVR took place 20 years after the implementation of section 504 of the vocational rehabilitation act of 1973. Section 504 likely opened the door for cases like mine. The statute served as an anti-discrimination clause for any federally funded vocational rehabilitation service. Prior to this legislation vocational rehabilitation was geared primarily towards injured veterans and civilian workers from other sectors of the economy. Persons with congenital impairments, thought to be more severe or difficult to work with, were often denied rehabilitation services. It was widely believed that they would not benefit from such interventions. Section 504 illustrates a fundamental fallacy of anti-discrimination statutes a with regard to equalizing opportunities for disabled people. While the law sought to end discrimination in the administration of vocational rehabilitation service, the operational paradigm of vocational rehabilitation quickly proved obsolete, given the expanding range of disabled applicants.

Traditional rehabilitation operates on a medical model of disability, positing the damaged or impaired body of the disabled subject as the source of failure. Embedded in this paradigm is the notion of the human body as a flexible and adaptable subject, whereas physical and social environments are not. Hence the philosophy and practice of rehabilitation seeks to minimize or eradicate the problem of impairment and enable those with designated impairments to function at their highest possible physical, social, and psychological levels. In other words, disabled people become objects to be cured, treated, changed, and made "normal" according to a particular set of cultural values. My direct experience with this phenomena is illustrative. My counselors at DVR assumed that all I needed to do was find an effective medication and secure employment in a field that corresponds with a positive match on a personality inventory. So convinced were they of the infallibility of medicine that they were unable to conceive of medications being ineffective in my case. What's more, they failed to consider the effect of my impairments with regard to neoliberal work intensification of all economic sectors.

The limitations of the traditional medically based model of rehabilitation has been documented by disabled activists worldwide since the 1960s (Hunt 1966, Sutherland 1981, Zola 1982) In practice, this model amounts to little more than a cruel on-going effort of attempting to put a square peg in a round hole. In fact, there is overwhelming evidence that rehabilitation and related interventions are extremely limited in what they can achieve with regards to enabling the disabled to attain economic and social parity with non-disabled peers in societies organized almost exclusively around non-disabled lifestyles. Yet, rehabilitation workers will continually be dominated by or allied to medicine and the treatment of disability (in the ICF) as a health, rather than political issue. The on-going and relentless subjugation of national governments by transnational corporate interests and monetary organizations and their ensuing prioritization of profit over people and secondly, the enormity of barriers, economic, political, and cultural, encountered by the disabled. The treatment of disability in the ICF as a health, rather than cultural issue maintains this status quo among rehabilitation workers.

Section 504 prohibits discrimination in federally funded rehabilitation settings. The statute was implemented to address once common practice of discrimination against rehabilitation clients deemed to show minimal promise of successful rehabilitation. But did this only complicate matters further? Too often principles of civil rights embodied in laws such as section 504 and the ADA are subverted by reliance on courts. The courts themselves rely upon an antiquated functional understanding of disability. This very paradigm has prevented disabled people from fulfilling aspirations implied by this regulation.

The traditional rehabilitation paradigm of integrating the disabled into the labor market is entirely obsolete. But what specific institutional entity to replace it out with is no easy question to grapple with. Could a system of self determined niche construction ever be formally institutionalized? Would it need to be formally institutionalized as such? Could valorization of non-working lifestyles, and acceptance of those unable to participate in economic production, effectively minimize the marginalization of disabled people? These are all questions that the disabled experience should illicit with regard to restructuring society's values and institutions.

Chapter 5 – Placebo Effects:

" Education either functions as an instrument which is used to facilitate integration of the younger generation into the logic of the present system and bring about conformity to it, or becomes a practice of freedom, the means by which men and women deal critically and creatively with reality to discover how to participate in the transformation of their world."
- Paulo Friere
Pedagogy of the Oppressed

It was now January of 2000, a new year harkened a new chapter in my life. Moreover, an entire decade had passed, as had an entire century, and an entire millennium. Four major layers of time were shed in the peeling back one smaller layer - the transition from December 31st 1999 to January 1st, 2000. I was electrified by a positive energy of hope and optimism. The snake has shed its skin to reveal a vibrant new exterior. The 1990s were over, soon to be a mere footnote in history. The decade of my tumultuous transition from adolescence to adulthood is now water under the bridge. This was the time for renewal and rebirth.

Will the partaking of collegiate education lead to the dawning of a new era for me? Or will it merely be a separate and distinct chapter in my ongoing efforts at social integration-efforts that ultimately lead to nowhere. Here I was, now in my mid 20s, decidedly an adult and at least theoretically healthy, able-bodied and easily employable. Yet why is it so difficult to simply gel with the norm? The glass bubble would just not break. Hard work had simply not been working. For three years now, every fiber of my being was poured into simply trying to secure good job and a place in society. Yet, an impenetrable shield remained – one that constantly barred my entry into the normal workaday world, despite my best efforts. Yet still, I still regularly imbibed the widely proselytized snake oil of hard work and determination as the sole salvation from poverty and marginalization which stem from disability.

Perhaps the secret to permeating that shield was simply heeding advice of those who knew me, rather than marching in lock-step on a path dictated by aptitude test results. The advice of Professor Gundersen at Green River Community College began to resonate seven years after the fact. Was he on to something in his suggestion that I was a promising student who would do well in college? Maybe Jill and Ivan at Jerry's Rock and Gem were astute in their frequent suggestion of teaching anthropology and archeology classes as a most fitting vocation for me. Certainly, there must be wisdom in following one's more deeply rooted interests and authentic intellectual orientation(s). This had to be the ticket to any semblance of a halfway decent life.

I now have an MA in experimental archeology, published work to my name and more will surely follow. My post grad school professional development has undoubtedly been stymied, due to my disability. However, higher education has surely enriched and enhanced my life in ways that would never have otherwise occurred. My ability to organize a writing project of the magnitude of this book, was made possible by skills and abilities that I developed in both college and grad school.

By 25, attending college seemed my only path to redemption. Knowing of many who attend college for the first time in their 40s; the mid 20s seemed to comfortably predate any imagined expiration date to do so. Yet the pang of urgency was still an ever present motivator. It was now or never. Even if successful college education didn't enable me to secure the specific occupation I aspired for, there must be other ways of using an academic degree in some socially useful way. There is much more flexibility with which a liberal arts degree can be utilized.

A lifetime of living in relative isolation, consequent to my disability has engrained a tendency to simply live inside my own head. I am frequently described as being pathologically disconnected from my immediate environment. For me, this tendency proves nothing short of an insurmountable difficulty in typical business situations where you must be at one with the here and now. Perhaps my pursuit of higher education can lead to a career where living inside my own head is an asset, rather than a liability.

Setting a pattern that enabled me to succeed academically in college was not that difficult. Hours spent reading, writing, and thinking on esoteric matters came very natural to me. The only caveat being that I need opportunities to maintain optimal health and balance out these sedentary activities with regular physical exercise.

My initial 2-3 weeks at Pierce College were a period of settling in and re-adjustment. This was the point where I learned that if I am to succeed as a full time college student, a number of conditions were imperative. Firstly, I must learn live inexpensively enough to subsist almost entirely on quarterly student aid refunds. Under no circumstances should I work more than nine or ten hours a week. Second, recreational and social activities were to take place only during breaks between quarters. Third, work on written essays was to be initiated at least three weeks prior to the due date. And finally time spent on math assignments should equal no less than four hours per credit per week rather than the recommended one hour per credit per week. For better or worse, this was the formula that successfully pulled me through an AAS degree, two BA degrees and an MA degree.

Part time study, which would have maximized the benefits of my college education, was simply not an option. Being funded by federal student aid meant that the only way to obtain student aid refunds sufficient to subsist on each quarter, was to attend full time. I would not get as much money as a part time student, which would necessitate working nearly full time in order to survive. For a student with a learning disability, working so many hours on top my coursework would more than cancel out any benefit of attending college part time in the first place. Trying to juggle the two very different activities would compromise your ability to do either, to any acceptable proficiency standard.

During my first quarter at Pierce College, my class lineup included English 99-Introduction to Composition, Math 51-Basic Arithmetic, and Anthropology 105-intro to World Prehistory. My initial rude awakening came while writing my first essay for the World Prehistory Class. My mistake was using the same approach to essay writing that proved effective in high school. This approach simply entailed treated the assignment as though it were a weekend project. This usually worked in high school but college is different. Standards and expectations are much higher. And meeting those standards with a virtually untreatable learning disability can be next to impossible. I began working on the essay over the weekend, prior to its Tuesday due date. By Sunday, I was very much over my head. Initially, I sought to write about the late Mesolithic appearance of ground stone woodworking implements in The British Isles and the development of this technology towards the Neolithic age. However my research skills were so limited that I could not secure a sufficient database of literature sources to do the topic any justice. Two days prior to the due date, I switched topics and wrote about two French Mousterian sites. One was named Combe Capelle and I can't even remember the name of the other site. The paper had no clearly defined thesis and at only a page and a half, it fell unacceptably short of the minimum 3 page length requirement.

Nearly comatose from over 48 hours without sleep, I hung my head in shame and regretfully submitted the worst essay of my entire collegiate years to Dr. McLaughlin. "I can't go back, I can only go forward - my next three essays will blow him away". This was the mantra that repetitively resonated in my head, helping to soothe the sting of justifiable embarrassment while transferring the ill fated project to its place of final judgment. I took solace in the resolution to accept whatever mark the essay is deemed worthy of, and simply do better on the next one.

That following week, returned our graded essays to each of us students. A modicum of relief was felt, in finding out that overall none of the students performed very well on that assignment. The class average was around 60%. I knew this because of the acerbic diatribe Dr. McLaughlin issued to the class while returning all essays to us. He even stated that some of the essays would have been comical if not for the fact that they were written by his students. Few of the students thought very highly of Dr. McLaughlin but he and I had a good rapport, despite my faux pas with the first essay. Based on prior communication, he knew I was a serious anthropology student. On the first day of class, he requested that all students introduce themselves by stating their name, personal/professional background and reason for attending Pierce College. This was where I mentioned my prior experience with stone tool manufacture and other primitive technologies. I also described my academic goal of ultimately earning a post-graduate degree in anthropology or archeology. Dr. McLaughlin was delighted to have someone with my background and aspirations in the class. So when he graded my ill fated 1st essay, his comments reflected suspicion that my performance on the assignment was an egregious but uncharacteristic blunder. Some of his comments were statements to the effect of "When did you begin writing this paper?" The essay failed by a substantial margin with only a 20% mark. I was even surprised that it was deemed worthy of that.

144

In this nascent stage of my first quarter, I attempted to maintain part time work as a landscaper on campus while going to school. Yet after the epic failure of my 1st essay in World Prehistory class, I had to report to Al Downs, the campus plant manager that I needed to quit my campus job. It was simply not possible to manage the job along with my studies. Mr. Downs was completely understanding of my need to terminate and it was a mutually agreeable decision. He needed someone who could regularly and consistently work more than 9-10 hours per week.

I went home that evening, barely conscious from having stayed awake for two consecutive nights. Miraculously, I managed to scrape together enough energy to complete a math assignment due the next day. By the time of completing the assignment, I was actually having hallucinations brought on by sleep deprivation. I became dissociated and confused in place and time. While lodged in my bedroom at my parents' house, I thought I was in the upper deck of the college library. Students in the building were typing papers using antiquated 1930s mechanical typewriters. All the while, Beethoven's 5th was being composed by a student orchestra on the 1st floor of the library. In my mind, this was where I was at, prior to falling asleep only to wake up at 10am and miss my first class. Nobody ever told me that college would be easy but it was a challenge I was abundantly willing to embrace.

I soon found the campus gym to be an indispensable resource. Not only did it better enable me to maintain a high standard of physical health, but also a positive mood and spirit. These were not just frivolous extras but were absolutely crucial to staying motivated to sustain the effort required for me to succeed in my classes. The Pierce College gym at the time was small and provisioned mostly with an assortment of antiquated Nautilus™ machines, along with more modern cardio-vascular equipment. But, during my first three quarters at Pierce College, it served its purpose well. In the Fall quarter of 2000, I joined a local branch of 24 Hour Fitness in Lakewood and began to once again exercise religiously, as I did in high school. After a little over a year, I lost 40 lbs, going from 220lbs to 180 lbs. I surpassed my high school standard of physical fitness, restoring youth and vitality once again.

Physical conditioning became a critical aspect of my life which I grew determined to never again dismiss or minimize. I made this mistake about a year after graduating from high school. This was what caused me to gain so much weight in the first place. If not for working diligently to maintain sound physical conditioning, I may well have incurred other medical conditions stemming from obesity and diabetes by the time of completing my 1st BA. I may not have even survived long enough to even earn my MA. Throughout my college years, balancing an effective health regimen along with my studies was always a very costly struggle.

After developing a strategy to balance academic work along with my fitness routine, the next order of business was to register for disability accommodations before it was too late. The deadline was fast approaching and I nearly missed it. Settling into a new life was very taxing of my time and energy.

I approached the receptionists' desk of disability support services, located in the registration and records office. I brought along a copy of my 1997 neuropsychological evaluation. Such documentation is necessary to determine my eligibility for disability accommodations under ADA policy. In the office, I was greeted by the receptionist, a rather fine looking Junoesque tangerine – haired lady. Her eyes widened and eyebrows lifted as she inhaled deeply while smiling sheepishly, placing her hand over her heart. "I'm sorry, just had to catch my breath for a second there. How can I help you?" Before I could answer, she interjected; "have I seen you somewhere before?" In response to her question, my imagination wandered to various locations where we may have encountered each other before. Let's see, Decatur High, Bates Technical College, no, certainly not Clover Park, hmm where could I have seen her. After a few seconds reflection, I gave up, stating "I can't think of where that might be."

"Come to think of it, I can't either. What can I do for you?

"I'm here to request ADA accommodation for a learning disability. I have a copy of my neuropsychological exam right here."

"The person you need to speak to about that is Jochim Benson and he's not in the office right now, but I can schedule an appointment for you to speak to him."

146

"Sure".

She grabs a logbook and lists some possible dates for me to come in. We agreed upon a date and she handed me a Post-it™ note with the date/time written on it. "Be sure to bring in that neuropsychological evaluation, when you speak to Joachim." Before I left, she asked, "How do you highlight your hair? It is the most gorgeous color I have ever seen."

"It's just natural sun bleaching."

"That's it? Well I hope this isn't too inappropriate to say, but it goes really well with your eyes."

"Thank you", I replied.

"You're welcome have a nice day."

"You too".

I walked out of the office, levitated with effervescence. An attractive woman expressed such interest in me-even in a situational context of revealing my disability. Disability is generally regarded as highly repugnant, even frightening to many people. But a part of me was still uncertain as to what to make of it all. Was it just innocent? She did have pictures of what were presumably her husband and children on her desk. Even as a harmless crush, it's very exhilarating.

The next day, I met with Joachim, and submitted all required documentation. During our meeting, I described to him what I felt were potentially the most problematic challenges with academic work. These mostly related to short term memory impairment, as well as deficits of concentration with their impact upon reading comprehension and mathematics. The following week, I came in for another meeting and was presented with a list of suggested academic adjustments. These included; the permission to tape record lecture sessions, access to the instructors lecture slides, as study aids, extended time (time and a half) to take exams, and the option of taking tests in a quiet distraction free environment. They really seemed nothing short of extreme measures, even though the rationale behind them made sense.

147

After submitting the list of accommodations to my instructors, I "tinkered" with each of them for the first half of the quarter. It quickly became apparent that the only academic adjustment I needed was the opportunity to take math tests in a quiet, distraction free room with extended time. With linguistically based philosophy, history, and social science classes, I could take tests under normal test taking conditions and even come out among the top scorers in the class. But all of the exams at Pierce College were multiple choice "fill in the bubble" types. For any written test it would have been necessary to take the test in a quiet room with time and a half.

The most effective strategy for my success in college was not even one provisioned by the campus ADA office. My most effective strategy for college success was simply my ability to live inexpensively, subsisting almost entirely on student aid monies. I never had to work more than 9 hours per week while attending college. Thus I was able to devote the effort required for me to earn stellar marks on coursework. For me, this in itself was beyond a full time occupation -often amounting to 70 or more hours per week. Such a regimen was imperative for me to complete essays to a high standard of quality and devote the many hours needed to adequately prepare for math tests. It was this approach enabled me to succeed only to the extent of maintaining a high GPA and earning my degrees in a timely manner. However, it did not lead to success in the realm of career development. With little to show for my higher education years aside from my degrees and a high GPA, I was never able to develop a competitive professional track record. These consequences became abundantly clear after earning my AAS at Pierce College. The needlessly competitive economy and society engendered by neoliberalism has virtually neutralized any class ascending effects of merely earning a college degree with a high GPA. The once proselytized passkey to the American middle class is now merely a bastion of false hope and empty promise for too many.

For the first two and a half years of my collegiate career, I steadily and diligently ploughed through mounding piles of assignments like a sturdy plodding ox following a carrot on a stick. My carrot was a high GPA at the end of each quarter and the hope it betrayed for a better future. It was my meager assurance that all my efforts were not in vain. At least this in itself should improve my track record and provide some chance toward developing a positive rewarding career, in which my disability poses the least restrictions. Surely,

148

just earning a college degree should confer some advantage over not having attended college in the first place. But how much of an advantage? The torments of my reality, the chronic sleep deprivation, making high marks but learning nothing, for they are not much different from the time honored fabled college experience. Yet for me, these hardships were intensified by the effects of my disability-intensified to an often unhealthy extreme.

Many students eventually become able to effectively manage a full time academic workload to the point of being able to balance coursework, internships and other extracurricular involvement. I never attained this mastery. The very nature of my disability negated this achievement. Yet so long as I was making the grades and able to maintain my exercise regimen, I was artificially content. But my contentment was nothing more than a mere placebo effect from seeing my hard work and effort pay off in some superficial sense. At least for a while, the snake oil advice emphasizing hard work and exceptional effort seemed to be working. Not yet aware of the ramifications of my mode of living/studying upon my professional development, I remained psychically anaesthetized. The power of popular cultural myth can be disastrously misleading .

During my second quarter at Pierce College, I took an anthropology class that completely changed my worldview. More specifically, my worldview changed in a way that ultimately led to my conscientization, years later while pursuing an MA degree in the United Kingdom. The instructor, Mike Avey was an ardent Marxist who vehemently discredited social Darwinism, and the competitive, hierarchical, dichotomous thinking, underpinning that philosophy. He explained variation and natural selection in ways that were not only intellectually comprehensible but also have potential to change popular conceptions of the natural world, for the betterment of society. For example, he described species variation as a color wheel, rather than the traditional more hierarchical and dichotomous models. The color wheel represents multiple spectral hues. Many problems arise in attempting to discretely categorizing one hue from another. The most basic problem is created, for example when trying to distinguish at what point does one color morph into another. For example at what point does purple become violet and violet become blue? Moreover, such distinctions can differ depending upon who creates them, making individual categories less objective and far more arbitrary than we realize. Yet the labels we use to distinguish can create a specific reality only in the mind of the beholder - a reality that too often ignores variation or potential variation that can occur within a recognized category. More importantly, these arbitrary distinctions form the basis for the oppression of subordinated classes of people, based on their perceived undesired difference from the dominant norm. Professor Avey was also very keen on pointing out popular misconceptions on biological theory that have been used to justify oppression and subjugation of less powerful social groups within society. For example, we often consider the wealthy and powerful as justly deserving their power which they supposedly acquired through their talents and diligent application thereof. Too often though, we neglect how even in a democratic meritocracy, social, political, environmental, and historic factors are far more influential in determining someone's lot in life.

Dr. Avey's teaching style was very egalitarian and student centered. He virtually never lectured and assigned each of us students to small discussion groups to which each group was assigned a central question pertaining to the class readings. After each group researched their items of inquiry, we would then meet as a class and discuss all of the questions as a class, with the instructor. In retrospect, I wondered if he may have been influenced in some way by the work of Paulo Freire. When I read Dr. Friere's work after getting my MA, much of it resonated with my reflections of Mike Avey's classes and teaching style. Mike Avey really tried to raise critical consciousness among his students. After taking Mike Avey's class, I saw the world through a very different lens.

Midway, through my first year of college, I was feeling a genuine sense of purpose, and a definite mission in life. My purpose in college was more than just doing what I liked or felt suited to. I now actually felt I was getting an education that I could generally use to make a difference. Many of my classmates in social science and history classes enjoyed studying with me. My input in class discussions was always greatly appreciated by both students and faculty alike. This was especially so when discussing some of the academic ramifications of my primitive technology practices.

This type of feedback affirmed in my mind that teaching anthropology had to be my optimal vocational niche. Though a long way from reaching that goal, my first 2.5-3 years of college were remembered as the happiest years of my life, even to this day. It was one of the few times that I felt like a legitimate member of society rather than a Bohemian outsider on the fringes of the norm. I was truly developing a life of my own and enjoying reprieve from the survival mode I was enmeshed in, since initiating my reintegration into society around 3-4 years prior. Now light years ahead of that, I had more than just enhanced purchasing power and a consistent daily routine. I also had the capacity to contribute and make a difference in the lives of others. During my first quarter at Pierce College, I actually enabled three of my classmates to pass the anthropology class with a better grade than they otherwise would have earned. One actually told me that she is convinced that she would have failed the class were it not for me. It was the first time that I knew what it was like to feel plugged in to the world around me. This new sense of connection, purpose and direction motivated me to sustain the intensely focused effort required for me to maintain my level of progress. Being financially dependent on federal student aid monies for my education meant that academic failure could ultimately lead to my funding being withdrawn and being placed in either academic suspension or probation.

In my first year at Pierce College, I befriended another LD student, named Victor. He himself had been on academic suspension and probation with financial aid. This was due to unsatisfactory academic performance on his part. His learning disability was of a type I could not quite identify. He had prominent motor deficits and was very awkward socially. E mail messages I received from him were laden with misspellings. His spelling difficulties were far worse than mine and he seemed to have a very limited attention span. Yet despite his many troubles with financial aid, he always managed to successfully appeal academic suspensions. In fact, this was an ongoing cycle for him. He would get on suspension, and successfully appeal, only to take classes for a few quarters before getting suspended and having to appeal once again. In fact, of the nearly two years I spent at Pierce College, there were only two quarters in which Victor and I simultaneously attended. We met in the late winter quarter of 2000 and he wasn't able to attend classes again until Fall 2001.

Victor was 10 years my senior but with his slight build looked very young for his age. In fact I actually thought that he was somewhat younger than I, perhaps in his early 20s. I met Victor in the tutoring lab, as we were both trying to master Dragon Naturally Speaking in hopes of improving our efficiency with written coursework.

In addition to an organic learning disability, he also suffered from both PTSD and an anxiety disorder. Both were the outcome of him being physically attacked while on guard duty in the Army. Those latter ailments certainly had an impact on his academic performance and ability to function effectively. In fact his disabilities were of a severity as to warrant approval for SSI. Furthermore, for reasons far too complex and multifaceted for a layperson to fully comprehend, he struggled much more severely in his academic coursework than I did. Unlike me, though, he could drive. Yet he also had a history of accidents and tickets for moving violations. His capacity to actually profit from his studies was markedly compromised. He had been attending college there on and off for nearly 20 years before finally earning his Associate's degree. By the time I knew him, he really had no clearly defined career goals, and was just attending college to occupy his time and to get the extra money. He started with every intention to improve his lot in life. Ultimately, however it turned out that attending college classes was the best thing for him to do with his time. He had nothing else to do. Over the course of his many years in college, he switched majors from history to computer science.

Though Victor was on suspension during much of the time I attended Pierce College, we would regularly stay in contact by talking over the phone and by e mailing each other. During the inter-quarter breaks we would go to the Tacoma Rifle and Revolver Club shooting range for informal target practice. I supplied the firepower, ammo, and range access via my membership and Victor supplied the transportation.

Victor and I maintained contact with each other for several years after our time at Pierce College. A few years after we both graduated, he moved to California following the death of his parents. We continued to email each other for the next three years but never could we visit. The last e mail message I sent him was just before I left for England to attend grad school. To this day, I can't help but wonder what ever happened to Victor.

My friendship with Victor was not unlike other friendships that materialized during my college and grad school years. Many of my closest and long enduring friendships I developed were with fellow neurodiverse and disabled students struggling to overcome the social hardship of their disability. Though our specific disabilities varied considerably, with regards to specific symptoms and overall severity, we all seemed bound together like molecules, ambling through the universe and forming bonds upon our encounter with each other. We would often exchange info on tactics and resources to help us succeed in college, including which instructors/professors were most ND friendly in their teaching approach. There almost seems to be a culture of neurodiversity-one analogous to the culture of blindness or deafness. We connect through a common bond engendered through our common experiences and similar perspective on life, resulting from both this factor and our unique neurological wiring and brain chemistry. With increased politicization of the various disability movements and growth of disability studies in academia, the college and university system could become a locus for political consciousness and mobilization of the various disabled populations.

Pierce College was where I also met Shannon-one of my dearest female friends, of whom I came close to forming my first romantic relationship with. Though I never really worked up the courage to ask her out, I think she may have been waiting for me to do that. I have very extreme difficulties in gauging as to whether or not a woman is interested in me as a potential romantic partner. So I was always too painfully shy to ask her out. But I was so deeply infatuated with her that any day I missed a visit with her seemed incomplete. Is this what true love feels like? I never really knew.

Fueled by caffeine, exercise induced endorphins, and lots of positive energy, I earned my AAS at Pierce College with honors one quarter sooner than anticipated. Following the advice of professor Mike Avey, I transferred to TESC, intent on doing an independent study contract, focused on experimental archeology.

In my final two quarters at Pierce College, I was all but completely exhausted from the effort required of me to keep up with my coursework while maintaining a respectable GPA. I could barely muster the energy to effectively research transfer colleges. Moreover, my transportation limitations, and limited internet access compromised my ability to visit campuses and do all of the legwork required for the process. Being the first person in my nuclear family to attend college, I was without the critical familial coaching from parents and other relatives to assist me in the process. I did not even understand what to look for in a transfer college. And even if I had more readily available internet access, it may not have done me much good. I was no nearly as skilled in navigating websites as I am now. It was all a proverbial stab in the dark.

With regard to academic offerings, according with my major, I was beginning to doubt my decision to enroll at TESC. But I knew of no other schools with an anthropology department that also featured the unique progressive approach of TESC. By my final year at Pierce College, I came to question conventional business oriented academia with its emphasis on product completion and time management. How can a person truly develop any reflective and critical thinking capacities when only focused on time and deadlines? Isn't development of reflective and critical thinking capacities more germane to the advancement of academia than expediency of product completion? After all how can society's knowledge truly advance when academia is structurally dominated by those whose only contribution is the ability to produce work quickly even if not the most groundbreaking work? And why restrict participation within academia only to those who can consume and produce knowledge quickly? Doesn't this reduce the array of different fronts from which groundbreaking knowledge and ideas can emerge, thus undermining the overall richness within academia?

The progressive Evergreen State College was where the seeds were sown that sprouted into my critical consciousness regarding political and sociological ramifications as to the struggles of many neurodiverse people in post modern western society. During my first quarter at TESC, I enrolled in a full time interdisciplinary program called health and human development (HHD).The program incorporated the disciplines of human biology, psychology, and sociology, and emphasized the ways in which these academic perspectives intersect with regard to the healthy development of the individual and society. Though not entirely relevant to my intended academic major of anthropology, I had a solid background in human biological and social sciences from Pierce College, so I knew that I could at least make it through the quarters in HHD until I got into an individual study program. In the program, we studied both physical and mental health and linked these to sociological health.

It was during that first quarter in which I was introduced to the social model of disability. This proved very libratory for me as a person diagnosed with a potentially disabling condition. Perhaps in a different cultural context, my unique way of thinking and functioning may not incur the dire personal hardship that it has. Cultural context notwithstanding, perhaps just some modifications in my

154

environmental circumstances could make a difference. This was a lesson that came to life for me as a second year undergraduate at TESC. I had far less difficulty with studies and with life in general at TESC. I certainly had not become more efficient in my ability to complete coursework. Neither was the coursework getting any easier. In fact the work at TESC really required a much higher level of critical thinking than any work I did at Pierce College. This was simply due to the more advanced academic level I was studying at. The standards for written work were also more stringent than any at Pierce College. The actual workload didn't decrease any. In fact, there were no more words written per quarter than at Pierce College. But why was I able to complete all of my work by its due date, maintain my exercise routine, do occasional archery or atlatl practice over the weekend, and find time to prepare actual meals from raw ingredients? The answer was simple. Olympia is a far more bicycle accessible town than are Tacoma and Lakewood. This meant that I had access to much more efficient transportation, meaning less time was consumed just in moving from point A to point B. In Olympia, I felt almost like I was enjoying a comparable life as the typical American adult who drives. Also the academic workload was distributed throughout the quarter in a way that usually resulted in students virtually never having two or more assignments due at around the same date.

After successfully completing my first two quarters at TESC, I was able to develop my own course of independent study for my remaining quarters at Evergreen. From the summer quarter of 2002, to the spring quarter 2003, my learning flourished. I could actually converse on the subject matters I studied. At Pierce College, I earned respectable marks and graduate with honors but did not truly learn anything. In the summer of 2002, following advice of Steve Kipling, my dorm mate, I enrolled in a program called Consciousness Studies. The professor for this program was extremely unconventional to say the least. He followed a practice of student centered learning to an extent that some might call extreme. Students in the program were encouraged to develop their own curriculum for study, surrounding themes pertaining to the philosophy of human consciousness. However, under the auspices of the program a student could really pursue any mode of independent self determined study that interested them, provided that they had a sufficiently defined plan of action and submitted reflective progress reports every week. I seized the opportunity, as there were many things I wanted to do, in the way of primitive technologies. Certainly few other academic institutions would afford such opportunities.

In the summer quarter of 2002, I enrolled in consciousness studies with the intent of exploring cognitive archeology in relation to obsidian use within the ancient Neolithic Anatolian "beehive city" of Catal Hoyuk. This was the first time that I was able to flintknapp in about three years. The quarter got off to a shaky start, impeded by a high maintenance girlfriend of whom I quickly managed to shake off my back. But once that was done and over with, I could get back in the swing of my routine and ultimately gain the respect of both my professor and many of my cohorts at TESC.

By the end of the summer quarter of 2002, I replicated 5 Neolithic Anatolian obsidian mirrors, each using different working processes, based on geological and ethnobotanical research of the early Holocene Anatolian plateau. Correspondingly, I wrote experimental reports for each respective replication. I also read voraciously about the symbolic life of the ancient inhabitants of Catal Hoyuk and the role that obsidian mirrors likely played in that aspect of their lives. Additionally, I researched the significance of Catal Hoyuk and of the Anatolian Plateau in the development and diffusion of Neolithic culture and Indo-European languages within western Eurasia. Once I worked out a few kinks in my personal life, I knew that I was going to profit immensely from student centered learning at TESC. This was what motivated me to put in 8-10 hours per day on my studies despite the absence of firm deadlines, tests and specific quantifiable amounts of products to complete. My activities that summer quarter set a precedent for being the most productive member of any group of students David Ruteledge had ever worked with.

The class meetings were very joyous and productive occasions. Attendance was completely optional, but I attended most sessions. It was always intriguing and inspirational to follow what other members of the class were doing and studying. The Evergreen State College is a very liberal arts oriented institution and many students worked on musical compositions, and visual arts such as charcoal drawings. The possibilities were endless. One student in particular, Angela was a singer-songwriter who composed and recorded numerous musical compilations while in the class. Her genera would best described as a dazzling style of indie folk, imbibing many thought-provoking philosophical and introspective themes. Angela and I communicated frequently with each other as

156

we were both intrigued by each other's work. This was her final quarter at TESC, as she was subject to graduate at the end of that summer quarter. Angela later went on to pursue music professionally. She had produced numerous CDs through small label recording contracts and had played in many local venues Her music was frequently aired on many college radio stations. For Angela, independent learning at TESC proved to be a worthwhile springboard to her musical career. Both her and I were lauded by the professor as being among the more serious and dedicated students in the class.

After completing my first quarter of self directed study at TESC, I knew that this was where my learning would flourish. By the end of the quarter, I could actually converse on topics related to human prehistory and could answer questions from the top of my head that students would pose to me. Often my answers would lead to lengthy monologues, giving the inquisitor more than they bargained for.

By this point, much of what I was learning at TESC was beginning to synthesize. I read a lot on the work of Howard Gardner, involving multiple intelligence (or MI) theory. Additionally, I became acquainted with the work of Paulo Freire and his concepts of student centered learning and problem posing pedagogy vs. the banking concept of education. In his highly influential book *Pedagogy of the Oppressed*, Paulo Freire refers to the banking concept of education, describing it as "fundamentally narrative in character". According with this traditional paradigm, the teacher is the subject and the students are passive objects. Education is thus seen as a process of depositing knowledge into passive students, trusted to receive that knowledge. Teachers are the epistemological authority in this system; students' pre-existing knowledge is ignored, aside from what was expected to be 'deposited' into them earlier. Freire also refers to a banking paradigm as regarding students as "adaptable, manageable beings". Thus the more they accept the passive role imposed on them, the more they tend simply to adapt to the world as it is and adapt to the fragmented view of reality deposited in them. The banking concept of education is essentially an investment towards maintaining the oppressive systems and power relations that sustain them. By contrast, the problem-posing model of education solves the student-teacher contradiction by recognizing that knowledge is not deposited from one (the teacher) to another (the student) but is instead formulated through dialogue between the two. Problem posing education refers to a method of teaching that emphasizes critical thinking for the purpose of liberation. Dialoguers approach their acts of knowing as grounded in individual experience and circumstance and learners make connections between their own conditions and those produced through the making of reality.

However, despite of my new found understanding that began to emerge, I remained focused primarily on my studies of prehistory and archeology-giving little thought as to any larger social or political issues. In fact I was still very much apolitical during this time-only concerned with my passion for prehistory and how to make a viable career out of it. In my mind, this was my own personal struggle, with no political or sociological ramifications whatsoever. Only years later, would I come to see the fundamental error in this way of thinking. For it is entirely a product of the oppressive system I grew up in.

In the interim break following that summer quarter at TESC, my friend and dorm mate Steve and I decided to rent a house in the small town of Hoquiam, 30 miles southeast of Olympia. We both desired a quiet, rustic small town setting close to opportunities to fish, hunt and target shoot. Since we were both independent study students, there was no need for either of us to be regularly present on campus. Steve, like myself, also had a number of specific learning difficulties and psycho-social challenges. Though his were manifest primarily as both dyslexia and bipolar I disorder, we were both feeling the same disillusionment towards conventional academia. Prior to being involved with independent study, Steve was feeling betrayed by the false promise of an inclusive progressive learning environment betrayed by some specific faculty that he dealt with at TESC. We were two chronic outcasts now in our own cliques-one of few that we could ever fit into. By this time, Steve became a frequent reader of the writings of Paulo Freire, relating his pedagogical experiences to Freire's pedagogical philosophies. Freire was very thought provoking and inspirational to Steve. After his readings, he would monologue intensely as to what he read and I would listen intently doing my best to make as much sense of it as possible. But at that point, much of it was still irrelevant and incomprehensible to me. The idea of student centered learning resonated with me, but only in a very concrete apolitical sense.

Steve's main interests were flamenco guitar, ethno-poetic writing and the philosophy of ethics. I spent the remainder of my time at

TESC studying paleoindian fluted point technologies-involving replicative studies of these. I also studied archaeo-metallurgy, involving copper smelting and smithing in both the old and new world. During my final quarter in the spring of 2003, I conducted pilot experiments on the use of ground stone atlatl weights and the likely role these played in North American prehistory as techno-cultural entity. This would become the subject of my Master's dissertation at the University of Exeter some four years later.

I graduated from TESC in the spring quarter of 2003. Steve remained enrolled as a student there for another year. I later came to wonder if his decision to stay enrolled at TESC wasn't a wiser decision. I graduated from TESC with my BA degree feeling, at 28, more empowered and renewed than I ever had in my entire adult life. I certainly had come a long way from the drifty, fantasy-indulging days of my early 20s. I was finally coming to life and truly coming into being as a contributing member of larger society. This was one of the proudest moments in my entire life.

•••

Knowing that ADA statutes were applicable to my disability, made the pursuit of a higher education degree seem much more approachable. This was my first instance dealing with ADA law. Before long, I began questioning the very logic underpinning the ADA. The statute especially lost credibility with me, given that for the most part, my academic adjustments in college were completely irrelevant to my situation. I couldn't help but wonder as to how effective such targeted programs could be in helping the disabled to integrate into society. Yet, I did not have the vocabulary to describe what I was feeling. My only thought was that such ADA accommodations were totally useless.

I earned my first two undergraduate degrees with a high GPA and positive evaluations from my instructors. Yet very seldom was it even necessary to use any of the academic adjustments that the ADA permits in cases like mine. Why should I? No such accommodations would have generated more time towards completing coursework. Not even extended deadlines would have been effective. Even with extended deadlines, the student is still required to complete the same amount of work before the quarter is over with. For neurodiverse learners, the opportunity to pursue adequately funded part time study might be more conducive to more optimal benefits from higher education. Yet student aid funding policy, typically militates against these arrangements. Perhaps this is one means by which ND students could benefit from an unconditional basic income.

Higher education, under capitalism is almost invariably structured in accordance with the logic of the market, centered on production. In the three and a half years it took for me to earn my AAS and 1st BA, I studied under two very different pedagogical paradigms. One, the conventional paradigm, rooted in capitalist institutional structure utilizes methods of compulsion and high stakes testing. The hierarchical ranking of performance resulting from this approach can sometimes pit students in destructive competition with each other. The other approach I partook, at TESC, was based on the teachings of Paulo Freire. Moreover this was a student centered model, grounded in Marxian critical theory. I succeeded in both scenarios. But I truly profited academically from my work at TESC. Moreover, my neurodiversity was no object at all in my independent contract study at TESC. There was no need to even consider disability accommodation. In this way, I was not a problem to be dealt with. I conducted my studies at TESC in a largely self determined manner that enabled me to take ownership of my learning. It was a slower, more self-determined flexible mode of academic work that de-emphasized quantifiable production of academic products. The teaching approach at TESC was more centered around the content and process of the student learning. In a sense, it were as though I had no disability at TESC. In fact, I was one of the most prolifically achieving independent contract students, my professors had encountered. I often think of this scenario as a microcosm to illustrate how a system that truly democratizes our institutions and economic productive processes, could enable more neurodiverse people to find a positive niche and be productive and thrive.

Civil rights legislation such as the ADA inadvertently, yet frequently posits the targeted demographic as a social problem, or creates, in the minds of many, an illusion of "special privilege" enjoyed exclusively by the demographic served by the civil rights legislation. The ADA is a perfect example of the failure of liberal civil rights. Yet such legislation is the only means by which capitalism can ensure some minimal level, if not a mere illusion of protectionism for the disabled. As I described in the introduction, disability is a socially created category. In the context of the modern world system, it is derived largely from labor relations, inherent to the economic structure of capitalist society. In this respect, disability is an aspect of one of the central contradiction of capitalism that Karl Marx identified. Marx postulated that the competitive nature of capitalism would lead to a concentration of capital in fewer and fewer hands. This condition creates an excess capacity and lack of aggregate demand. In its drive for increased competiveness, workers whose lives don't lend themselves to efficient production face unemployment, poverty, and social marginalization, Thus oppression of the disabled is one of the social preconditions, necessary for the capitalist class to accumulate wealth. Disability politics that do not acknowledge disability as an outcome of such exploitative economic relations are at best fundamentally flawed strategies for reform. Worse, they serve as forms of bourgeois ideology that prevent this realization from being seen. This is not to say that civil rights legislation is not worthwhile. I am simply saying that under capitalism, such legislation will, for the most part remain effectively toothless. The ADA does not dismantle the exploitative capitalist labor relations that society's institutions are based on. It is these exploitative relations that lead to productivity demands for which disabled people will rarely satisfy. Moreover, the ADA will not change the structures of educational institutions which are designed to ensure conformity to norms that center around capitalist productive interests.

The goals of the ADA are fully compatible with neoliberal policies emphasizing ending dependency and increasing productivity. These politics are underscored in the ADA legislation itself. Congress specified three major goals when it enacted the ADA. These include; eliminating arbitrary barriers faced by disabled persons, ending inequality of opportunity and reducing unnecessary dependence and unrealized productivity. In theory, the ADA promotes the inclusion of disabled persons in the majority workforce and higher educational settings through the establishment of constitutional laws and regulations which are geared to creating 'equal opportunity' in the labor market or education. More specifically, it hypothetically serves to create opportunities for disabled people by 'leveling the playing field' and requiring the organization or institution to accommodate impairments on the job, unless doing so would cause undue hardship for the organization. Thus, under the ADA, entitlement to accommodation is no entitlement at all. Disabled people's quasi-civil rights would be tolerated by the anti-government and anti-regulatory political interests as long as the ADA cost the federal government next to nothing, was largely voluntary for business with no quotas or affirmative action and promised to get people off state funded entitlements.

An entitlement to accommodation would be too politically unfavorable. Such legislation would be perceived by others as a privilege to the disabled. Even in it's current state, without such entitlement clauses, ADA law is very often regarded as such. In a competitive capitalist market economy, targeted civil rights legislation, only further creates an, us vs. them mentality of disabled, vs. non-disabled. What is more, the ADA perpetuates a false illusion of equal opportunity.

The false perception that equal opportunity exists for the disabled, further solidifies the widely held myth that the disabled can achieve economic and social parity with their non-disabled counterparts if only they put forth the required effort. Placing the onus upon any oppressed group to advance their own situation, only feeds into a culture of silence that impedes social reform.

CHAPTER 6 - THE QUEST FOR DIGNITY

"Lack of respect, though less aggressive than an outright insult, can take an equally wounding form. No insult is offered another person, but neither is recognition extended; he or she is not seen-as a full human being whose presence matters.

When a society treats the mass of people in this way, singling out only a few for recognition, it creates a scarcity of respect, as though there were not enough of this precious substance to go around. Like many famines, this scarcity is man-made; unlike food, respect costs nothing. Why, then, should it be in short supply
-Richard Sennett,
Respect in a World of Inequality

Throughout my final three quarters at TESC, I began investigating various graduate school options. Yet by that point, I was really burned out on college and ultimately decided to take about year or two off before commencing with grad school. Academically, I was entirely ready to pursue an advanced degree. Still, I wanted to get out into the "real world", establish some financial footing, and pay off some undergraduate student loans, before heading off to grad school.

For much of my adult life, my disability left me very cloistered from the normal labor market and the real world in general. I had no understanding of market forces and their ramifications upon the world of work. In my profound naivety, I believed that retail associates earned a living wage with full medical benefits. I applied for a sales associate position in the hunting and fishing department at GI Joes, ultimately landing the job. For the time being, working in a retail sporting goods store, seemed simple and minimally demanding. Such working conditions would enable me to use my spare time to focus on independent research projects, and publishing the results. Having published work to my name would certainly improve my prospects for grad school acceptance. With all factors considered, working at G.I. Joes seemed a reasonable interim reprieve, until I was ready for graduate school. With only a BA degree, there are few career options for someone with my

163

academic background, emphasizing experimental archeology and lithics studies.

Many of my colleagues at TESC, including my roommate spoke critically on the business practices of large corporations like Walmart, and their myriad consequences, including detrimental environmental, economic and social impacts. Yet I remained largely insular from these discussions. For at the time, these were issues, largely irrelevant to my own little world. I was much too focused on my own rehabilitation into society. Moreover, I regarded my rehabilitation as an entirely personal, apolitical project. My then apolitical mentality was undoubtedly a product of the baseless, folkloric message of personal responsibility that society imparts onto the disabled. We are conditioned to believe that our rehabilitation is entirely a personal struggle with no social or political ramifications. This message, I believe is the biggest obstacle towards more widespread and effective political mobilization among the disabled. Too often, struggling with a disability means being consumed with a single minded focus of simply improving one's lot in life. Yet these extraordinary efforts are frequently in vain. And too often, the diligent effort we must invest towards our own rehabilitation, itself, becomes a distraction toward optimally developing our political consciousness. Such was my reality all throughout much of my undergraduate years. But the inherent fallacy of this way of thinking, became abundantly clear after a few months on the job at GI Joes.

My first month on the job at GI Joes passed by quickly, even blissfully. I had nearly full time hours and virtually could not believe that I was getting paid to work there. All of the customers I dealt with were pleasant and gracious and most of the situations were well within my capacity to deal with. During my second week, our store manager was impressed that I sold two expensive gun safes and two high end hunting rifles. I got along well with all of my co-workers and supervisor and I had every confidence of eventually publishing some of my work and gaining admission into a graduate program. Much of my time was spent rummaging through some of my TESC writings to determine which ones could be re-formulated into a journal article. Having published work with only a BA should certainly give me a leg up towards grad school admissions.

Before long, however, my position at G.I. Joes quickly became a nightmare. Eventually, the emotional toll of working retail completely rendered me nonfunctional outside of work and just barely functional at work. For the most part, I was too depressed to do little aside from going to work and doing bare minimum physical exercise to maintain health and physical conditioning. Though highly depressed much of the time, I was determined not to allow my physical conditioning to deteriorate. Good physical conditioning is imperative, given my modes of transportation. Being unable to walk or bicycle for any significant distance would literally cripple me. Worse yet, I did not want to develop type II diabetes like my mom and sister have.

After a little more than a month of working at GI Joes, difficulties stemming from both my disability and severe mismanagement of the company were abundantly problematic. As employees, we had very scant training and most of our equipment was either in short supply or barely operable. A perfect example of this problem was the paucity of fully functional data scanning guns or LRTs. We were using LRTs that were close to 10 years old and completely unreliable. This basic inadequacy often made it impossible for many of us to perform essential functions of the job such as producing pricing labels or doing individual price checks for customers. I have seen many a customer walk away angry because so much of the merchandise lacked appropriate price information and often sales staff were without any means to even perform an expedient price check.

Even basic supplies such as paper and writing instruments were extremely scarce. Many of my co-workers who were most capable of dodging customer wrath were not necessarily those who were most resourceful at meeting customers' needs despite our paucity of resources. Rather, they did so through employing a variety of artful dodging tactics. Either they could look busy and dodge customers, or they seemed to have a knack for "pulling" answers out of thin air. The answer did not have to be truthful-just sound truthful and sincere enough to satisfy the customer for the time being. As long as they smiled appropriately and spoke with the right command, the customer would usually walk away, disappointed but at least would not usually display any overt rage. It seemed like a special trick that I could not quite figure out how to pull off. Maybe I just wasn't devious enough to make it work. But sometimes this tactic would backfire, and unfortunately with repercussions upon those bearing no responsibility for the customers ire. Many times I have bore the brunt of verbal abuse from customers who had been previously misinformed by one of my co-workers. Often this would place me in situation where I would have to solve problems on the spot that I was unable to effectively solve, given available resources. It was as though we were expected to perform miracles.

My lack of deceptive capabilities, were a tremendous disadvantage in this line of work. Perhaps this was especially so, given the extent of mismanagement inherent to this particular company. One has to be at least a little bit deceptive and cunning to cut corners and to formulate seemingly plausible answers for customers, on the spot, from thin air. But deception and guile are not skills I can actually master. I simply cannot speak unless my words are backed by something real. Not only is this a matter of simple honesty and integrity of character, but my thought processes are too concrete.

This was my very first taste of corporate culture and I was far from a good fit. The corporation is truly an institution where the inability to act immorally can be a very real work disability. This example should elicit the question as to who are truly the sick ones in our culture. Is it the movers and shaker that we so highly regard, or is it the many diagnosed persons who struggle to fit into a world built on the deceptive and immoral endeavors of these movers and shakers.

Many of the difficulties I faced while working at GI Joes were the result of multi-level mismanagement. Mismanagement and short staffing were problems which several co-workers complained about. Yet despite the many faults of management, there were in fact numerous obstacles I faced that were inherent to my disability. Retail and customer service work typically involves solving problems in fast paced and unpredictable environments. This places a premium on the ability to think on one's feet, multi-task and respond effectively on the spot to novel unexpected situations. Depending on the diagnosis, these are all capacities that are effectively precluded by the unique neurological wiring in many neurodiverse persons. I had numerous instances where some aspect of my disability resulted in my inability to meet customers' needs. For example, if a customer spoke too fast or did not enunciate clearly, it would result in miscommunication.

My naturally slower, more deliberate and methodical mode of communication meant that I might spend more time assisting customers than what was practical. In our understaffed store, this created situations where a customer would become irate in waiting

166

to be helped, consequently lashing out at me for not assisting them more expediently. I became very depressed while working there. This was yet another occupational setting where I was nothing more than the proverbial square peg in a round hole. Sure many of us have experienced this at some point in our professional lives. But for me it was now growing abundantly clear that this is my constant reality. I had not felt so lackluster since Jr. High. Is there a place for me anywhere in this world of ours?

Often my depression became alternated with feelings of intense rage and hatred. I harbored many violent fantasies about physically harming customers who had verbally abused me. Mentally, I gorged myself on these fantasies. They often became obsessions. In my off hours I would canvas the GI Joes parking lot and the entire south end of the Lakewood Towne Center, where the store was located. I actually hoped to encounter one of the customers who had insulted me on the job. My plan was to confront them, and initiate an argument. I would then egg them on further in an attempt to provoke them to the point of physically attacking me. At which point, I would draw my legally licensed Walther PPK handgun, fatally shoot them and then build a self-defense claim. Often, I would also fantasize how satisfying it would be to fatally torture them by shooting off all of their appendages with buckshot from a 12 gauge shotgun, causing them slowly bleed to death. That would give those petty, week, pathetic crybabies something to piss and groan about! Mass shooting sprees were another subject of obsessive fantasies. It was very tempting to open fire on the entire shopping complex where the store was located, sparing only those of whom I knew and had a positive rapport with.

After about 4 months of working at the store, I was increasingly at odds with Miles, the new store manager. He picked up on my difficulties but did not fully understand them. He attributed them all to basic aloofness and indifference on my part. But I was in fact, putting forth my best effort. Yet my best efforts were simply not cutting it. There is a very finite extent to which a cat can be reasonably expected to act and behave like a dog. And is there any occupational niche within the neoliberal social fabric where my natural functionality is not a problem? Miles did not have this level of understanding. He issued a written reprimand for my inefficiency. After the reprimand, he and I had a conference with him and we settled our differences amicably.

167

By this point my hours at the store were declining rapidly-often to as little as 12 hours per week. This seemed to be about the average for the sales floor staff at the store. They were trying to cut costs, using this mode of skeletal staffing. The store was looking increasingly like a ghost town. There was minimal customer flow and virtually no sales staff present. Most of my co-workers also had part time jobs elsewhere, but I knew of few other options that wouldn't be even more problematic for me than working at GI Joes.

I supplemented my hours at GI Joes by doing art modeling at both Pacific Lutheran University and the University of Puget Sound in Tacoma. The art modeling work was entirely within my capabilities. Yet still my total working hours fell short of full time. At least the artists I worked with really enjoyed working with me as a model. The positive feedback I received as an art model, had something of an ameliorative effect on the pangs of derision I was subjected to at GI Joes.

It was becoming obvious that I needed to get into a grad school program ASAP. But how? I purchased many GRE preparation materials and dilligently studied for the GRE exam while not at work. GRE preparation kept my mind in check and even provided a modicum of the type of intellectual stimulation I need, but was not getting through my work. Though too depressed to do much else, at least studying for the GRE gave me the feeling of moving forward. It became a shell that I would slip into, affording an escape from the bleakness that GI Joes had cast upon my world. I was too emotionally fragile and broken from all of the negative customer interactions and could do little else but work on my GRE and grad school application materials. At times I would feel the urge to do some recreational flintknapping or to work on a given academic experiment. But I just couldn't. I was too miserable and depressed to work on anything that did not have a more direct effect towards moving me forward in life. At that point, getting into a graduate program was my top priority. It was my vehicle out of the miserable slump I was in. My world was growing darker and I needed an exit.

By January of 2004, I was laid off at GI Joes and it was a relief. Now all I had to do was remain laid off and collect unemployment until I could get into a grad school program. So during my time of unemployment from GI Joes, I supplemented my meager unemployment benefits by modeling for art classes in the Tacoma area. Again the positive feedback from the artists was germane to my healing from the trauma incurred at GI Joes. Being laid off also meant that there was more time to work on my GRE and compile application materials for grad school applications.

But this extra time off also meant that there was more time to ruminate and perseverate over the many hurtful interactions I encountered at GI Joes. At times, these would be so intense as to put me into a fit of rage. Sometimes, I would spend days on end randomly roaming the woods surrounding The Evergreen State College campus. Often, I slept overnight in the woods, not wanting to return back to my home and to my new reality.

One evening, while using the computers at the Pierce College library to send e mails, the idea dawned upon me to do post-baccalaureate study in the event that grad school does not pan out. I superficially browsed the web site of Central Washington University and made an impulse decision to get on the FAFSA (Free Application for Federal Student Aid) web site and apply for financial assistance. I was at the pinnacle of desperation, operating under a dire survival mode. I simply cannot go back to working retail, but what other options are there? Successfully completing post-baccalaureate work, under a traditional academic curriculum, should improve my likelihood of getting into a graduate program.

Thus far, the feedback I received from the anthropology graduate program at Washington State University was not promising. Hence post baccalaureate study was starting to make more sense. I initiated the application process for WSU in October of 2003. By February 2004, all of my materials were in order with the exception of my GRE scores. The chair faculty of the program informed me that they were impressed with all of my experimental work at TESC. Their main contention was that my background lacked well-roundedness. They were also concerned as to my lack of training in statistical methods. The department chair advised that statistics are a major component to the work in their program. Based on my review of other grad school web sites, it was easy to envision that other graduate programs would decide similarly. The all seemed to have the same focus.

As days turned to weeks and weeks became months, I studied the GRE for hours on end, every day. I tried to give equal attention to all facets of the test, but paid special attention to the math battery. Given my lifelong hardships with mathematics, it only seemed logical to do so. Before long, I called Prometric testing center in Puyallup and asked when their next GRE session would be. They gave me the most recent date of March 15th and I registered for that one off the bat. By that point, I already invested 6 months preparing for the test, on nearly a full time basis. By March, I was ready as I ever could be.

My test day soon came and it was nothing short of a relief to have reached an end-point in the entire process. Before entering the testing room, the proctor took my photo and all required stats. Those included educational level and personal information such as the presence of specific disabilities. I left all personal effects at the proctor's desk and entered into battle, armed only with a few pieces of scratch paper and some meager writing instruments. It was a computerized test. As the hours dragged on, I eventually completed the test, well before the passage of my allotted time. It was all done and over with. I can only accept any outcome of the test, knowing that I tried my hardest and did my best.

Weeks later, my GRE results were mailed to me and they did not surprise me a bit. My verbal scores were in the 76th percentile and my essay scores were in the 86th percentile. In sharp contrast, my math scores were only in the 5th percentile. Such low math scores could never be anything but a barrier to admission into a graduate program.

As weeks and months passed, decisions were rolling in from the five graduate programs I applied for. Not one of them offered a place. But I did apply for post baccalaureate study at CWU. By this point, it seemed certain that this was where I would be in the Fall of that year.

In late May of 2004, I was notified of my acceptance at CWU. In my highly distressed and compromised mental state, the prospect of incurring further student loan debt concerned me very little. I grew increasingly better informed of the various student loan discharge strategies, so I knew that there were ways out. One option of particular interest was the disability discharge. With a strong well documented argument, supporting an inability to pay off my student loans due to my disability, it is possible to have all or a portion of the debt discharged. And in the meantime, doing post baccalaureate study would at least shield me from ever having to work another customer service job. What is more, it could serve as a highly viable

170

gateway to graduate school. Given my disability, grad school seemed key to my only viable career option of a college lecturing post. So though it incurs more debt, earning a graduate degree is the only way I can get into a career that would enable me to pay off that debt. With no plan of ever having kids, and no likelihood of ever owning a motor vehicle, my student loan payments should be fairly manageable, provided that I get into a full time tenure track college lecturing post. And if I don't, I'll just pull a legal maneuver to discharge all of my student loans.

With my acceptance at CWU confirmed, I began researching private scholarships that may offset any student loan debt incurred at Central. Now, all I have to do is remain on unemployment, until the start of my classes. This ensures that I have plenty of time to research and apply for scholarship opportunities, prior to being officially enrolled at CWU. Still lacking home internet access and being less efficient with information technologies than I have since become, researching scholarships required full time effort to make it halfway fruitful. It became a full time occupation for me, even though I ultimately found that there were no scholarships that I qualified for.

By this point, my occupational limitations were becoming increasingly evident. I never imagined that a simple learning disability could incur such hardship. All that I learned at TESC about the social model of disability and the many criticisms railed against economic globalization now began to resonate with me. I was gaining something of a crude understanding as to my impairments and the limitations they pose in the social and economic context I inherited. But years would pass before I had the opportunity to truly reflect upon these. My survival mode at the time was highly antithetical to such reflection.

I was spending much of my time at the Evergreen State College library in Olympia, doing research on scholarships and performing a minimal tokenistic job search to satisfy the requirements of employment security. All I could do is remain on unemployment until school starts. However, by the late spring of 2004, I was called in for an interview with Sears and Roebucks in the Sea Tac mall in Federal Way. Okay, so my deliberately absurd answers to some of the application questions weren't sufficient to deter them from calling me in for an interview. My only hope now was to deliberately blow the interview.

I came to the interview dressed in Khaki Dockers, running shoes, and an olive drab short sleeved shirt. I didn't shave that morning and left my hair down. I didn't want my intent to seem too obvious, but also wanted to render my chances of getting hired there to an absolute irreducible minimum. Working at Sears would be worse than GI Joes. Its larger size, and higher volume customer flow, means that the pace of work is likely to be more intense. I deliberately tried to present poorly by answering questions with evasive statements like "I don't know" or "beats me." I also slumped forward in my seat. Yet in spite of my best efforts, I was hired on the spot and had to take the job. Employment security law stipulates as such. Damn! I should not have told the interviewer that I was collecting unemployment. My intent must have been too obvious. The job was for a full time merchandising position at the store. On top of the fast pace and multi-tasking, much of the job would require frequently scaling ladders while handling awkward and unwieldy merchandise. Hence, my equilibrium and motor impairments would preclude my ability to safely perform the work.

The training at Sears was far more extensive and in-depth than with GI Joes. I attended the first two days and had no difficulties with the training. It even seemed plausible that the more adequate preparations might make this job somewhat easier than working at GI Joes. But climbing ladders and stairs was such a frequent requirement for this job. This alone renders it out of my capabilities. Had someone inquired as to my ability to perform this job function, I could have explained this and avoided being hired. But nobody even asked about my ability to perform such essential functions. Besides, what customer service job does not involve its fair share of negative customer interactions? By this point, I was still far too fragile from working at GI Joes. I could not even withstand one disparaging encounter.

On the third training day at Sears, I approached the store manager and explained that I just could not do the job and only applied for it to satisfy employment security's stipulations for unemployment eligibility. I elaborated by explaining my range of impairments and their corresponding difficulties. We both agreed that they were completely insurmountable in the type of work environment at Sears. I asked if there were any more feasible positions for me at the store, given my impairments. She could not think of any. We both amicably agreed to my dismissal.

172

I reported to Employment Security that I had to quit the job for reasons related to my disability. My report emphasized the frequent stair and ladder climbing, with regard to my motor and equilibrium impairment. I also disclosed my inability to effectively multi-task and work in fast paced environments. I explained how all of these limitations were attributable to specific organic impairments, and enclosed copies of my 1997 neuropsychological evaluation. After all, their policy does stipulate that disability related limitations are a valid reason to quit a job and remain on unemployment benefits. I was certain that my reasons would fall squarely within their criteria.

Approximately two weeks after reporting my departure from the job, I received a notice from employment security in the mail. Their decision was that I did not have a valid reason for quitting the job. They completely ignored critical facets of my disability that I clearly spelled out to them. Rather, they oversimplified my argument to make it seem as though I merely found the work unpleasant, as opposed to not safe or feasible, given my disability. Consequently, my unemployment benefits were discontinued. I also had to pay back a $160.00 over-payment of unemployment benefits collected while they made their determination. From that point on, I was forbidden from collecting unemployment for the next 7 years, or whenever my income met or exceeded 7 times that of my prior earnings-whichever came first. What could I do? I only had about $150.00 in my bank account. It was in the summer of that year and there was no art modeling work to do. After reading the letter carefully, I saw that clients had the right to appeal any such decision that they disagreed with. There was a way out. Perhaps I can appeal before any overpayment becomes due. I called employment security and established a graduated payment plan of $40.00 payments per month. Instead of having $160.00 due in 30 days, I only had $40.00 due in that amount of time. I paid the first payment well before the due date, and summarily began working on an appeal. Devoting the effort towards developing an appeal, completely diminished the time and energy needed for me to continue researching scholarships. I resented having this bomb dropped on me when I was legally and morally in the right. My parents gave me $100.00 to spend, knowing that I was totally broke. I also received my paycheck for the three training days I spent at Sears. Should I use these monies to pay off the rest of my alleged overpayment, just to get them off my back? No, I must appeal. There was no reason to cave in to corporations and state institutions that do wrong.

173

One day, in late June, I was browsing GI Joes, shopping for new angling gear. One of my former co-workers in the fishing and hunting department informed me that they needed additional summer help in the store. He asked if I would be interested in working there again, until school starts. Were I not so broke and indebted to employment security, my answer would have been a firm "no". But given my desperation and knowing that I would be moving to Ellensburg to start school in less than three months, I reluctantly agreed.

I re-submitted my application, went through another interview and drug screening and was hired on again at GI Joes. Okay, now I will have some funds to make payments on my benefit overpayments and to cover moving expenses for moving out to Ellensburg. The new store manager Ed, and the new Field and Stream manager, Tom were much nicer than the former boss I worked for last time. This made a tremendous difference. I worked there for another ten weeks before moving out to Ellensburg, to start school at CWU. Luckily, no hurtful customer interactions occurred during that time. When I left, I was determined to make GI Joes the last customer service job I would ever work. Yet this is no easy undertaking in the new economy. But my resolution to never work customer service was really not a matter of choice. I simply could not work customer service any longer. I was only able to remain hired at GI Joes, on a part time basis, due to my product knowledge of angling and archery gear. Few other employees had that type of knowledge. If not for my product knowledge, I could easily have been fired due to general performance inefficiencies. Not to mention, the long term emotional toll that the many negative customer interactions has taken upon me. The damage remains with me to this day. I have not fully recovered from it and am now much more hypersensitive, hostile and defensive than I ever was. I have a much more suspicious outlook towards others than I ever did and many things offend my sensibilities more readily than before. I'm not the same person I was and probably never will be. My experiences while working there really set back much of my progress in psychosocial development that occurred during my years at both Pierce College and TESC.

In July 2004, I confirmed my acceptance at CWU and enrolled in my classes online. A decision made from a knee-jerk and misguided solution to my predicament now came to fruition. It's a done deal now. So what can I do to make the most of my time here to ensure

174

that I transition immediately from post-baccalaureate study to my MA program. Three weeks prior to the start of my classes, I got to meet with a faculty member for an advising session and we had a lengthy conversation about flintknapping and lithics studies. I even began to discuss with him, my hypothesis on North American ground stone atlatl adjuncts in a post Pleistocene ecological context. The professor was impressed with my hypothesis. He seemed enthusiastic to have me as a student in the anthropology department. I was looking forward to once again having a place to go where I truly belonged. The positive reception I got from the CWU faculty was very encouraging.

In late September, my classes started. I found an affordable room to rent in a house with two clean, quiet, and responsible roommates. All was well. I still had about $80.00 remaining of my balance, with Washington State Employment Security. My appeal fell on deaf ears. I moved to Ellensburg about a week prior to the start of my classes and was able to enjoy some pheasant hunting and trout fishing with one of my housemates.

Attending the campus orientation for disability support services was rather moving. Most of the students at the orientation were just like me. Nobody could tell that any of us were disabled, based on physical appearance. There was not a single wheelchair, cane, walker, or service animal in the room. Is this the new face of disability in our time?

I did my best to remain optimistic, given all I had been through that year. Yet my optimism could only last for so long. Three weeks into my first quarter at CWU, I slipped into a serious depression-one made me suicidal and nearly unable to commence with the normal duties. I harbored serious doubts as to my success in a traditional academic setting, taking upper division classes. My doubts were brought on by what would normally have been completely innocuous occurrences in one of my classes. It was like the final catalyst added to a highly volatile mix. One major issue was with a professor for one of my anthropology classes. I sensed that the professor was dissatisfied with my input in class discussions. Yet her criticisms were very vague, and never specific. In a sense, they felt like nothing short of elitism - tinged, passive aggressive attacks against me. She had such rigid and narrow expectations of how students should respond to questions and discussion topics. Her attitude struck me as very narrow minded and I often wondered how well she was even processing what I was saying. My observations and experiences in that class were a stark contradiction to the principles and aims of any truly progressive and inclusive pedagogy. What is more, I always thought of anthropologists as being a particularly progressive, humane, and open minded lot. It was a class on museum studies. Initially, I was very interested in the subject. There is much applicability of experimental and replicative studies to museum work.

But that professor's attitude caused me to disconnect and lose interest in the subject matter. One day, in a moment of hostility, I e mailed the professor, stating that I no longer wished to participate in class discussions and was growing disillusioned because my input never seemed adequate for her. I felt awkward coming to class that next day. Hoping to initiate some discussion, I asked her if she received my e mail and she said no. It was a Friday and I only had one other class to attend that day. It was a 1 pm anthropology lab class.

After the class, I tried to settle down and work on assignments. Yet I simply couldn't. The combination of agitation and depression were sabotaging my efforts. I spent most of my time in the campus computer lab randomly surfing the web, trying to take my mind elsewhere hoping to ease my angst. I even forgot that the following Monday, there was an assignment due in that troublesome museum studies class. I left the computer lab in the early evening and wandered aimlessly throughout the town of Ellensburg. I was still upset over the frosty reception I was getting from the professor in my museum studies class. It's not as though we all intend to major in museum studies. How egocentric of her to expect us all to be as dedicated to her subject matter as she is. The only reason why I even took the class was to fill a time slot on my schedule to satisfy a full time credit load. I was practically forced to do so by the department of education. My walking and rumination eventually lead me to Jerroll's where I bought a new scientific calculator. I then went to the Starbucks further east on 10th avenue. At the Starbucks, I was able to focus somewhat more effectively on my studies. I stayed there for a few hours, before writing a check for the final payment to Washington Employment Security. I then sealed it in an envelope and mailed it off. Before long, it was dark. Days were getting shorter, making depression come much easier. I walked out of Starbucks consumed with hopelessness. Why don't I just end it all? This would be so easy to do with a single painless shotgun blast to the head. I do have the means to commit the act. Then all of my struggles would have ended.

I wandered aimlessly through campus, contemplating the best way to end my life. Everything just suddenly hit me like a ton of bricks and I randomly broke down and cried. But I know that I have friends and family who would be devastated if I killed myself. But I really don't want to live anymore! Why me? Why?

I walked to the health and counseling office about an hour before they closed and was able to do an intake and crisis intervention. I set up appointments for subsequent therapy sessions. We agreed to have all of my firearms and ammo kept in a safe place until a mental health professional opined it was safe to do otherwise.

During that initial session, I spoke to the crisis intervention counselor. Naturally, our conversation shifted to matters pertaining to the inordinate occupational hardships incurred by my disabilities. More specifically, I described these with a sociological perspective I was gaining, which attributes much of my functional limitations to the global capitalist system I am functioning in. But it all seemingly went in one ear and out the other. In retrospect, it came as no surprise. The earth flag in her office, the Buddha statues, and other eastern religious motifs all betrayed the very liberal capitalist mentality I was railing against. Her voice even took a somewhat irate tone. She insisted that there is no basis in reality to my assertion that my disability limits me to such a narrow range of vocational options. Yet my entire adult life experiences illustrate otherwise. Did she really think I was so stupid as to believe such baseless platitudes? How arrogant is that? But I kept my mouth shut and said nothing. It really wasn't the time nor place to debate the matter. The immediate concern was crisis intervention.

All of the counseling staff at the CWU counseling center were truly representative of all that is wrong with the mental health professions. For whatever reason, the field seems to serve as nothing more than a professional haven for narcissistic pseudo-intellectual charlatans. Many of them advance in their career only through talking a good talk and by playing the game of cronyism.

Like so many of society's institutions, clinical practice, including psychology and psychiatry is practiced in accordance with the values that sustain capitalism. This entails only focusing only on the faults of individuals and families, rather than on society and its structures and institutions.

The health and counseling center also set up an appointment for me to see the medical doctor at the center. Days later, I had my medical appointment, and the doctor gave me a sample pack of Zoloft. Yet I was too terrified to take it, and ultimately refused to do so. My fears were based on many accounts I have known of people becoming violent, agitated, and even suicidal from taking the drug. I could not bring myself to do it. Besides, medication was not the answer. A fitting and respected place in the fabric of society was what I needed.

Both the severe depression itself and undertaking the rigmarole of seeking the treatment, caused me to forget about the assignment that was due in my museum studies class. I called the professor and left a message on her voicemail, explaining what had happened. I explained that I was going through a severe episode of depression which caused me to space out the assignment. In my voicemail, I also stated that I was getting treatment for the depression and asked if I could turn in the assignment a day late for reduced credit. To my recollection, this was the late assignment policy stipulated in the syllabus.

That following day in class, I received my first graded essay from the museum studies class. Much to my surprise, this assignment scored a 97%. This put me in much better spirits. Maybe I will do better than I think. At the end of that class session, the professor approached me, asking if I had a few minutes to talk after class. We each stepped outside of class. The halls were empty with most of the students having already settled into their next classes. "How are you doing? she asked. "Okay" I responded, meaning I was doing a little better, now knowing that I have better chance in succeeding in the class than I thought.

> "I got your message yesterday and yes you turn it in
> on Tuesday, and I won't count it as late. You can
> place it in my box."

"Thank you", I replied.

She then told me that she knew what I was going through as both of her sons had learning disabilities and that she herself was given to bouts of depression.

"I appreciate your understanding".

"Is there anything I can do to help, with your studies in this class ?", she asked.

"No" I responded. "I just really began to disconnect because I was getting, what seemed to me, indications that I was just not meeting certain standards. But now that I see that this may not be the case, I'm in much better sorts now. And by the way, I really apologize for that one email that I sent that may have came across as rather hostile and derisive. I hope that you weren't offended."

"No, I wasn't, I understand what you are going through. But just be aware that most professors do not take too kindly to students who overtly expressing a lack of interest in their class. To them it reflects on their ability to teach and they're not thinking in terms of the student who has no real interest in the subject matter."

"I understand. Plus I must say that much of what I'm going through right now is the result of everything that happened to me over the past year, with my employment situation and the challenges that I'm facing in getting into a graduate program. Grad school seems to be my only ticket to a halfway decent life".

"Well, let me know if there's anything I can do to help".

"Thanks, I will".

I then returned to my next class. After that instance during my 1st quarter at CWU, everything very much looked up. I maintained a high GPA and earned the respect of my colleagues and professors. I just followed the same formula for a high GPA that worked during my freshman and sophomore years at Pierce College, This formula basically entails working 60-70 hours per week just on assignment

179

completion, maintaining an exercise routine for physical and mental health, forego any extracurricular work or internships, and pull an all-nighter here and there as needed.

During my first year at CWU, I was also participating in group counseling offered through the campus health and counseling center. Yet this did little to alleviate my bout of depression. My success in my classes and the new friends I was making had more to do with the improvement in my spirits than any treatment I received. There really is no 'treatment', *per se* that will improve my condition or its secondary consequences. By this point, I was growing fully cognizant of this fact. I only followed through with the treatment to acquire a clinical history which would contribute to my case for SSI, should that become necessary.

I sensed that I did not have a very good rapport with the counselor, Randy Robinette. There was always an uneasy tension between the two of us. He did not understand my unique proclivities as a neurodiverse individual. I felt that his prescribed treatment modality (i.e. group counseling) was really not applicable to what I was going through. By this point, I was gaining a sociological perspective on mental health issues. At times, this perspective expressed itself during group counseling sessions. I inadvertently reminded Dr. Robinette of his professional inadequacies and he resented me for that. He asked questions of me during the counseling sessions that took a somewhat hostile or defensive tone.

Once, when I made a point as the difficulties I encounter because institutions are not structured and developed to take account of the struggles of LD adults, he quickly and abruptly interrupted to ask; "How do you see it manifest in this group?" "I was unsure how to answer his question as it was completely irrelevant to the point I was making. Before I could formulate a response, he quipped, "maybe not at all?" I answered "yes" because I knew that that's what he would rather hear, and it was the quickest way to end the conversation. But I think my statements made him defensive and he was trying to gauge my awareness of his limited knowledge on the matter.

The group counseling sessions I took at CWU only solidified to me that my struggles were largely sociological problems, not personal or medical problems. Dr. Robinette often conducted the dialogue of each counseling session in relation to general over-arching themes, such as "acceptance", "resilience" etc., etc. I spent most of my time in these sessions simply trying to generate something to say that I thought would satisfy what he was looking for in a response. His stupid themes were completely irrelevant to my situation. Dr. Robinette's approach was not atypical of those employed by many in his profession. Typical in the way that they think they can implement a "one size fits all" approach as if the clients are nothing more than blank slates stamped from the same mould and should respond the same way for a given treatment. If the patient fails to respond accordingly, it must be the function of their primary or some secondary disorder (i.e. *their* personal shortcomings). Seldom are any professional or institutional shortcomings taken into account. In other words, it is not a client centered approach. Similarly, capitalist academia is not student centered. Both institutions fail many of those of whom they attempt to serve.

Before long, in almost the blink of an eye, I completed my first year at CWU. Once again, it was time to research grad school options. Now aware that many overseas and Canadian graduate programs do not require a GRE for admission, applying to such an institution must surely be my best bet. I knew that my low GRE math scores would be nothing short of a bad mark, diminishing any probability of acceptance into any US post graduate program. What's more, I had long established a very specific interest in the experimental research of lithics technology. No graduate programs within Anglophone North America offered much in the way of postgraduate studies pertaining to experimental archeology. After much exhaustive research, I discovered a Masters in experimental archeology program offered at the University of Exeter in the United Kingdom. Traveling overseas to the UK for graduate school seemed a daunting endeavor, but by that point, I was willing to try anything that would lead to postgraduate admissions. A Masters if not a PhD was my only ticket out of a lifetime of welfare dependence and despair.

CHAPTER 7 – CONSCIENTIZATION:

"How can I think outside the box if nobody will let me out of it?"
-Anonymous

In knee-jerk reaction to wanton and crass emotional violence that marked my 1st (un)real world job, I retreated back to collegiate life at Central Washington University. This was not only a retreat from a perverse reality, unfortunately accepted as the normal workaday world, but a springboard to grad school. Ultimately, I used it as an effective means to both ends. My one and only passkey to a decent life was finally in my hands.

But still, was I only kidding myself? What would an MA degree be but more symbolic capital, leading to no real professional advancements? By this point, the desire to finish what was started was my only motivation to complete my MA. It was growing abundantly clear to me that a PhD was of utmost necessity, even for teaching at the junior college level. In my first two years of college, many professors told me that an MA was sufficient credentials for most college lecturing posts. Four to five years later, this was no longer the case. Were the fast track demands of credentialism and rapid degree inflation rendering a given set of credentials obsolete in such a relatively short period of time?

After earning my MA, spending another 3-4 years in pursuit of another piece of paper was looking increasingly impractical, if not counter-productive. This is especially so, given how corrosive I have found conventional academia to be with regard to my actual learning and career development. Pursuing a PhD would be nothing more than an intensified version of the same game I had been playing all along-spinning my wheels to complete absurd quantities of academic products with respectable marks, yet learning nothing, even depleting crystallized knowledge, placing me at even greater professional disadvantage. The only way that earning a PhD might be a worthwhile undertaking would involve doing so, through a progressive student centered program. Yet, there did not be such a program available, with an emphasis on experimental archaeology.

183

Moreover, could I even physically survive the process of working towards a doctoral degree? Save for part time study, the workload demands of a PhD program would mean negating regular physical exercise to afford more time to keep up with the higher volume workload. Reduced physical exercise combined with frequent consumption of easily prepared calorie dense convenience foods would more readily prove a fatal lifestyle for me. Naturally slower basal metabolic processing makes me highly susceptible to weight gain. Were I to survive the game long enough for my PhD, come to fruition, I would probably be 100 lbs heavier and suffering from both diabetes and severe hypertension. My physical mobility would be even more compromised as I would no longer have the physical conditioning required to walk and bicycle effectively.

Besides, am I really suited for teaching, after all? This may have been so when I first began college education. But I am no longer the person I was. Working at GI Joes has permanently impacted me in a very negative way. The frequent abuse from customers has made me even more withdrawn, hypersensitive, disconnected, even more potentially hostile than before. Moreover, the negative emotional effects brought on by the constant survival mode I have been in all of my adult life have now taken a major psychological toll. By that point, it had been over a decade into my quest for a virtuous place in society. Yet, my virtuous place is one that does not exist under neoliberal capitalism-at least not in the established economy. Consequently, much of my life has been consumed in nothing more than a relentless cycle of running in circles and collecting degrees with high marks, but achieving little more. My ultimate goal has been nothing more meager than escaping the poverty and despair which too often accompany disability. Yet, under global capitalism, such a goal for any neurodiverse person would typically be nothing more than a vanishing mirage.

It was becoming abundantly clear that the two-headed neoliberal snake of work intensification and underemployment had slithered its way into the academic sector as well. Colleges and universities depend more and more on underpaid adjuncts and only a small handful of overworked full time faculty. There is no way possible to secure an academic lecturing post, where one enjoys a 30-40 hour work week, working only at a single location, making bike/foot commuting viable.

The cognitively corrosive effects of time pressure and sustained sleep deprivation were growing more apparent during my second year at CWU. By that point, my academic presentations were becoming more disorganized and tangential. It were as though my basic crystallized verbal capacity was diminishing. Progressively increasing workloads, and resulting chronic sleep deprivation of more advanced classes was showing a negative effect on the time required for me to prepare a focused, and engaging academic lecture. No longer could I converse spontaneously and in depth on anthropological subjects as I was able to do at TESC. The more demanding pace of my final post baccalaureate year was virtually exacerbating my disability. This trend would only continue and intensify in grad school.

Besides, what is archeology but an interesting subject to converse on at a party? Can it make a difference in someone's life? In some isolated instance, perhaps, but not on any grand and significant scale. What has it done to alleviate oppression and suffering around the world? Little that I know of. It certainly has done nothing to improve the lives of the disabled. In fact, as I further advanced in my study of archaeological anthropology, it grew increasingly clear how structurally ableist the field truly is. There are no opportunities within the field for one to work steadily, in solitude at one's own pace. And as with many other professions, advancement in this one, is highly dependent on playing the competitive game of organizational politics and maintaining a sizable social network. Invariably this will disenfranchise many neurodiverse individuals. Such structural ableism excludes many who can potentially make a difference in society. Undoubtedly, this is a legacy of the highly ableist social Darwinian culture from which the discipline originated. Mike Avey at Pierce College was certainly one of a kind. He was no facile liberal. Professor Avey was a true Marxist who managed to implement a truly inclusive student centered teaching method within a traditional academic institution. Alas I would only discover in my quest for grad school admissions, that in the field of anthropology, professor Avey was an exception rather than the norm.

By the time of confirming my acceptance to the University of Exeter, disillusionment was dampening my once inviolable enthusiasm. My decision to proceed was largely motivated by the mere desire to achieve a goal that I had thus already invested so much effort, time, and energy toward. Perhaps I could make some good come of it. Moreover, I needed some justification for my impulse retreat to

185

CWU. Bailing out was not an option. Besides, living in England could be rather interesting.

In the summer, preceding the start of my MA studies in Exeter, England, I managed to secure enough art modeling work, throughout the Puget Sound region. I earned enough doing art modeling to generate effective survival income, given the circumstance of staying with my parents in Tacoma. By this time, I was also consulting regularly with SSI attorneys in my locale. My intent was to assess the likelihood that someone with an MA would be approved for SSI on the basis of a mere learning disability, and psychosocial dysfunctions. One attorney told me not to even bother. His recommendation was that I continue to do art modeling until I am able to secure a lecturing post. The majority of the attorneys I spoke with, opined that it would be difficult, but not impossible. The challenge would be securing the right evidence to construct an argument proving that my disability causes the work related hardships that I claim. This would especially the case with trying to reconcile earning an MA degree with an inability to drive a car, keyboard effectively, and the extraneous amount of time required for me complete any given task. One attorney cautioned that because my range of difficulties, are not commonly associated with specific learning disabilities, I must furnish as much non clinical evidence as possible. In particular, he recommended obtaining multiple independent witness statements, attesting emphatically to my marked slowness and inefficiency with even basic low exertion manual work. After having consulted with at least five attorneys, most opined that winning SSI would be extremely difficult but not impossible. However when asked if any of them would actually be willing to take on my case, only one expressed a willingness to do so. At the end of my free office visit with this attorney, I promised to contact him immediately upon my return to the US after completing all coursework for my MA program. This was the time to have all of my ducks in a row.

By that point, I still held onto some hope of being able to teach undergraduate anthropology classes. However, I knew just how scarce such positions were and how drastically the occupation had changed. Through the informal survey of SSI attorneys, I was somewhat assured that at least there was some feasible safety net, in the event of not promptly securing a full time lecturing post. Also, with all of the art modeling I had been doing during the summer of 2006, I was making plenty of contacts among artists in my locale.

Art modeling could surely serve as a source of survival income until either winning SSI case or securing a lecturing post, whichever came first.

Most of the artists and art instructors I worked with enjoyed working with me as a model and the nature of the work is such, to not be precluded by any aspect of my disability. There are no real pace requirements to art modeling and no demand of frequent spontaneous social interaction. If only more jobs could be like that. Most of the artists and students I worked with were always so respectful and appreciative of my efforts.

It was rather fortuitous that I was not working full time that summer. Given my disability, the processes involved with obtaining my passport, student visa, and applying for federal student aid monies for overseas study, required the effort of full time job. The forms and documentation required to apply for these things were quite extensive. Plus this was the first time I had done this. With only three months to spare in getting everything in order, I really had to burn the midnight lamp on this project. I could not even conceptualize as to where I needed to go, in order to obtain the information and resources to fill out much of the paperwork. The agencies seemed to have assumed that everyone had been through this process a few times before or knew someone who had. Even with working on this project for hours on end, every day, I just barely managed to get everything in order, required to travel overseas.

After all of the rigmarole, it was finally time to fly out to Exeter, England and remain there for the next nine months. With a combination of borrowed, earned and donated funds from different sources, I bought my plane ticket and booked a reservation for the Globe Backpacker's Hostel in Exeter. In late September, 2006 I boarded an economy class flight to England. All of my possessions were contained within both a Green canvas US military parachute bag and a green canvas German military surplus mountain pack. After an 18 hour flight, I arrived in Exeter and took a cab to the hostel, merely 5 or 6 miles from the airport. I could have easily walked that distance were it not for the weight of my luggage. I rode in the back of the cab, judiciously watching the meter as we drew closer to my destination. We arrived at the hostel and I paid the cab driver the fare and grabbed my bags before exiting the cab. "Welcome to England sir, please enjoy your stay in our country", the cab driver stated before driving off. Well, here I am! This is England!

187

I rang the front doorbell of the hostel and the door was opened by one of the receptionists. I walked up to the front desk to confirm my reservation. "My name is Allan White, I'm from the USA, I booked my reservation last week on the 19th".

"Oh yes, there you are", the receptionist said aloud, thumbing through the pages of a nearly 2 inch thick logbook. "I have you booked here for a week, is that correct?

"Yes it is, I replied"

"That will be 50 quid sir".

I withdrew my neck pouch from which I extracted a £50.00 British Sterling note and handed it to the receptionist. By this point, all of my US dollars had been converted to Sterling at the JFK airport in New York. After printing my receipt, she led me up the stairs and down a hallway to the men's bunker area. She also showed me where all amenities were located such as the bathrooms, showers, and kitchen. Given my aversion to living in such close quarters with others, I had to find more permanent accommodation, ASAP. The place was like a human chicken coop. I certainly had no intention of staying there longer than a week. But for the price, it served its purpose adequately.

Within three days of perusing the local Express and Echo want ads and making phone calls, I found an affordable room for rent in a working class brick townhome, located on E. John Walk, in Exeter. The neighborhood seemed highly reminiscent of the show "Coronation Street". It was quintessentially British, from an American perspective. Rent totaled around £240.00 monthly which was comfortably affordable on my £ 800.00 per month student financial aid budget. As with my undergraduate years, I was fortunate enough to have, by chance, found a room to rent in a house with two responsible housemates, named Chloe and Dianne. Chloe was taking art classes at Exeter College, and Dianne worked full time at a fashion boutique.

Classes were to begin in less than a week. This left adequate time to familiarize myself with the town of Exeter and the unique peculiarities of living in a different country. During this time, I was able to figure out where to find food that suited my diet as well as opportunities for recreation, and where to shop other goods and services.

Graduate school was where I ultimately developed a life changing critical consciousness of the world. My critical consciousness was based on my lifelong subjugation as a differently abled person. Paulo Freire describes critical reflection upon one's lifelong circumstances as essential to promoting one's critical consciousness or "concientization". The exclusion and unapologetic social snobbery I was subjected to at the hands of some of my colleagues on the course proved a decisive factor in developing my critical consciousness. Reflection upon my experiences and learning at TESC was also germane to facilitating this transformative process. My shift in consciousness as a post-graduate student set my life focus in an entirely new direction.

At TESC, I did not really think of myself as a marginalized person. At that time, I was still laboring under the paradigm of the dominant class – a paradigm which dictates that disability is an exclusively individual and medical problem that the afflicted person must work harder to overcome. Overcoming disability meant securing a comfortable life niche and earning acclaim from others. So strongly ingrained was way of thinking, as to impede my politicization and development of critical consciousness. Though I had been indirectly exposed to the work of Paulo Freire, my indoctrination by the dominant class was far too strong. But such indoctrination could only maintain its stronghold over my conscious for so long.

The experimental archeology program at the University of Exeter was developed in accordance with a pedagogy developed for the quintessential neurotypical, "well-rounded", unimaginative extroverted learner. Moreover, the program's structure, and underpinning pedagogical philosophy tended to privilege students coming in with little or no prior firsthand experience with primitive technologies. Basically those who are too consumed with following their massive social circle, without ever taking the opportunity to develop and cultivate authentic interests of their own; will most likely excel and profit most optimally from the program. Professor Bradley, was the only professor there who did not seem threatened by students who had their own interest sets. However, he had no influence over the overall program structure.

189

The practical module within the program was especially problematic. The structure of this module, which constituted 50% of the students overall grade, was perfectly illustrative of the elitist, competitive, and non-student centered orientation of the program. The module was designed in a way that there were lectures intended to introduce specific technologies such as lithics, pottery, basketry, etc. Students practice these technologies, both on the lecture days and on their own time. Students are expected to only devote attention to the technologies that were lectured on in class. I had years of prior experience with a range of Stone Age technologies, yet this approach did not bode well with me. I found it stifling and counter-productive. I had long developed multi-faceted interests with specific technologies such as lithics, woodworking, and Stone Age weapon systems. I resented being academically coerced into devoting even some minimal amount of attention to studying technologies such as basketry, pottery, metallurgy, which I had no interest in or academic orientation towards. Yet my grade depended on it. It was a waste of my time and effort, and nothing more than an intrusive hindrance to my learning process. I must approach new and foreign subject matters and skills much more slowly and gradually. And in the time-span allotted by the structure of the practical module, I could not have adequately assimilated these new and foreign subjects even if I wanted to. It would have been better if students could simply create their own practicum based on their specific interests and prior experience. There is every potential to make such a graduate program more student centered in this way.

The culture of hierarchy and one-upmanship was a prominent and toxic feature to the program. To hold learners accountable to communitarian benchmarks based entirely on performance in rigidly prescribed range of skills, by narrowly defined criteria naturally fuels such a corrosive culture of invidious comparison. The petty competitive one-upmanship mentality in that particular program was abundant. On the course, there were always comments as to who can do what better than whom. Some of the faculty even fed into this mentality by becoming directly involved with such comparisons. With the exception of Dr. Bradley, it was clear that the rest of the faculty had their favorites. More specifically, some faculty resented students who had any prior experience, well defined authentic interests, or "thought outside the box" too much.

In a contrasting scenario, when learners are allowed to pursue their own interests it naturally leads to regarding others as individuals, valuing them as such. Such a culture of unconditional positive regard was the dynamic I witnessed in the student centered programs I took at TESC. We each valued and respected the uniqueness of each individual learner. This condition is critical to developing an inclusive pedagogy that enhances the development of the individual learner. But unless society's reward structures can function in a more human, person-centered way, it is highly doubtful that such a paradigm shift could ever become widespread in our pedagogical institutions.

The types of ancient technologies I have long gravitated to are ones that have also proven relatively feasible to master, given my motor deficits. Flintknapping is a perfect example of this. A lot of flintknapping is a skill performed largely with gross motor movements. This is particularly true of percussion flaking and the pecking of ground stone implements. Likewise, Stone Age woodworking mostly involves chopping, hewing, whittling and scraping. Again those are largely gross motor actions. Pottery and Basketry, on the other hand, both involve a lot of finer motor manipulation. Therefore, my effective mastery of those skills within the time period allotted in the program was virtually impossible. I never had much interest in those particular technologies anyways, and never even foresaw myself focusing on them for my academic work. It was the typical non-student centered approach, by which students are nothing more than mere blank slates to write on and all stamped from the same mould. My TESC mentors David Ruteledge and Raul Nakasone would be appalled by it all.

The practical module of the program accounted for 50% of the total grade. Thus my intermediate merit rating in the practicum brought my overall grade down slightly.My overall grade went from a distinction to a high merit rating. Many of my other marks in the program were solid distinctions. I could not optimally accommodate many of the foreign subjects (eg pottery, basketry, metallurgy) that were being imposed upon me. Also, as a full time neurodiverse student, I found it nearly impossible to effectively balance work in the practicum, with the copious amounts of theoretical writing from other modules. Part time study was not an option for international students. Were that the case, I could have easily come out of that program with a high distinction, especially if the program were more student centered.

The practical module of the program had every opportunity to be structured in accordance with a more student centered model. And it would work, given that most, if not virtually all graduate students arrive into their program with some long-standing, if not well pronounced interest. There are no "undecided" majors in grad school. In the case of the MA program I took, it would have been more student centered if students could design their own practicum, specifying their learning objectives, based on their own interests. This is essentially what I did during most of my time at TESC. Any graduate student should be capable of accommodating this mode of pedagogy. The student could then work independently towards their stated learning objectives, in relation to whatever particular interest they may have within experimental archaeology. With this approach, the learner is more likely to take ownership in their learning and profit more as a result. An approach such as this is more likely to engender a culture of respecting the uniqueness of each individual learner, rather than a culture of hierarchical comparisons and quasi objective value judgments.

Socially, my experience during the first semester of my MA course was reminiscent of what I encountered while participating in a community based assessment at Half Price Books and Music, years prior. Most of the bullying tactics were indirect and passive-aggressive such as ignoring, shunning and refusing to talk to or even acknowledge me. Never have I been treated this way in other academic settings. The major culprits were two other international students. One of whom was a fellow American, named Via, a bisexual libertarian, in the midst of a lesbian phase. I later realized that my major transgression against her was nothing more sinister than introducing myself to her on the first day of the program, upon realizing that she too was American. In her patent egotism, she took my mere outgoingness to be unwelcome sexual interest in her. This made her immediately hostile towards me. The other problem child was Tine, a Norwegian pseudo-intellectual who was well versed in copious facile platitudes on archaeological theory and philosophy but held no genuine wisdom of her own. They did everything in their power to make me feel excluded and left out whenever the class convened as a group.

A redeeming factor to the entire situation was that I formed a very close alliance with a fellow neurodiverse student, named Andrew Young. To this day, Andy remains one of my closest friends I could ever have. Were it not for Andy and his support, I may have quit the program

Andy's entry to the world of neurodiversity was by agency of a head injury which he sustained while serving as a law enforcement officer. Basically he had been ran over twice in a row by a suspected drug dealer he was attempting to arrest. While Andy was pursuing him on foot for some distance, the suspect was eventually able to gain access his getaway vehicle which he summarily used to run Andy over, making an attempt on his life. By Andy's account, the suspect ran him over once, then saw that Andy was still alive, so he backed up and ran him over again. It was during the second time Andy was ran over that resulted in the severe head trauma which left him in a coma for over a month. It's nothing short of miraculous that he even survived such a devastating attack. Along with the head trauma, Andy also sustained some severely torn ligaments in one knee and extensive fracturing of the right maxillary bone in his face. That latter injury needed to be fused together with titanium plates. Consequently, the introduction of these foreign metallic elements to his natural bone tissue continues to cause residual problems with recurrent infections that require treatment with antibiotics.

Though Andy survived his injuries, he was left with a permanent case of epilepsy, for which he now must take phenytoin to control his seizures. As a side effect of the medication, he suffers from lapses in both long term and short term memory. Andy's seizures are triggered by various sources of visual stimuli including; flashing lights from sirens, or the image display older model computer monitors, featuring convex screens as opposed to newer monitors with flat screens. Like me, he also has severe difficulties with organizational ability and is prone to forgetting, and misplacing things. In general, we have very similar symptoms, though for different reasons. We also had many of the same ways of looking at the world and similar ways of conceptualizing academic problems and solutions which seem to rely heavily on visual conceptualizations. It was our similarities in basic psychological processes and our commonality of research interests, emphasizing ground stone tools, which facilitated and solidified our connection to each other. Like myself, Andy too was studying archeology as part of his rehabilitation; building a career according with his interests and residual abilities not precluded by his impairments.

The man who ran Andy over was later arrested and convicted of the attempted murder of a police officer. He was given the maximum sentence under British law, which is life in prison. In a final and fitting act of incidental justice, Andy's attacker died in prison, from a drug overdose, deemed "suspicious". His death occurred eight years into his sentence. According to Andy, the autopsy report revealed that the level of heroin in his blood was too high to have been self injected. The coroner deemed it likely that an outside culprit must have deliberately administered the lethal dose, making the case a likely homicide. Yet no suspects were identified and apprehended. At any rate the man simply died as a natural consequence of his lifestyle.

Andy was truly one of a kind and I very much looked up to him. At least once a week, the two of us would get together and have a little two person 'knap in", to develop our flintknapping skill. We were the most accomplished flintknappers in the class. I was helping him to improve his flaked stone knapping ability. He had less experience in this area than I did. We would often have very intellectually stimulating and thought provoking discussions on stone tools and ways of interpreting lithic finds. From Andy, I gained a greater understanding of archaeological theory and how it pertains to experimental methods. At least somebody accepted and believed in me. With the exceptions of Tine and Via, I actually got along very well with my other colleagues at the University of Exeter. But any time Tine and Via were present during any gatherings of the class, they always managed to wall me off from the rest of the group. But whenever they were absent, the others were much more open and accepting of me. The influence of those two psychopaths was unbelievable.

Ultimately, I reached a point where I quit joining the rest of my colleagues for coffee break in the grad student lounge. Mostly their conversations consisted of little more than very inane, non-academic banter anyways. Andy never liked attending these occasions either. The two of us would get together and have our own separate coffee breaks where we felt we could hold more sustentative academic discussions.

After the fourth week of the course, I sent Andy an email in which the subject matter eventually led to my perception of some of the attitudes and personalities that I was observing. Sensing that Andy too felt a modicum of separateness and isolation in the class, I was curious as to whether or not his observations were in any way similar to mine.

In his reply, he noted witnessing many of the same things I did, with regard to petty unwarranted intellectual snobbery. Later that evening we sat down at the Boston Tea Party café on Queens Street in Exeter. What an ironic name for a place in which an American and a Briton would meet. While at the café, we both had a good chat about what each of us was observing and experiencing. We cross-checked with each other's observations and found many consistencies. In Andy's case, the source of exclusion and discomfort came from different students than those of whom I named. Yet he too, held a very low opinion of Tine and Via, simply due to the general arrogant haughty attitude he saw in both of them. We talked at great length about Tine in particular. He divulged to me that she made a number of derisive remarks about my slower rate of speech and sometimes repetitive content of speech[13]. Andy purportedly rebuked Tines remarks by explaining to her that my speech characteristics were symptoms of dyspraxia. He then elaborated to tell her that if she were to actually listen to what I say, that there is often real gravity to much of my analysis on stone tools.

Our meeting was the starting point from which Andy and I made a plan of action to talk with professor Bradley about what we were each experiencing. I e mailed Professor Bradley about what Andy and I discussed. He agreed to speak with each us individually on the matter. Apparently, there was a policy at the university prohibiting the discussion of disability related matters with more than one student present. I could sort of see the rationale behind the policy but didn't quite agree with it. Nonetheless I agreed to address the issue with Professor Bradley on the terms he put forth. We set a time of day for Friday of that week.

For the remainder of that week, I stayed away from the main (Streatham) campus as much as possible. I even quit attending lectures for a while. I simply worked independently on both essays and projects for the practicum module. After discovering the specific motive for the exclusionary tactics used against me, I could not bear to so much as even lay eyes on either Via and especially Tine again.

On the agreed upon date for the meeting with Dr. Bradley, I went to my locker, located in the Laver building on the Streatham campus. I

---

[13] This tendency becomes more pronounced when I am subjected to a lot of multitasking and time pressure.

needed to collect some materials for one of my projects. My intent was to go to campus, grab what I needed from my locker, then abscond, without having to encounter either Tine or Via. Yet I would not be so fortunate. While in the hallway of the rear entrance, I was rummaging through my locker, sorting through what I needed. Via entered the building, walked past me and said "good morning". I said nothing back just as she did for the first two weeks after we just met. She just walked on without questioning my response as I hoped she would. She then went straight to the experimental lab, dubbed the "playpen". This was where she was working on a set of bronze smelting bellows.

Almost immediately afterward, Tine came out of the playpen, approached me in a friendly manner, like she never did before. "Hi Allan, is that you making all of that noise?" Her question was in reference to the sounds of me rummaging through the raw materials contained in my locker. Seething inside, now aware specifically of her attitude towards my mild speech impairments, I simply refused to respond and acted like she was not even there- just as her and Via had always done with me. I hoped that she would get the idea and just walk away. But she didn't. She continually pressed at me trying to get me to respond; "Allan, Allan, Allan," she kept repeating. I became like a coiled viper on the verge of attack. Eventually, I switched tactics.

Knowing that Via, her closest cohort was just around the corner in the playpen, within hearing range, and her tutor Alan Outram was in his office just feet away from the lockers, also within hearing range, it was the perfect opportunity to humiliate her by haranguing her right in front of her tutor and closest colleague. After about her third or fourth attempt to engage me in conversation, I ultimately struck. Looking her squarely in the eye, I asked point blank: "So I talk funny do I?" Her voice grew softer and lower and in a sheepish tone replied, "No I don't think you talk funny". Knowing that polyglots often cannot effectively deceive in a weaker second language, I knew I could get her to fess up in front of her tutor and colleague, with regard to what her comments about my speech impairment. Though Tine had entirely functional proficiency in English, her command of the language seemed as such that she could not convincingly lie in it. I knew that if I pressed her just a little, she would likely fess up on the spot. I then responded by saying:

"Well I won't reveal my source, but I understand

196

that you have made disparaging remarks about my slower labored speech resulting from my dyspraxia- a neurological impairment that I have no control over. I always wondered why you and maybe a few other people around here seem to treat me as though I'm diseased. Now that I know the actual reason, it's even that much more pathetic-especially coming from supposedly educated people!"

Tears welled up in her eyes, and her voice choked up as she broke down, admitted wrongdoing and rendered a tearful apology. Her remorse was heartfelt and I must have made an impact. She fought tears, saying:

> "That was really stupid of me, I feel like absolute crap; you can say anything about me you want!".

> "I never have in the first place. When I have a problem with someone, I'll deal with them directly, rather than gossip about them like some immature adolescent".

> "You're more moral than I am", she replied.

> "Yeah, and let's just say that I'm not as dumb as you think", I retorted

My intent was to make the point that I am more aware of social circumstances than she seemingly expected. Before I could finish making my point, her crying intensified and she abruptly interjected:

> "I do not think you are dumb at all! You are a smart man! You always say clever things about stone tools! I'm really sorry, okay? I did not mean to upset you!"

> "Apology accepted. But though I accept your apology and forgive this particular transgression, I'll just leave you with some parting food for thought. You and some others around here should consider yourselves lucky that this miserable excuse of a grad school isn't held at a university in my native country-you want to know why?"

197

"Why?"

My voice grew dim and I gazed her squarely in the eye, as I replied:

>"Because there I have access to guns! You know
>the mass shooting sprees like Columbine and
>such that you Europeans like to attribute to
>our American gun culture? Well that's just how
>much rage that has been boiling inside of me -
>so much that I could easily do something like
>that. You see my point?"

>"Yes", she replied sheepishly.

>"You see; guns don't kill people, its people who
>have been shit on, disrespected, and treated
>like garbage who kill people!"

With her voice quivering nervously, she attempted to shift the focus of our conversation to one of the class readings on lithics. But still not in the frame of mind for an amicable academic discussion, I didn't say much. She exited the conversation and walked into the playpen. Soon, I could hear her bawling to Via about the exchange that took place between her and I. "Did you hear what he just said to me?" She shrieked crying and still distressed. But not much more could be heard after that. I took what I needed from my locker and went to the Students Guild Building to hang out and do some light reading until it was time for Dr. Bradley and I to meet.

After it was all said and done, I felt really bad about having brought Tine to tears. I felt compelled to go back and apologize. Yet I thought that there were lessons that needed to be learned and considered apologizing as something that potentially softens the message. So ultimately I never did apologize. She was clearly in the wrong and even owned up as such. So why should I apologize?

I returned to the Laver building about two hours later to talk to professor Bradley about everything Andy and I discussed. I explained exactly why I was feeling so alienated, as to consider exiting the program. He was very empathetic and did not try to discourage me from doing so, should it come to that point. Perhaps he had a general sense of the social dynamic between myself and Tine and Via and how it all hampered my ability to integrate into the

198

class. Yet it was nothing he could really put his finger on nor do anything about. I told him about the exchange that took place between Tine and I earlier. He was rather shocked and appalled by my actions, deriding them as overly confrontational. He reminded me that Tine was a rather sensitive person who was likely very hurt and humiliated by my words.

At that point, I wondered if I may have reacted too harshly with Tine and considered other alternative ways that I could have handled the situation. But she always seemed so pompous and uppity that I saw no other way to reach her than to use the abrupt and aggressive tactics that I did. After confronting Tine, however, both her and Via seemingly respected me more and treated me much more civilly and inclusively. Perhaps they just didn't want any trouble from me. Socially, everything improved for me in the program, from that point onward.

In the latter term of the second semester, I found out that Via had actually received a number of official reprimands because of her attitude. She could never hold her tongue when it came to snide remarks and her behavior seemed to be costing her professionally. A few years after our graduation, I found out through Via's Facebook page that she was still working at a Whole Foods store in Overland Park, Kansas. It was the same job she held prior to the start of her graduate study in Exeter. The "Survivor-reality show" mentality did not seem to take her very far.

During the second semester, my social difficulties diminished in the program. Yet still, it took every fiber of my being to remain enthusiastic about the academic work. It was not that I didn't like archaeology anymore, but the curriculum structure was such that I could not truly express my full potential, nor maximize my learning. It was very stifling to an extent as to have a very detrimental impact on my academic and professional growth. Further, I was going through a lot of internal conflict as to my aspirations in the field of archaeology. This, itself hampered my ability to proceed with my studies. While I still maintained interest in archaeology, another field of inquiry was becoming a competing, perhaps even stronger interest.

Reflection on all that I learned at TESC about the social model of disability became very illuminating, given what I was going through. All of what was studied at TESC truly began to resonate with me while perusing an MA at the University of Exeter. Up until that point, I simply dismissed the social model of disability as another example of lofty politically correct thinking, applied to another facet of the human condition. It was only when working on my MA, that it dawned upon me that my life has been living proof as to the validity of the social model of disability. It were as though no matter how much effort I had put into developing my career, I was getting very little in return. There was always some invisible barrier, keeping me from moving beyond a certain point. In studying the social model of disability, those invisible barriers became glaringly visible.

College lecturing posts only go to those who have a much more competitive professional track record than myself. Simply earning a postsecondary degree with a high GPA is not good enough anymore. One must have in their track record, a number of extracurricular involvements, and even some publications to their name. But I could never develop any competitive track record due to both the structure of traditional academia and my inability to drive. The ability to drive, would enable me to do more in a day and rack up more professional achievements. Were I able to attend both college and grad school part time and conduct my studies in the same self determined student centered manner that I did at TESC, I might have had the time to publish articles and conduct academic lectures. Such activities would have been highly conducive to advancing my academic career.

A less competitive, materialistic, and less rigidly and arbitrarily structured culture is one that is far more conducive to fostering tolerance of functional variations among individuals. In such a culture, nobody would feel that those speaking at a slower rate, costs them unduly. By this point, I truly began to recognize myself as disabled but only to the extent that disability itself is merely the result of the culture one inhabits. This newfound understanding and the plight of others in my boat, made the subject of archaeology seem far less important. At times, I even felt disillusioned with archaeology, regarding it as a trivial subject, only of interest to petty individuals with small minds and big egos. By this point, my normal visits to the university library were increasingly marked by distractibility. Offerings in their collection, pertaining to disability studies were more appealing by this point. But I could merely skim and browse those books. I could not read any of them given the time pressure from my coursework. By this point I was being pulled in two different directions, intellectually. There were times toward the end of the program that I grew to perceive the subjects of archaeology and prehistory as frivolous and elitist-merely something of interest to people with sufficient wealth, privilege and comfort that they can afford to focus on such trifles. Moreover, the time constraints, imposed from without, which prevented me from immediately partaking of the disability studies readings, registered as nothing short of a form of oppression.

Too often the advice given to neurodiverse people is to build a career based upon a strong interest set. Yet for all the faith invested in such folklore, nothing is acknowledged with regard to structural barriers inherent to many fields that bar professional entry or advancement of neurodiverse people. As I argued in the introduction, today's occupations in all sectors of the economy, demands a level of flexibility, sociability and versatility that many neurodiverse people simply cannot meet. Interest and ability, alone are not enough to make it in most professional fields. You now have to know how to play the game and this is what stymies the professional development of many neurodiverse adults-even in occupations correlating with their particular interests and abilities.

By June of 2007, I completed all main coursework largely with respectable marks. I then took a flight back to Tacoma, Washington, to complete my Masters dissertation. This was the final piece of work, required for the program. My dissertation dealt with the topic of functional attributes of weighted atlatl systems. Ground stone atlatl weights are an aspect of the North American archaeological record that I grew passionate about. Prior to grad school, it was a technology I had done a good deal of prior informal experimentation with on my own time. I had briefly addressed this topic as part of my undergraduate studies at TESC.

Basically, North American archeologists have identified ground stone artifacts commonly believed to have been weight bearing adjuncts attached to an atlatl. Though not currently a major topic of debate, in North American prehistory, the functional significance of this technological entity remains uncertain. In essence, I briefly reopened an experimental archaeological cold case.

Using an experimental approach of my own design, I tested several different weight loads and found that accuracy improved substantially with a load of 50-100g. Beyond a certain load, however, the effect of drag would have a negative impact upon accuracy. However, I cautioned that this does not mean that atlatl adjuncts weighing more than 150g would be impractical and thus not likely to be used in this manner. I formulated a secondary hypothesis that the optimal weight load would most likely depend upon the individual atlatl user and his/her respective level of conditioning towards working against specific weight loads. This factor, I argued, may possibly explain some of the vast size and morphological variation among these artifacts.

After about four grueling months of dragging my feet slowly but surely plodding along, and two deadline extensions, I ultimately completed my dissertation in October of 2007. It was not nearly as high a quality of product as I envisioned and I was ashamed to even have turned it in. I cut many corners and left out much that seemed excessive. I still regretted those omissions but nonetheless my dissertation was completed. I printed out a copy at the Kinkos/Fedex off of Steele Street in Tacoma and sent it to the University department of Archaeology and Earth Sciences. It's done, over with and off my back. By that point, I jumped for joy and would have skipped home from Kinkos/Fedex, were I not so tired.

On the way home, I stopped by the Half-Price Books and Music, across from Kinkos. I was intent on securing a copy of Paulo Freire's *Pedagogy of the Oppressed.* A seed planted at TESC, was soon to germinate and grow. I found a copy of the book and purchased it without hesitation. I had less than $100.00 in my checking account and was uncertain as to where my next monies would come from. Still, it was a worthwhile purchase. I then walked across the street in the blustery autumn torrents, to Borders Books and Music where I read the book over some coffee and a pastry. Revived by emersion in the cold autumn rain, harsh winds, profuse consumption of caffeine and my quest for a new paradigm, I sat in the café and read the book cover to cover in one setting. My reading session lasted from about mid morning until the store's 10pm closing time. As I read the book, I made note of ideas and concepts that resonated with my experience. One in particular was the dialectic between the oppressor and the oppressed. My entire being had completely transformed. My concientization was now in full force.

From actually having read *Pedagogy of the Oppressed,* I was able to put many of my prior life events and struggles in their historical, social, and economic contexts. My superficial success in higher education, years of following rehabilitation advice that never worked, and the culture of disrespect, I encountered in grad school, all had one thing in common. They were all symptoms of a needlessly competitive social order, inherent to a diseased neoliberal global capitalist world.

In his groundbreaking work, *Pedagogy of the Oppressed*, author and pedagogue Paulo Freire describes the process of conscientization. Conscientization refers to the achievement of critical consciousness. This is an educational tool that engages learners in questioning the nature of their historical and social situation. Thus, concietization, or critical consciousness is crucial for ending oppression. Freire refers to this as "reading the world". Critical consciousness proceeds through the identification of "generative themes" Friere identifies as "iconic representations" that have a powerful emotional impact on the daily lives of learners. In this way, individual critical consciousness helps end the "culture of silence" in which the socially dispossessed internalize negative images of themselves, created and propagated by the oppressor in situations of extreme poverty. Liberating learners from this mimicry of the powerful and the fratricidal violence that results therefore is a major goal of critical consciousness. This is the objective of conscientization. Through the process of conscientization, one is able to break through prevailing mythologies to reach new levels of awareness, in particular, awareness of oppression, being the object of others' will rather than a self-determining "subject". The process of conscientization involves identifying social and political contradictions in experience through dialogue and becoming part of the process of changing the world. In essence, this is the significance of concientization to the learner.

The words of Freire resonated with me and shifted my entire conscience. Never have I read a book with such intense and unwavering focus. His ideas and concepts truly moved me, like nothing I have ever read before. It was a rebirth and the most divine inspiration I had ever known, virtually akin to a spiritual awakening.

I wished I had bothered to have read *Pedagogy of the Oppressed*, while an undergraduate at TESC. At least my friend and roommate planted a seed in the form of his frequent renderings of the books subject matter. My post – grad school reading of Freire's work was the catalyst that enabled me to identify who the oppressors were in my life and the contradictions of my existence to that of the oppressor.

What are the oppressors I have identified and what are my contradictions to them? Simply put, the oppressors are the myriad global capitalist institutions and the needlessly harsh, competitive, fast paced social order borne from them. In their quest for global economic hegemony, these entities have set the pace, tone and tempo of society at such a freakishly rapid and chaotic pace, that many neurodiverse people especially cannot cope. Hence, we remain relegated to a marginalized existence. Our very survival, is too often dependent on the acts of false generosity through targeted government programs that treat us like a social problem, provide us with means to merely physically survive, and filling us with false hope of a better existence. Yet these acts of false generosity do nothing to alleviate the very conditions, responsible for our marginalization. What good are opportunities for job training, rehabilitation, and education if the world of work itself is simply unapproachable. What good are toothless ADA policies if most employers are unwilling or unable to provide the accommodations stipulated by them? What good are mere educational opportunities if the space simply does not exist in society's structures and institutions to develop a niche where you can succeed, thrive, and gain respect? The contradictions were now all too clear. The brainwashing and illusions were no more. The mental anesthesia was wearing off.

I began my college education with a specific vocational goal of teaching undergraduate anthropology and archeology classes. This could have been my only ticket to a comfortable existence. By the time of earning my MA, however, it was no longer a viable career option for me. The growth of on-line teaching, hence the need to learn computer functions quickly, and over reliance of adjunct faculty, changed the nature of this occupation drastically. Given those transformations, college lecturing was no longer a good fit for me. What is more, I was left so traumatized by my brief interlude in the normal workaday world as to render me too unstable for any occupation requiring even the level of social interaction involved with college teaching. It took all of those years of chasing a mirage to realize what I had basically known since I was 14. Society, with its current structures and institutions cannot create a place for me. I must forge my own path.

My epiphany following a careful reading of *Pedagogy of the*

Oppressed, led to a new intellectual curiosity. It was a curiosity that would compel me to demystify the jargon of the oppressor to enhance my knowledge on the subjects of politics and economics in order to better make sense of the world that leaves so many neurodiverse men and women impoverished, marginalized, and subjugated. My journey of informal re-education began with lighter readings of popular books by Michael Moore, Juliette B. Schor, and John deGraff. Eventually, I began to partake of finer-grained more scholarly readings on neoliberal global capitalism, as well as the institutional and cultural transformations, stemming from these. Through my studies, I grew increasingly more enlightened that a less arbitrary and less oppressive social order is possible. Such a new order, not only liberates the differently abled but also the normally abled from this life of servitude and drudgery. As Paulo Freire argues, these are the very conditions necessary for true liberation to occur. We, the neurodiverse and other disabled people must come to an understanding of the transformative and libratory processes which we individually and collectively possess.

Prior to earning my MA, I was very much apolitical. I cared only about indulging my intellectual curiosity and taste for the esoteric through the study if human prehistory, and the practice of primitive technologies. At that stage, I recognized my disability insofar as it was merely one of life's challenges to overcome. However, the sad reality that many disabled people at some point realize but never explicitly acknowledge is that the most heroic of individual efforts can only take one so far in "overcoming" their disability. Is this a result of their personal shortcomings? Most certainly not. It's a problem with global capitalism. This realization was the basis of my concientization. It was through my conscientization that I fully came to terms with and accepted my disability. But this attitude of acceptance was not one from the standpoint of giving up and not trying. Rather, acceptance of my disability came through recognizing the vital element that disability is to the human condition. For one may be disabled, but in the broader scheme of human existence, they are most certainly not defective or worthless.

It was only through my process of developing critical consciousness and understanding neurodiversity in its current economic and political context that I came to this realization. The glib speech and empty platitudes of psychotherapists did nothing towards those ends. For they were nothing more than empty words, devoid of meaning, context, and lacking any grounding in historical

205

experience. In my ongoing development of critical consciousness, I came to realize my unique social niche as a member of a new echelon of disability in America.

•••

Now, when I knap a stone tool or fashion an atlatl and spear set for throwing practice, there is a much different intent to these activities. Today, I am motivated by the dedication to craft, as Richard Sennett describes in various contexts in much of his work. I practice primitive technologies today, not with the intent of addressing questions pertaining to the archaeological record, or developing survival skills. I do it just for the sake of doing something well for its own sake. I am taking back, something that the system stole from me, in my efforts toward rehabilitation. During my years spent in college and graduate school, the tireless efforts exerted often left me too depleted of time and energy to do little aside from academic coursework and exercising to maintain my health. Years on end would pass without being able to do any flintknapping, or other technologies, diminishing proficiency at these crafts that I worked so hard at attaining. It was much more than a simple lament of work time cutting into play time. Craftwork that I had put years into perfecting and developing a mutually beneficial partnership with, had been robbed from me. Of especial cruelty was that it was coercively robbed from me with the false promise of a better life that scarcely materialized. I have now recaptured that space to rekindle that partnership.

Chapter 8 – Preserving Neurodiversity:

"It is no measure of health to be well adjusted in a profoundly sick society."
            -Krishnamurti

"We need to say no to the neoliberal fatalism that we are witnessing at the end of this century, informed by the ethics of the market, an ethics in which the minority makes most profits against the lives of the majority. In other words, those who cannot compete, die. This is a perverse ethics that in fact lacks ethics. I insist on saying that I continue to be human. I would then remain the last educator in the world to say no, I do not accept history as determinism. I embrace history as a possibility [where] we can demystify the evil in this perverse fatalism that characterizes the neoliberal discourse in the end of this century."
            -Paulo Freire

In the introduction, I describe the social model of disability, positing that disability is primarily a social construct. More to the point, disability is the product of disabling barriers and social institutions which impede daily lives and long term aspirations of disabled people. Relevant to such a paradigm is concept of neurodiversity, coined in 1997 by Autism advocate Judy Singer. An obvious implication to this re-conceptualization of brain difference is that systemic social and economic injustices and contradictions of neoliberal capitalism are a prime causal factor for the work disability, economic hardship, and social exclusion incurred by many with even relatively minor neurological impairment.

In sharing my personal story, I hope to have further illuminated the multitudes of economic and social injustices, with regard to their especially deleterious consequences upon neurodiverse persons. The inordinate struggles many neurodiverse adults face in securing a positive niche in life, must not be glibly dismissed as "personal hardships" or challenges that one must simply work harder to overcome. The unique hardships we face are symptomatic of a fundamentally diseased neoliberal world in which unfettered market

207

competition is the driving force of all human endeavor. Dismantling the present hierarchical and competitive social order is of utmost importance, not only for the preservation of neurodiversity, but for the betterment of human culture, society and our institutions.

Neurodiversity, like any other form of diversity, is critical to the health, vitality, and continuity of the human species. Analogously, biodiversity in general is regarded by most scientists to be a necessary precondition the health of species and ecosystems. Gene variations that carry deleterious traits may also carry many advantageous traits. And a deleterious gene variation, may also prove adaptive as a species evolves with its environment. Likewise, Behavioral and cognitive differences, resulting from neurological variations that prove disabling in one context, may be perfectly normal, perhaps even advantageous in another. Hence from a strictly bio-evolutionary standpoint, this is why it is so critical for society to embrace neurodiversity.

Yet there is much more than a mere biological impetus for the preservation of neurodiversity. Humans are cultural animals and like biological and organic structures, cultural institutions evolve over time. This is why preserving neurodiversity must be guided by a cultural precept as well, as well as a biological one. From a cultural standpoint, the various expressions of neurodiversity are critical to the enrichment and flourishing of culture and society. Moreover, as cultures change over time, there is no telling what unique behavioral patterns might become culturally valued, given future institutions and cultural practices.

When viewed from a cultural standpoint, preserving neurodiversity takes on a meaning that supports actual inclusion and social integration of the neurodiverse. To use a strict biological premise, it could be argued that the preservation of neurodiversity is achieved simply in allowing the neurodiverse to physically survive, free from overt persecution. By extension, one might argue that doling out public assistance to neurodiverse persons unable to work, further maximizes these ends. However, the very institutions which provision such targeted assistance too often only serve as instruments of oppression for the disabled. Moreover, equal opportunity and anti-discrimination statutes such as the ADA theoretically serve to facilitate full social integration of the disabled yet do nothing to deconstruct the concrete labor relations that promote exclusion and marginalization of the disabled. More poignantly, as I hope to have illustrated throughout my story, the power structures of capitalism all too readily convert equal opportunity statutes such as the ADA, into weapons for justifying existing oppression of the disabled. Yet in the cruelest of ironies, such quasi-civil rights legislation remains concealed under a facade of equal opportunity. In this way, they have only enabled oppression and suffering to continue, stagnating the promotion of full inclusion of the disabled. Simply put, without economic justice there can be no social justice.

As previously stated, the preservation of neurodiversity, must involve social reform which facilitates the optimal cultural expression of neurodiverse people. Promotion of neurodiversity to this level entails more than mere social acceptance of neurodiverse conditions and those afflicted with them. The frequent exclusion suffered by many neurodiverse people, often relegates us to a materially impoverished and socially marginalized existence, where mere physical survival becomes life's primary focus. The consequent survival mode that many neurodiverse adults become enmeshed in is antithetical to our optimal self enhancement, and personal expression. No enlightened and progressive civilization should accept this. As biological diversity is central to the health, vitality, and continuity of any species, the cultural enrichment of our species depends on the diversity of individual expressions within human culture and society. When any segment of the population is excluded from the discourse of cultural development, it creates a very stagnant discourse. A different perspective on the world, introduced for example by one with a neurological impairment, potentially enriches discourse and provides a unique opportunity for rethinking our assumptions about the world. This is the essence of what I mean by accepting and preserving neurodiversity not just as a biological entity but as a cultural entity as well.

The unmitigated marginalization of neurodiverse persons, speaks poignantly to the need for an entirely new social contract and not just a revision of it. Campaigns seeking to promote awareness and understanding are no effective solution to our oppression and suffering. Private individuals can only devote so much effort towards increasing personal awareness and social consciousness. Neoliberal capitalism and its institutions create a highly competitive social order that is highly antithetical to individuals behaving in an enlightened socially conscious manner. Such competition breeds alienation which leads to rifts and divisions among societies members. This maximizes oppression and marginalization of the disabled under capitalism. Even with the most widespread disability awareness possible, the fact remains that the unplanned, competitive nature inherent to capitalist production demands efficiency standards for which the labor efforts of many disabled too often fall short. Moreover, the prevailing market hegemony produces a culture in which one's intrinsic worth depends on their capacity to produce and consume within the parameters of capitalism. Disabled people as a whole, will invariably be marginalized, under such a system.

It is important to remember that the present order is not the resultant of natural preordained laws of the universe. Rather, it is a product of mutable cultural institutions, which must be reformed for the sake of developing a humane and just civilization for all. In the foregoing discussion, I canvass the prospects of an unconditional basic income for America. This I believe is the most critical initial step towards dismantling the global market hegemony and creating a more neurodiverse friendly society. I personally do not consider the basic income to be a miracle panacea, and "cure-all" to the many ailments of capitalism. However, I do regard it as the first and most important step in the right direction towards a more humane and progressive civilization.

In general, what we need, is a top down redistribution of wealth, from capital to labor sufficient to liberate the working classes from the necessity to work for their basic survival. In other words, we need a more even the balance of power between labor and capital. This precondition is an essential element of any society where the disabled can best thrive, not just merely survive. These ends are crucial and necessary for preserving neurodiversity not just as a biological entity but also as a cultural entity. As discussed in the introductory chapter, time famine, work intensification, and the accelerated tempo of life, brought on by the new economy is largely resultant of a gross imbalance of power between labor and capital. Hence liberation of neurodiverse people is embedded in the larger mass struggle against the stronghold of the global corporate hegemony.

An unconditional basic income may be the most powerful initial step towards achieving a more favorable balance of power between labor and capital. This fosters a subordination of the economic sphere to other aspects of life, creating a culture where all can reach their

210

utmost human potential. An unconditional basic income would give workers greater leverage in negotiating for better working conditions, making the workplace more democratic. In this way, there is potential to strengthen existing movements toward shorter working hours and perhaps even curbing work intensification. These structural changes in work can easily facilitate an overall slower temporal environment, engendering a society that confers better life prospects for neurodiverse adults.

It is crucial to bear in mind that a basic income in itself, does not guarantee that society will change in certain ways. Basic income proponents envision many different future scenarios. The important point here is that such a policy possesses the capability of loosening up the current market stronghold over society, making various different lifestyle options possible. In this way, it enables prospects for social change that wouldn't otherwise exist. A basic income coupled with advancement of the neurodiversity movement and heightened political consciousness among the neurodiverse, might even usher in a new era in western civilization.

Imagine entire communities of educated, politically conscious neurodiverse individuals, no longer coerced into attempted conformity to restricted, narrowly defined roles imposed on by the market. Given the abundant creativity common among neurodiverse individuals, could a basic income facilitate a proliferation of novel artistic expressions within society? Could we see unprecedented developments in technologies which enable the neurodiverse to express their talents? With neurodiverse adults free to explore what works best with regard to environmental conditions, might we see neurodiverse communities cropping up in key geographic locales? Prime locations for such a "mass exodus" might include quiet, low stimulation, bicycle/pedestrian accessible locales. Small college towns would be a perfect example.

The concept of basic income is garnering popularity and support among social thinkers and economists alike. However, there is equally strong opposition to it. Work disincentives, inflationary pressures and presumed astronomical costs are common objections to basic income schemes. Such objections, however are based more on fears rooted in culturally based preconceived notions and folkloric ideals, rather than sound economic theory and social insight.

Most economically feasible basic income schemes could never be sufficiently sizable to completely obviate work incentives. Given opportunities to work and earn more, most people will invariably do so. Nobody chooses to live in poverty, unless unable to do otherwise. Data gleaned from experiments designed to test for possible work disincentives created by basic income, support this argument. For example, a recent pilot experiment conducted in a Namibian village illustrates this case.

The Namibian pilot experiment was conducted from January 2008 to December of 2009 and took place in a Namibian village located in the Otjivero-Omitara area. In the experiment, all village residents, below 60 years of age received an unconditional BI grant of $100.00 Namibian dollars per person per month. Receipt of this grant was not contingent upon work requirements, eligibility criteria or, means testing. During the experiment, researchers observed no detrimental effects upon work incentives. In fact, the results stood in stark contradiction to popular criticisms of basic income proposals. The majority of participants were able to increase their work-both for profit, and family gain. Self employment in the village, increased as well. Businesses such as bread baking, brick making, and dressmaking opened and employed many villagers. Other social and health benefits were evident. For example, childhood nutrition improved markedly. By July 2008, rates of underweight children dropped by 25%. School attendance also improved. Parents were able to prioritize the purchase of school uniforms and the stronger financial situation overall enabled the school to improve its teaching material for the pupils (e.g. buying paper and toner) The school principal reported that dropout rates at the school were 30%-40% before the introduction of the BIG. By July, 2008, these rates were reduced to 5%. Economic and poverty related crime (e.g. illegal hunting, theft, and trespassing) fell by over 20%.

Fears of rapid inflation are another popular argument against a basic income. Yet there is no reason to believe that a basic income would necessarily trigger inflation. Most BI models merely involve re-directing wealth in society. Whereas a key cause of inflation is the production of excess currency in relation to the amount of goods and services on the market. Conceivably, a BI could even have ameliorative effects upon inflation. More money in the hands of the average person means more consumption, and subsequently increased production of goods and services, without the need to borrow (i.e. debt). The US dollar is a fiat currency that is essentially

212

based on debt. Thus more debt stimulates the cycle of money production responsible for inflation. In this way, its possible that a basic income would reduce consumer borrowing, while stimulating spending. In this scenario, the production of money is more likely to be more proportional to the amount of goods and services produced, thereby calming inflation.

Contrary to intuition, a basic income is also theoretically a more cost effective alternative to our current plethora of specific targeted welfare programs. With automated cash transfer technologies, the IRS could electronically transfer basic income funds into individual bank accounts, eliminating the printing and mailing costs of paper checks. With a basic income cash transfer, there is no need for a large administrative bureaucracy, to administer funds, and enforce both means and eligibility requirements. This is another aspect of the BI that makes it more efficient and cost effective than the current welfare state. The government would be saving money, meaning perhaps less need to borrow. Again, less borrowing means less need for the Federal Reserve to print more money, meaning less inflation.

Where basic survival is not inextricably linked to labor market participation, the cultural inclination to ascribe intrinsic moral value to work is greatly diminished. In this way there is less stigmatization of persons who would normally be tenuously connected to the labor market. Such marginalization breeds an entire host of destructive and costly social problems. Diminished competition among individuals in society, not only fosters trust and cohesiveness, minimizing alienation, enabling us to move toward an ethos of true respect for both oneself and for others, regardless of one's natural talents and abilities or lack thereof.

The material conditions essential for a more equitable, less competitive society are now present. The past 40 years have witnessed increased productivity gains, attributable largely to more efficient automated production. As such, it is now possible to produce more with less of the human element involved in the production process. With productivity dividends distributed more equally among society's members, the economic sphere of life can potentially take a much more subordinated role. In 2004, Juliet B. Schor, posited that between 1969 and 2000, the overall index of labor productivity per hour increased from 65.5 to 116.6. Thus the average worker in 2000 could produce nearly twice as much as in

1969. Had the productivity dividend been used to reduce hours of work, the average American could be working slightly more than 20 hours per week, and still live comfortably.

The social ramifications of more efficient production have long been endorsed by the late sociologist Yoneji Masuda (1905-1995). Masuda once described a future "computerized" in which "free time" replaces "material accumulation" as a critical value and overriding goal of society. He argued that while the Industrial Revolution was primarily concerned with increasing material output, the information revolution's primary contribution will be the production of greater increments of free time. This would give human beings the "freedom to determine voluntarily" the use of their own futures. According to Masuda, the transition from material values to time values marks a turning point in the evolution of our species. As Masuda asserts; "Time value is on a higher plane in human life than material values, as the basic value of economic activity. Whereas material values correspond to the satisfaction of physiological and material wants, time value corresponds to the satisfaction of human and intellectual wants". In other words, the hyper paced temporal environment that disables many neurodiverse people is primitive, antiquated and is not even necessary to fulfill society's production needs. What is more, it impoverishes society culturally, socially, and intellectually.

Not only is production more efficient, but further economic growth no longer yields the gains in physical quality of life that it once did. In *The Spirit Level-Why Greater Equality Makes Societies Stronger,* authors, Richard Wilkinson and Kate Pickett, point out that the developed nations are at a moment in history, in which economic growth and increases in average income cease to contribute further to the wellbeing of individuals. For the vast majority of people in the developed world, the difficulties of life are no longer about filling our stomachs, having clean water and keeping warm. As living standards rise and countries get richer and richer, the relationship between economic growth and life expectancy weakens. As most of the OECD nations have prospered, inequality has risen in those countries. The contrast between the material success and social failure of the wealthier countries is a critical signpost. According to Wilkinson and Pickett, this trend suggests that if we are to gain further improvements in the real quality of life, we must now shift attention from material standards and economic growth to ways of improving psychological and social well being of entire societies. According to Wilkinson and Pickett, a critical aspect of fulfilling this

214

objective is leveling out the stark inequality that marks those many developed nations. Creating a much slower temporality and leveling out inequality are two slightly different but interrelated related goals that would arguably satisfy the ends of improving the psychological and social well being of entire societies.

Leveling out inequality and the transition to time value as opposed to material values, creates an overall less competitive culture. Less competition and time pressure improves everybody's psychological well being. Perhaps this is one project for which an unconditional basic income may prove to be effective transformative agent.

The idea of an unconditional basic income is not a new one and has proponents from virtually all points on the political spectrum. There are just as many proposed funding strategies as there are political philosophies supporting the idea. There are two main widely known basic income proposals. One simply involves funds derived from taxing both income and capital gains, and the other involves the high taxation of rents paid for the use of natural resources. The latter model is commonly referred to a citizen's dividend (CD) and is advocated by many with libertarian leanings.

The social logic underpinning basic income advocacy is indeed striking. The entire population as a whole potentially benefits from a basic income, not just the elderly and the disabled. For example, a BI would make single income households more economically feasible, allowing one parent to devote full time effort towards rearing the children.

One obvious benefit of a basic income to the disabled is its capacity to more efficiently and humanely provide financial assistance for those with a mitigated or non-existent capacity for gainful employment. It is a much more humane system for various reasons. For one, its universal distribution means that there is less stigma associated with receiving it. Moreover, it is administered anonymously without face to face interaction with a social service agent, obviating the need to divulge one's circumstances to a total stranger. It thus protects the dignity and autonomy of those stricken with poverty that frequently accompanies disability. It is also much more humane because there is no need to wait, often years before being deemed eligible, while a large bureaucracy debates the merits of your case. This is a cruel, degrading and demoralizing process that has driven many Social Security applicants to commit suicide. I personally know SSI recipients whose stress induced behaviors have alienated friends and relatives while enduring the long waiting game for award of benefits. One should never have to suffer so tremendously, simply for being unable to work.

For neurodiverse persons, the basic income can more readily serve as a catalyst to enable niche construction, thereby promoting our own self determination in life. With no penalty for additional earnings, and no tiresome bureaucracy with which to contend, any disabled person may freely choose to find work, on their terms, or create their own niche outside the normative labor market. Examples might include working as a freelance artist, activist, writer, etc.

With regard to cash transfer programs, the very concept of disability-based eligibility requirements should now be regarded as obsolete. The changing nature of disability in the developed world, means that determining disability among contemporary disabled populations is much more complicated than was the case generations ago. The present welfare model of most industrial nations, is rooted in a point in history, in which being disabled, often meant being largely dependent on others for personal care and unable to do anything. Today's disabled populations are different. The implications of these differences with regard to most appropriate social protectionisms are enormous. Many of the people, officially regarded as disabled in modern society are exclusively and specifically "work disabled". As previously discussed, changes in the labor market and society have rendered many relatively mild neurodiverse states highly disabling with regard to work. Outside the sphere of work, however, most neurodiverse persons function just fine without assistance from others. Growth in the sector of disability, often termed "work disabled", contributes significantly to the overall population of disabled individuals. Also, many other disabilities that were once much more pervasive, now constitute primarily as work disabilities. New technologies and medical breakthroughs facilitate greater independence and bolster functional capabilities for many afflicted with sensory and physical impairments. Optical magnifiers and speech recognition, for example, now enable many visually impaired persons to use computers more effectively than what might otherwise be the case. Yet, despite technologically enhanced capabilities, many such persons remain unable to effectively compete in the modern labor market. It's easy to envision how one who is unable meet his/her basic personal care needs, without

216

assistance, would be unable to work. Yet it is exceedingly more difficult to determine work incapacity among impaired persons with other functional capacities fully intact. A tragic consequence to this is that many disabled people are wrongly deemed capable of work and subsequently denied assistance.

The very system of eligibility requirement, built into current disability support schemes, also breeds suspiciousness and hostility towards the disabled. The suspicion and hostility is typically rooted in the perception that such benefit programs are susceptible to abuse from malingerers or that they represent a special privilege enjoyed exclusively by anyone with a medically determinable impairment. Such feelings among the general public, further marginalize the disabled, often hampering our efforts towards inclusion, independence and self determination.

So how is a basic income possible and how would it even work? Most BIG proposals are government programs to ensure every citizen's basic economic security. Under such a proposal, all adults would receive, without means test, work requirement, or eligibility standards, an income sufficient for food, shelter, and basic necessities. In this respect, many BIG proponents refer to the plan as "Social Security for all". This grant is paid at a fixed level, irrespective of whether the person is rich or poor, lives alone, or with others, and is willing to work or not. In most BIG proposals, it is granted not only to citizens but also to permanent residents, who have lived in the country for 5 or more consecutive years. Incarcerated persons would be ineligible for a BIG.

Implementation of the BIG would entail that each adult who files an income tax return receives an annual BIG much like a "refundable tax credit" (RTC). Like the RTC or SSDI, the BIG would be available to every adult, rich or poor. Social Security and the RTC both enjoy wide support, due to their universally applicable nature. For this reason the BIG too could potentially enjoy popular support among the general public. By contrast, the NIT (Negative Income Tax) plans of the 1970s would have gone only to those in need, much like means tested welfare which does not enjoy wide support. A smaller income grant, less than subsistence level is a "partial" BIG. The late Basic income advocate, Allan Sheahen proposed that one approach to introduce the BIG would be to enact a BIG first at a level below subsistence (eg around $3,000.00 to $5,000.00 per year) and then increasing it over time. Here are some other points as to how a BIG

217

would work.

- BIG advocates differ as to whether or not children should receive such a cash grant. However, inclusion of children is a compromise any BIG proponent would be happy to make. Meanwhile, we can still retain or increase the current RTC of up to $1000.00 per child per year.

- All other income (except the BIG) is taxed.

- Most BIG plans would be administered by the IRS and each recipient's grant is electronically deposited monthly into a bank account, similar to the way the Social Security System presently operates. This is a very efficient and cost effective mode of payment.

As with other similarly wealthy nations, there is ample wealth in the US to fund a basic income. Our 2011 net worth was $58.1 trillion. According to the 2010 census, the US population was 308.7 million. This averages out to $188,200 for each man, woman, or child in this country. Our 2011 GDP was $14.7 trillion, an average of $47,643 per person. Moreover, Sheahen describes 173 separate tax loopholes (officially called "tax expenditures" in the current tax code, that could theoretically be eliminated to help pay for a BIG. Additionally, there are more than 100 welfare programs that would be obviated by a BIG and their elimination would go a long way towards financing the cash grant. Thus a BIG of $10,000 per adult is more than feasible.

With regard to a specific taxation model to fund the BIG one described by Sheahen simply involves a fair revision of the income tax code. Here are the major points of Sheahen's proposal:

- Eliminate 80% of all tax loopholes:
    As Sheahen explains, there are 173 tax loopholes which cost the federal government $1,025 billion. Eliminating 80% of these would save $820 billion per year. Specific examples of these include; individual tax breaks such as deduction on home owner mortgage interest, property taxes, charitable contributions, as well as corporate tax breaks, such as accelerated depreciation on machinery, deferral on income from foreign corporations, and employee contributions for medical premiums and pensions

- Eliminate the standard deduction and personal exemption from the tax code:
    This would save an additional $300 billion

- Cut more than 100 welfare programs which would not be needed under a BIG:
    Examples include; the earned income tax credit, unemployment compensation, Supplemental Security Income (SSI), and a variety of programs with heavy administrative costs. This could potentially save $400 billion.

- Cut the defense budget from the current (2011-possibly more now) $689 billion per year, to its 2000 (pre-Iraq war era) level of $295 billion.
    This saves another $394 billion.

According to Sheahen, the total savings of these cuts is potentially $194 billion. Just from the savings incurred from those cuts, it is possible to redirect the resulting revenue to citizens, in the form of an unconditional basic income. Such a BI could be awarded at a level of $10,000 per adult-just slightly below the official 2010 poverty level of $11,139 per person. Additionally, Sheahen also describes how certain simple tax revisions would eliminate the (estimated 2011) budget deficit of $1267 billion. These sources of savings are as follows:

- Reverse the Bush tax cuts of 2001 and 2003. This could generate an estimated $104 billion per year.

- Reverting to higher income tax rates of 1994, which were 2.3% to 12% higher than 2010 (or most current) rates. This generates an additional $30 billion.

- Further simplification of the tax code: eliminate separate tax rates for "married but filing jointly", "married but filing separately" and "head of household". With the BIG being granted on an individual basis, there is no need for a variety of tax categories. By using single tax rates from 1994 at 1.2% to 31.7% higher than the "married but filing jointly" rates, this raises an additional $60 billion.

- Adding a surcharge of 20% for incomes over 1 million could generate an additional $129 billion.

- Extend the 12.4% payroll tax to all earned income, not just those under $113,700 a year. This could raise another $220 billion.

- Establishing a tax of ¼ of 1% (.0025) on all stock transactions. This would raise an estimated $100 billion and also lower the number of tax trades, bringing stability to a volatile stock market.

- Institute a 2% tax on wealth above $80,000 per individual. This plan was originally described by Bruce Ackerman and Anne Alstott, in their book *The Stakeholder Society*. This would generate $450 billion a year.

- By raising the current tax rate on capital gains from 15% to 35% (the same rate paid by workers) this would raise an estimated $88 billion a year. Under such a plan, 75% of the tax increase would be borne by the richest 1% of taxpayers.

- By hiking the estate tax rate up to 65% for estates over $500 million, this would generate $7 billion a year. IRS data shows that only 0.6% of deaths in 2008 resulted in estate tax liability. Of the 5,500 estates expected to pay any taxes under the updated (2009) rules, only about 100 or 1.8% of these estates will have a majority of their assets in a small business or farm. And of those 100, the vast majority have sufficient cash to pay the tax.

According to Sheahen, the above tax revisions potentially generate an additional $1,188 billion in additional revenue to the treasury. This would have been an adequate sum to wipe out the 2012 deficit of $1,267 billion. With the 2014 budget deficit projected at around $514 billion, or less than half of the 2012 deficit, Sheahen's proposals would be entirely adequate to eliminate the deficit and provide a basic income for all Americans. Addressing the budget deficit would make an unconditional basic income more feasible and economically sustainable.

I discus Mr. Sheahen's proposals in great detail because I believe his model to be the most sensible and feasible Basic Income plan ever devised for America. Sheahen based his proposal upon easily verifiable sources of revenue that anyone can confirm for themselves through any official source. His proposed tax revision is not a highly radical one and I think it could easily gain approval among the general public. However, with many powerful constituencies and lobbies supporting them, eliminating the various social programs, made redundant by the BIG might be a hard sale among voters and members of congress.

Some have argued that a Negative Income Tax (NIT), would, in theory serve the same function as a BIG. The NIT was a plan devised by free market economist, Milton Friedman and debated in congress throughout the 1970s. However the purpose of the BIG, by most definitions is to provide guaranteed income to all people, regardless of whether or not they have other income from work. The NIT would provide that income only to those who are employed but lack sufficient other income from work. So, for the purpose of a true BIG, the NIT fails to satisfy the aims and philosophy of an actual guaranteed income program. Most BIG proposals advocate for a cash grant just above poverty level, and thus high enough to survive on but low enough to ensure an incentive to work to earn more. The following chart graphically illustrates how an exemplary basic income model would work in practice:

Income	Tax	Tax Credit (BIG)	Net Tax	Net Income	Tax Rate
0	0	10,000	-10,000	10,000	0
10,000	1,500	10,000	-8,500	18,500	0
20,000	3,000	10,000	-7,000	27,000	0
30,000	5,450	10,000	-4,550	34,550	0
40,000	8,250	10,000	-1,750	41,750	0
50,000	11,050	10,000	1,050	48,950	2.1
100,000	26,390	10,000	16,390	83,610	16.4
500,000	178,639	10,000	168,639	311,361	33.7
1,000,000	376,639	10,000	366,639	633,361	36.7
2,000,000	972,639*	10,000	962,639	1,037,361	48.1

Note: *Includes a 20 percent surcharge on incomes over $1 million
Source: Sheahen, 2013, pp.90

There are other proposals for funding a BIG. For example, Rep. Jan Schakowsky, a democrat from Illinois proposed the Fairness in Taxation Act (HR 1174). At the time of this writing, the bill remains pending in congress. This referendum would tax income over 1 million at a rate of 45% and income over 1 billion at a rate of 50%. This bill would also subject to higher taxation the capital gains and dividends that millionaires report. These sources of wealth are currently taxed at only 15%. Representative Schakowsky's proposal would subject these sources of wealth to the same tax rates that apply to ordinary income. Similarly, Moshe Adler, professor of economics at Columbia University and author of *Economics for the Rest of Us*, proposes a graduated scale. The tax rate on $1 million earnings would pay 39.6% and the 2nd million, 40.6% and the third; 41.6%. A family whose income exceeds $53 million a year would pay the maximum rate of 91% on each dollar above this sum-the same rate as what it was during the Eisenhower years (1953-1961).

One particularly esoteric proposal that I believe warrants consideration nonetheless, involves taxing the use of land and natural resources to a high level and using the revenues collected to fund a citizen's dividend (CD). The even handed sharing of such wealth generated from natural resources is commonly referred to as geonomics. Geonomists argue that because nobody creates natural resources, any wealth derived from them should rightfully be shared equally among all. Modern Geonomic practice is defined by Jeffrey Smith of Portland, Oregon as follows:

> *"a kind of economics that tracks the flow of "rents" that follows all the money that society spends on the nature it uses". Rather than reduce or repeal property tax on both buildings and land, replace it with a tax, fee, or dues at a high rate to recover the annual rental value of the land. The recovered rents could then be dispersed (either fully or partially) as dividends to residents (similar to Alaska's oil dividends) or to citizens (as Kuwait once did). Such a geonomic policy could deflate the cost of living so that rent dividends could play a role as a hefty basic income."*

The term geonomics, translates from Greek as "earth share". Contemporary geonomics is theoretically influenced by the work of economist Henry George (1839-1897). George's seminal 1879 work *Progress and Poverty* sold about 3 million copies and is still in print and available at the following website: www.progress.org. Geonomics is an economic philosophy and ideology which holds that people own what they create but that things found in nature, most primarily land belongs equally to all. Hence, according to Geonomic thought any citizen of a defined geopolitical entity should be made a part owner of all natural resource commodities found within its borders.

One present example of geonomics in practice is the Alaska Permanent Fund Dividend (APFD). The APFD is based on Alaska's oil revenue and has been available to all Alaska residents since 1982. Alaska distributes a variable portion of its oil royalties to every Alaska resident of at least one year. The annual amount of the grant fluctuates with the cost of oil. In 2011, every man, woman, and child received a check for $1,174.00 or about $4,696.00 for a family of four. In 2012, the grant was $878.00, the smallest dividend since 2005. The Alaska Permanent Fund remains popular among Alaska residents. In 1999, residents voted 84% against an initiative to curtail it. No legislator would even think to advocate it's repeal. The fund is one of the reasons why Alaska has one of the lowest poverty rates in the US, why it is one of the most economically equal state, and in fact is the only state in which equality has been rising for the past 20 years. People don't view this dividend as a handout, but as a reward for collective ownership. This, in essence is the philosophy behind Geonomics.

Portland Oregon based geonomics advocate Jeffrey Smith proposes that land and other natural resources could be taxed at a high level. Other suggestions of similar revenue sources have included fees from government created monopolies (such as broadcast spectrum and utilities), collective resource ownership similar to the APFD, mineral extraction, airway corridor use, space orbits, universal stock ownership and pollution taxes. Geonomic purists argue that the extraordinary returns from natural monopolies should accrue to the community rather than a private owner. Subsequently, were this to happen, no other taxes or burdensome economic regulations should be levied. Some geonomic advocates claim that the flow of rent alone, in society is substantial enough that were it collected and distributed equitably, the former disadvantaged would no longer need targeted welfare programs or other public cash transfer programs to assist them.

I personally am skeptical as to the potential to fund a CD sufficient to serve as a substantial basic income and completely obviate the need any social spending funded through taxation. In my own research, I have yet to find objectively verifiable sources, indicating what actual percentage of GDP natural resource rents constitute. Geonomy advocates often concede there are no exact figures to confirm this but roughly estimate the percentage of FIRE (Finance, Insurance, and Real Estate), economically considered closely related to rent, at over 40% of the GDP. More official sources,

223

however, namely the Bureau of Economic Analysis, attributes only 22% of total GDP to the FIRE sector. As such, it remains questionable as to how much of a BI could be financed through a geonomic scheme-especially in a nation as large as the United States.

One aspect of the geonomic model of a CD that has many positive ramifications for the impoverished and disabled is its potential to deflate the cost of living-particularly with regard to real-estate. Such an effect has been historically observed in the case in Denmark during the 1950s. When the Danish government taxed rural property, large family estates were broken up into small family farms, yielding surplus food production, hence lowest food prices seen in a long time. The same thing happened in Taiwan, when their government made a geonomic shift. More recently, in the 1990s, when Pittsburg taxed urban land more than buildings, it had the most affordable housing (on home sites) of any major city in America. Aspen, Colorado currently even funds it's low income housing subsidy program through land taxes. Taxing land (or otherwise recovering its rent, through dues or fees) drives down land price. As the tax on land rises, the price of land falls, which is why realtors and speculators often argue against the geonomic tax shift from buildings to land. Yet where government has made this shift, it has lowered the price of land, which in turn trims mortgages, reducing the amount of debt in society. Less debt means that there's less currency produced and slower inflation. In an economy with the minimally useful amount of debt, coupled with the more efficient means of production afforded by techno-progress, the cost of living-even in current dollars would continue to fall. Deflationary effects on real estate prices, along with the narrowing of income gaps, are two compelling reason to base part of a BIG on rent revenues. That reason alone could be one benefit of incorporating a geonomic CD as supplemental to a BIG derived largely via income taxes, as described by Sheahen.

Proponents of geonomics are mostly libertarians (i.e."geolibertarians") who advocate for equitable and just ownership of all natural resources and decry the redistribution of confiscatory taxes on capital investment and labor as oppressive and unjust. As I will discuss later, it is worth noting that contrary to popular expectation, some of the most adamant proponents of basic income are libertarians who support the proposal on the grounds of social justice. Geonomists and Georgists argue that a tax on land is

224

economically efficient, fair, and equitable and that such a tax could generate sufficient revenue so that other taxes (e.g. taxes on profits, sales, or income), which are less fair and efficient can be reduced or eliminated. Geonomic purists tend to proselytize a single tax on land value to be a progressive tax since it would be paid primarily by the wealthy and would reduce economic inequality.

Perhaps a BIG, may usher in the level of economic justice needed to ensure that no one, regardless of their natural endowments or family and social position is without the basic necessities of life. Perhaps more importantly such a level of economic justice is imperative to improve everyone's odds of securing a comfortable life niche for themselves. I envision a BI, based on the work of Sheahen, sourced from tax code revision and re-directing government spending, implemented in tandem with a Citizens Dividend (CD), derived from wealth created from natural resources as most beneficial. Cost of living would be deflated to a point that the basic income cash transfer would enable most people to subsist reasonably well regardless of their connection to and increasingly more forbidding labor market.

Predictably many basic income proponents tend toward socialism and social democratic leanings. The primary interest in basic income within both political camps, is with social welfare and reducing inequality. However, some of the most vehement advocates of a BIG are also small government thinkers who view this policy as a means to streamline a welfare state and minimize the role of government in the lives of individuals. One conservative scholar Charles Murray supports the proposal of the federal government providing a nearly $10,000 yearly grant to every adult, with no work requirement. His primary rationale is that such an income transfer would involve no large expensive bureaucracy to support and no red tape to manage. In 2006, Murray published *In our Hands: a Plan to Replace the Welfare State*. In the book, Murray advocates a universal grant of $10,000 per year in lieu of the existing welfare system, including Social Security and the myriad state administered welfare programs. The gravamen of Murray's argument contends that money is always more efficiently and productively spent in the hands of private individuals rather than the government. Accordingly, the poor should be free to make their own choices as to how their monies are spent. For these reasons, basic income is very strongly promoted by people associated with political views that are generally opposed to public provision of welfare services. Hence

225

there is wide support for the BI among libertarians, economic liberals, and anarcho-capitalists. Among those economic schools of thought, the basic income is exhorted as a strategy to reduce the amount of bureaucratic administration, presently abundant in many contemporary welfare systems. Many libertarian proponents also view a BIG as a means to mitigate fiat-currency inflation.

In libertarian political circles, a more recent BI debate was ignited by Jessica M. Flannigan in an April 30, 2012 post in the Bleeding Heart Libertarian blog. Professor Flannigan is a self-described anarchist from the University of Richmond who opposes a system of property rights "that causes innocent people to starve". Accordingly, she postulates that all libertarians should support a universal basic income on the grounds of social justice. In her post, she cited a paper by the philosopher Matt Zwolinski of the University of San Diego in the December of 2011 issue of the Journal of Basic Income Studies. Zwolinski's paper also contained many papers by libertarians supporting the basic income concept. While Zwolinski acknowledged that most libertarians reject explicit redistribution of income, he pointed to several libertarians, including the economist F.A. Hayek and Milton Friedman who favored the idea of a universal basic income. More recently, Matthew Feeney, columnist of the libertarian magazine *Reason* wrote favorably about a recent Swiss proposal in November 26, 2013 post, lauding it as a complete replacement for the existing welfare system. This proposal, if passed would guarantee every Swiss citizen a yearly income of 30,000 Swiss Francs ($33,000) whether they work or not. In October of 2013, Generation Basic Income succeeded in gathering the 100,000 signatures required to put a ballot initiative before the country's voters. A vote will likely be held on this Swiss basic income initiative in another two or three years. Matthew Feeney believed the Swiss proposal to have merit and might even save money. He was especially critical of the paternalism of the current welfare system and the denial of autonomy to those living in poverty. Feeney quotes:

> *"Instead of treating those who often through no fault of their own, have fallen on hard times, like children who are incapable of making the right choices about the food they eat   or the drugs they may or may not choose to take, why not just give them cash?"*

Feeney also cited Thomas Paine in support of his proposal. Pains

1797 pamphlet, *Agrarian Justice*, proposes a social insurance system for young and old financed by a 10% tax on inherited property. Paine would have given everyone 15 pounds, at age 21 and 10 pounds per year to everyone age 50, for the remainder of their life. These are significant sums that are difficult to calculate the value of in today's dollars. However, using the on line *measuring worth* calculator, 15 pounds in 1797 would be the equivalent of $17,500 today. According to Paine, the purpose of giving young people a grant was in compensation for the loss of their natural inheritance in land, which had been seized by the state and given or sold to particular individuals for their exclusive use. Many modern libertarian economists adhere to Paine's assertion that everyone today suffers from past injustices in terms of property rights. According to this argument, a universal basic income might be appropriate reparations for this injustice.

A basic income bill has even been introduced to the US congress. On May 2, 2006 congressman Bob Filner (San Diego) introduced the Tax Cut for the Rest of us Act. It was given the number HR 5257. The preamble to the bill read "*To amend the Internal Revenue Code of 1986 to provide a basic income guarantee in the form of a refundable tax credit for taxpayers who do not itemize deductions*".

The bill was referred to the House Ways and Means Committee. The plan was simple, it removed the lines for the standard deduction and personal exemptions from the federal tax credit at the bottom of the form. All tax rates would remain the same. A standard tax credit of $2,000.00 for each adult and $1,000.00 for each child would create a tax cut for everyone with an income under about $60,000 per year.

Congressman Filner's bill was the 1st basic income bill ever introduced to the US congress. Some congressional aides and nonprofit groups thought that HR 5257 was "brilliant". Others liked the idea, but felt that the cost-estimated at an annual $186 billion was too steep. And still others questioned the practicality of "paying people not to work". The bill garnered only one co-sponsor-congressman Jesse Jackson Jr. of Illinois and it failed to get out of the House Ways and Means Committee. Despite the abysmal failure of HR 5257, it illustrates that there are at least a few mainstream politicians who are willing to support it. It is not just an esoteric idea of radical political activists and rogue social thinkers.

In many personal discussions with friends and acquaintances, I have frequently encountered many a knee jerk negative reaction to the BIG idea. It seems everyone knows at least one wretched person, for whom the thought of giving taxpayer money to that person is simply unconscionable. For this reason, a $10,000 basic income might be a tough sale. But to reject such a proposal based on such personal observations, is completely erroneous reasoning. There is no evidence to conclude that a basic income will have any effect towards enabling such individuals to continue living as they do or that such a redistribution scheme would make social deviance any more common among the general population. In fact the narrowing of income gaps and reduction of poverty might well have an ameliorative effect on social deviance. Antiquated as it may now be, the work ethic is a deeply ingrained value in American culture. Thus there will always be strong knee jerk reaction to the thought of paying people not to work or "getting something for nothing".

In America, the EITC, the CTC, and the Alaska Permanent Fund are examples of policies, similar to a BIG that are currently in effect. Because we already have such similar policies in effect, perhaps a comprehensive BIG may not be as farfetched as one might imagine. Given its small but broad spectrum political support, with increased awareness, it may not be inconceivable to garner enough popular pass a BIG bill in congress at some point in the not too distant future.

Getting back to the topic of neurodiversity, our advocates should at least give serious consideration of the basic income debate. Those neurodiversity advocate who support such a proposal, should consider joining forces in promoting an unconditional basic income for America. One obvious reason is the plain and simple fact that neurodiverse adults are disproportionately represented among both welfare caseloads and among the growing legions of the working poor. Many proponents of the BIG regard it as potentially a more efficient and effective way to reduce poverty and narrow the increasing income gap that continues to swell. This is only one reason why neurodiversity advocates should give serious consideration to basic income debate. Equally compelling and perhaps every bit as crucial is the potential for the basic income to actually work as a catalyst to promote niche construction, not just merely provide income support.

In his book, *Neurodiversity: Discovering the Extraordinary Gifts of*

228

Autism, ADHD, Dyslexia, and Other Brain Differences, Dr. Thomas Armstrong defines the principle of niche construction which holds that success in life also depends on modifying your environment to fit the needs of your brain. This is the sixth principle of neurodiversity. The (pseudo) individualistic mores undergirding capitalism proselytize the primary responsibility of individuals to adapt to the world around them. In other words, everyone must adapt to the structures and institutions and valorized modes of living that sustain capitalism or fall to the wayside. Yet in reality, the world is incredibly large and this complex culture of ours, features many subcultures or micro-inhabitants all with different requirements for living. If individuals can only discover their particular "niche" within the great web of life, they are then more able to find success on their own terms. A basic income potentially affords neurodiverse persons that space to do so. In other words, it makes multitudes of different lifestyle options more feasible.

The term "niche construction was first used widely by biologist Richard Lewontin, an Alexander Agassiz Research professor at the museum of Comparative zoology at Harvard University. Dr Lewontin describes niche construction as the process by which an organism alters it's own (or another species) environment to help increase its chances of survival. A beaver building a dam is an example of niche construction as is a bird building a nest, or a rabbit burrowing a hole. When animals migrate, they are seeking a favorable niche within which to flourish. Each of those activities assists the organism in achieving its basic needs-gathering food, protecting offspring, keeping clear of prey, seeking shelter from inclement weather and thus raising the likelihood that it will pass its genes on to the next generation. Scientists are just beginning to appreciate that niche construction may be as important to evolution as natural selection. In the book *Niche Construction: The Neglected Process in Evolution,* Oxford lecturer F. John Odling Smee and his colleagues write:

> *"Niche construction should be regarded after natural selection, as a second major participant in evolution. Rather than acting as an 'enforcer' of natural selection through the standard physically static elements of, for example temperature, humidity, or salinity because of the actions of organisms, the environment will be viewed here as changing and co-evolving with the organisms on which it acts*

selectively."

What this can mean for neurodiverse individuals is that instead of being coerced to attempt to adapt to a static, fixed, or normal environment, it could be possible for them (and their caregivers) to alter the environment to match the needs of their own unique neurochemistry and functionality. In this way, the neurodiverse can be more of who they really are".

Thomas Armstrong and other neurodiversity advocates metaphorically liken the potential for niche construction among neurodiverse adults to survival strategies employed by other members of the animal kingdom. Examples of which may consist of nests, holes, burrows, paths, webs, dams, migration patterns and more, meaning that niche construction for human beings must likewise be diverse. The capacity and opportunity to make such choices about lifestyle or career is critical in determining whether a person suffers as a disordered individual or finds satisfaction in an environment that recognizes ones strengths. For NDs, being stuck in an unsuitable occupation and/or living environment carries far more severe and damaging consequences than diminished happiness. It can make the difference between optimal functioning and being truly disabled in the utmost sense of the word.

One may conceive of niche construction as simply neurodiverse persons finding careers/occupations in the labor market suited to their residual abilities and personal interests. A highly known example is the proportionately high representation of individuals with autism spectrum disorder in computer software fields. Dr. Thomas Armstrong points out that there are a higher percentage of people with autism living in and around silicon valley in California than in the general population. Neurodiversity advocates further postulate that positive niche construction must necessarily include career and lifestyle choices, assistive technologies, and other life enhancing strategies tailored to the specific needs of a neurodiverse individual. Unlike public welfare or private charity, a BIG has the potential to actually enable an array of lifestyle options, outside the confines of the current market hegemony. And indeed for many neurodiverse adults, this may be their only avenue to secure a role in which they can at least feel socially useful.

A basic income makes possible the partaking of non-market

oriented work such as volunteering, home food production, caretaking, and self determined creative pursuits for personal enrichment or potential profit, etc. In this way, a wider array of positive life prospects and legitimized social roles become possible. With a BIG, any neurodiverse person who struggles with social integration now has the financial means to create their own niches, relative to their unique functionality-that is, lifestyle options divorced from the established labor market and traditional social environments. Moreover, they can seek out such ventures without the risk of losing the financial support to do so. Means tested benefits do not readily afford this opportunity for the disabled. In this way, a basic income would actually open up a new avenue of integrating the disabled into society-one operating on the principle of niche construction which may be much more humane and efficient than traditional modes of vocational rehabilitation. The traditional rehabilitation model, frequently amounts to nothing more than attempting to fit a square peg into a round hole. Niche construction is more self-determined and focuses on our potential, not our difficulties. Traditional rehabilitation often incurs unrealistic expectations on the part of client and employer alike. Too often it also leads to occupational placement in menial work that does not enable neurodiverse people to truly blossom for both their benefit and the benefit of society.

Moreover, positive niche construction for neurodiverse adults is highly dependent on available resources that are of highly variable accessibility. To a large extent, this is true for everybody, but for neurodiverse persons this is more strongly the case. Mitigated personal resources in the form of versatile, multi-faceted talents, which can be deployed in variable settings, make it far less feasible for a neurodiverse person to overcome any socio-economic and cultural disadvantages they may have been born into. An unconditional basic income, would to a great extent, mitigate such inherited social and environmental disadvantages. For example, an ND person who is virtually unemployable due to innate features of their disability may then be free (via basic income) to cultivate their talent at a particular craft Then ultimately such a person would have the initial startup capital to develop a home based business, based on that craft. If such a person is unable to drive due to his/her impairments, a basic income may afford them the freedom to relocate to a locale with better public transit and safer bicycle access, enabling them to enjoy a level of physical mobility that they would otherwise been unable to enjoy. Mobility is critical to

231

productivity.

With a basic income, any disabled person with other earnings, still has basic income benefits, making it easier to pay taxes which contribute to the overall BI fund. In this way, a BI is potentially more self liquidating. This differs greatly from most current eligibility and means tested benefits where earnings are deducted from benefits and income over a certain level completely disqualifies the client from such public assistance. These deductions never take into account capital to earn the money and interest on the money and so they act as built in poverty traps for many disabled people. With a BI, the disabled only have more money and resources to invest towards niche construction. In this way, the basic income is potentially more empowering for the disabled, making it a possible catalyst to full social integration of the multitudes of human potentials in existence.

A BI should also be combined with a paradigm shift in pedagogical practice at all educational sectors from grade school to higher education. Our current system is largely dominated by methods that emphasize pressure and compulsion. This should be replaced by a student centered model, based on multiple intelligences, which encourages independent exploration and self determination.

Consider the benefits of a BI, to neurodiverse college students. With an unconditional basic income, adequately funded part time college/university attendance becomes more feasible. Federal student aid policies currently award more money for full time academic attendance. As such, full time students receive a larger refund check each quarter. Part time attendance, funded by federal student aid would result in such a miniscule refund as to necessitate working at least part time. For many neurodiverse learners such arrangements are simply unworkable, and even negate any benefits of part time college attendance. For an ND college student, the opportunity for part time enrollment, without having to work, would mean that he/she is also able to derive more from his/her studies, rather than languish for years as a "professional student" just to fulfill one's time and have a means of social support. With a technical, AA, or BA degree, it is eminently possible for the ND person to put his/her education to work in order to construct an occupational niche divorced from the mainstream labor market. Dropping out of the established labor market may ultimately become the only avenue for many NDs to express their talents, as the labor market becomes

232

more demanding and more untenable for those lacking natural abilities in key areas. A basic income also enables a person to make better, more balanced decisions with regard to life and career planning. If one has greater freedom and flexibility not to work for his/her basic survival, they are less apt to make poor career and life planning choices, just to have a means of financial support.

For neurodiverse adults, optimal niche construction with regard to life and career planning is far more complicated than it is for the average person. This is for two primary reasons. For one, because of specific functional compromises NDs must more thoroughly evaluate which occupations place least premium on areas of functional limitation. Such options may not be readily available for some time. A basic income would enable an ND person greater financial means to weather those times and perhaps use such as an opportunity to enhance themselves and by discovering coping skills and treatments to improve optimal functioning. For many neurodiverse people, a poor occupational fit is more than an unpleasant experience. It can be very damaging and detrimental to their personal development and self enhancement so critical to optimal niche construction.

A basic income affords individuals more time and opportunity to think, plan and evaluate life choices-including those surrounding higher educational decisions. These latitudes would give NDs the option of choosing schools that are a better fit with regard to instructional methods. Perhaps this could lead to greater numbers of ND college students seeking more student-centered options, similar to what I was able to enjoy at TESC. The self determination that such educational paradigms foster would serve as a useful skill in developing one's own niche outside the established national economy. This should be regarded as a critical skill for ND adults.

One might think that certain neurodiverse states are so severe as to preclude anything other than the most menial work, if that. This is especially considered to be the case with intellectual disability in particular. However, such conceptions are increasingly proving to be untrue. In his book, *Neurodiversity*, Dr. Thomas Armstrong, describes extraordinary cases of niche construction, in the form of artistic entrepreneurship among intellectually disabled adults with Down's syndrome, or Trisomy 21. For example, Clara Link the professional photographer travels to regional and national conferences for her work. Another such example is Sujeet Desi who

233

plays multiple musical instruments including the violin, the piano, clarinet, and bass clarinet. He has traveled locally, nationally, and internationally, sharing his talent with others. Such cases are indeed extraordinary. Yet, given more equitable access to the right resources, they could become more commonplace and may even contribute greatly and positively to society's cultural enrichment.

Currently the concept of neurodiversity operates mainly in the realm of social activism and is far from being a widely acknowledged or accepted paradigm in conceptualizing neurological difference. Our current social and economic order essentially necessitates the marginalizing and often ineffective medical model and facile civil rights legislation in responding to neurological difference. Only by dismantling the current global market hegemony, can true inclusion of the neurodiverse be achieved. Inclusion, not only in pedagogical institutions and in the labor market, but inclusion in the processes in cultural and social development and more importantly inclusion in the hearts and minds of the general public as fully worthwhile members of the human race. Creating the material realities that affords a valued and fitting place for all persons, regardless of their natural endowments is *Sine qua non* to making neurodiversity a social reality, rather than a mere political construct.

Armstrong, Thomas. *Neurodiversity*. Cambridge: DaCapo,
    2010. Print.
Barnes, Colin, Len Barton, and Mike Oliver, ed. *Disability
    Studies Today*. Malden: Blackwell, 2008.
Barrett, Allison, MA, Michelle K. Derr, PhD, Jacqueline F.
    Kauf, MSW, and LaDonna Pavetti, PhD. "Mental
    Dodsorders and Service Use Among Welfare and
    Disability Program Participants in Fee For Service
    Medicare." *psychiatryonline.org* 5.61 (2010). on line
    journal. 8 August 2012.
    <http://www.ps.psychiatryonline.org>.
Bauerlein, Monika, and Clara Jeffery. "All Work and no
    Play:The Great Speedup." *Mother Jones online*
    July/August 2011. online magazine. 21 08 2013.
    <http://www.motherjones.com/policies/2011/06/speed-
    up-american>.
Brault, Mathew W. "Disability Among the Working Age
    Population 2008 and 2009." American Community
    Survey Briefs. 2010. 12 09 2011.
    <www.census.gov/prod/2010pubs/acsbr09-12.pdf>.
Cook, Richard. "A Bailout for the People: Dividend Economics
    and the Basic Income Guarantee." *The 8th Congress of
    the US Basic Income Guarantee Network and 2009
    Eastern Economics Association National Conference*.
    New York, 2009.
deGraff, John, ed. *Take Back Your Time*. San Francisco:
    Berrett-Koehler Publishers, Inc., 2003. print.
Feitshans, Ilise L.JD,ScM. "Diversity and Human
    Rights:Protections for Neurodiversity and Physical
    Disabilities Under International Human Rights Law."
    New York: Columbia University, 01 November 2006.
Ford, Martin R. *The Lights in the
    Tunnel:Automation,Accelerating Technology, and the*

Economy of the Future. Acculant Publishing, 2009. PDF file.

Freire, Paulo. *Pedagogy of the Oppressed*. New York: Continuum, 1993. Print.

Green, Francis. *Why Has Work Effort Become More Intense?Conjectures and Evidence About Effort Based Technological Change and Other Stories*. Department of Economics.University of Kent at Canturbury, 2002. PDF file.

Marx, Karl and Friedrich Engels. *The Communist Manifesto*. New York: New American Library, 1888. Print.

Masuda, Yoneji. *The Information Society as Postindustrial Society*. Bethesda: World Future Society, 1980. Print.

Mays, Jennifer. "Income Support for People With Disability." *The Social Change in the 21st Century Conference*. Center for Social Change Research, Queensland University of Technology , 2005.

McGee, Micki. "Neurodiversity." *Contyexts* 11.3 (2012): 12-13.

Nadel, Mark, Steve Wamhoff,and Michael Wisement. "Disability,Welfare Reform, & Supplemental Security Income." Social Security Bulletin. 2003/2004.

Oliver, Michael J. *3-Disability and the Rise of Capitalism*. University of Leeds, 1999. PDF File. <Disability studies.leeds.ac.uk/files.library/oliverp.ofd.oliver3.pdf.>.

Parjis, Philippe van. *Interview with Phlippe van Parjis* Christopher Bertram. Imprints, 1997.

Pickett, Kate, and Richard Wilkinson. *The Spirit Level:Why Greater Equality Makes Societies Stronger*. New York: Bloomsbury Press, 2011. ebook.

Russell, Marta and Ravi Malhorta. "Capitalism and Disability." *Socialist Register* 38 (2002): 211-228. PDF File.

Schorr, Juliet B. *The Overworked American:The Unexpected Decline of Leisure*. New York: Basic Books, 1992. Print.

Sennett, Richard. *Culture of the New Capitalism*. New Haven: Yale University Press, 2006. Print.

—. *Respect in a World of Inequality*. New York: W.W. Norton and Company, 2003. Print.

—. *The Craftsman*. New Haven: Yale University Press, 2008. ebook.

Sheahen, Allan. *Basic Income Guarantee:Your Right to Economic Security*. New York: Palgrave MacMillan, 2013. Print.

—. *Guaranteed Income:The Right to Economic Security*. Van Nuys: GAIN Publications, 1983. Print.

—. "Its Time to Think Big: How to Simplify the Tax Code and Provide Every American With a Basic Income Guarantee." *USBIG discussion paper #144*. April 2006.

Smith, Jeffery. "Land Equity:Public or Private? Can Geonomics Lower the CPI to Stretch the BI?" *The USBIG Track within the Annual Conference of Eastern Economics Association* . New York, 2011.

Smith, Jeffrey J. "Can a Citizen's Dividend Replace Welfare." *The USBIG Track in Eastern Economic Association Conference*. New York, 2007.

—. "How to Make a BO Inflation Proof While Also Raising Wages." *USBIG Track Within the Eastern Economic Association Annual Conference* . New York, 2008.

Sutherland, A.T. *Disabled we Stand*. London: Souvenir Press, 1981. print.

tenBroek, Jacobus, and Floyd W. Matson. "The Disabled and the Law of Welfare." *California Law Review* 54.2 (1966): 809-839.

Townsend, Peter. "The Restoration of Universalism: the Rise and Fall of Keynesian Influence on Social Development Policies." United Nations. United Nations Research Institute for Social Development (UNRISD), 2002.

Trout, J.D. *The Empathy Gap*. New York: Viking, 2009. Print.

USA. Social Security Administration. *Historical Background and Development of Social Security*. n.d. 23 03 2012. <http://www.ssa.gov/history//briefhistory3.html.SSA>.

USA. United States General Accounting Office. "Disability Rolls Keep Growing while Explanations Remain Elusive." Report to the Chairman Committee on Finance,US Senate and Chairman Committee on Ways and Means, House of Representatives. 1994. print.

USA. US Census Bureau. "Distribution of Selected Characteristics of Individuals 15 Years and Older by Disability Status." 2010. PDF File.

<http://www.census.gov/people/disability/publications/di sab10/table_A3.pdf>.

USA.Social Security Administration. "Annual Statistical Report on the Social Security Disability Insurance Program." 2011. PDF file.
<http://www.ssa.gov/policy/docs/statcomps/di asr/2011/di asr pdf>.

Van der Veen, Robert and Philippe van Parjis. "A Capitalist Road to Communism." *Theory and Society* 15.5 (1986): 635-655.

World Health Organization (WHO). *International Classification of Impairments,Disabilities, and Handicaps*. Geneva, 1980.

Zola, I. *Missing Pieces:A Chronicle of Living With a Disability*. Philedelphia: Temple University Press, 2003. Print.